TORMOD VAALAND BURKEY, PhD, studied ecology and conservation biology at Princeton. He is a biodiversity specialist, conservation scientist and environmental activist, as well as a birder, diver, sea kayaker and sailor. Tormod loves animals with a vengeance and longs to experience wildlife untrammeled by habitat degradation and persecution. He has struggled since childhood with the difficulties of saving endangered species, the natural world and the beautiful places on earth from human beings' ignorance and greed. He lives in a cabin on the banks of the river Glomma, Norway, with 'his' cat Kitty, and writes for a diversity of publications and media outlets.

Praise for *Ethics For A Full World*

Tormod Burkey would like to save the world because he cares deeply about it, and from the perspective of ecology and evolutionary biology, saving the world seems the right thing to do. Much like Daniel Kozlovsky's 1974 book, *An Ecological and Evolutionary Ethic*, Burkey makes a strong case that modern science provides a foundation for deciding how we should treat non-human species and the earth as a whole, even if we can't derive 'ought' directly from 'is.'
— Reed F. Noss, Provost's Distinguished Research Professor, University of Central Florida, author of *Forgotten Grasslands of the South*.

Tormod Burkey's *Ethics For A Full World* is one of the shortest, sharpest, clearest and most compelling descriptions of the causes and cures of our environmental bankruptcy that I have ever read.
— Lloyd Timberlake, author on environment and development issues.

Dr Burkey's extraordinary book touches on psychology and neuroscience, evolutionary biology, ecology, dynamic systems theory, statistics, economics, philosophy, ethics, conservation biology, history, law, religion and political science. A cure for narrow-mindedness, this provocative book should be required reading for politicians — and those who vote for them.
— Brian Czech, President, Center for the Advancement of the Steady State Economy, author of *Shoveling Fuel for a Runaway Train* and *Supply Shock: Economic Growth at the Crossroads and the Steady State Solution*.

People charge that I have abandoned science to become an 'activist.' What nonsense! Tormod Burkey's brilliant concise synthesis of the

sciences helps us understand why, for the sake of young people and all life on our planet, we must appreciate wisdom emanating from a broad perspective of all scientific disciplines, including philosophy and ethics.
— James Hansen, Director of the Program on Climate Science, Awareness and Solutions at Columbia University's Earth Institute, author of *Storms of My Grandchildren: The Truth About the Coming Climate Catastrophe and Our Last Chance to Save Humanity*.

Tormod Burkey has produced a fine, concise book which should enlarge the discussion on what in my view is the most important need of humanity, an 'ETHICS FOR A FULL WORLD.'
— Paul Ehrlich, Bing Professor of Population Studies Emeritus and President of the Center for Conservation Biology, Stanford University.

Your writing on this is the best I've seen, even going back a while. I think something might have been possible if we had tackled the problem in the 1980s but we have reached a tipping point now. Careerist have ruined our movement. And this is a tough time to be seeking the truth.
— Mike Roselle, Founder, EarthFirst!

'... Those of us who still see other species as our brothers and sisters, trapped in time and space on the same planet, desperately trying to survive the reckless behavior of our one ignorant species, are ready for the kind of ethics Burkey calls for, and that he recognizes are key to our survival.'
— Rod Coronado, indigenous biocentrist and former saboteur for Sea Shepherd, Animal Liberation Front, Earth First! and founder of Wolf Patrol.

ETHICS FOR A FULL WORLD

OR, CAN ANIMAL-LOVERS SAVE THE WORLD?

TORMOD V. BURKEY

CLAIRVIEW

Clairview Books Ltd.,
Russet, Sandy Lane,
West Hoathly,
W. Sussex RH19 4QQ

www.clairviewbooks.com

Published in Great Britain in 2017 by Clairview Books

© Tormod V. Burkey 2017

This book is copyright under the Berne Convention. All rights reserved. Apart from any fair dealing for the purpose of private study, research, criticism or review, no part of this publication may be reproduced, stored in a retrieval system, or transmitted in any form or by any means, electronic, electrical, chemical, mechanical, optical, photocopying, recording or otherwise, without the prior written permission of the copyright owner. Inquiries should be addressed to the Publishers

The right of Tormod V. Burkey to be identified as the author of this work has been asserted in accordance with sections 77 and 78 of the Copyright, Designs and Patents Act, 1988

A CIP catalogue record for this book is available from the British Library

Print book ISBN 978 1 905570 85 0
Ebook ISBN 978 1 905570 86 7

Cover by Morgan Creative featuring photograph © nialat
Typeset by DP Photosetting, Neath, West Glamorgan
Printed and bound by 4Edge Ltd, Essex

*To Edward Abbey – old Cactus Ed.
And Hayduke, Doc Sarvis, Bonnie Abbzug, and Ol'e Seldom Seen.*

Contents

Preface	1
Ethics For A Full World	7
Why Are We Not Acting To Save The World?	25
We Need A New Ethic	79
A Different Ethic	97
On The Tragic	119
Afterword: Can We Save The World?	137
Notes	151
Index	180

Preface

'The social tree is diseased because of the decrepitude of its philosophical roots; it will do little good to treat the withering branches.'
— Daniel Kozlovsky (1974)[1]

Before addressing a complex issue, we as citizens sometimes need to take a broad overview of the situation and make sure we know what the overarching and underlying problems really are. Large and important problems, the kind that can occur in a full world, are such issues. The issues that most urgently need our attention are the ones that (potentially or actually) exhibit tipping points – critical points in their underlying dynamics where the system switches into an entirely new regime, one from which it may be impossible to emerge. Such nonlinear dynamics and discontinuities are common in natural systems. 'Interesting' issues also have transboundary, international, dimensions, because internal issues are more easily addressed – those are more likely to be solved, indeed they may be well under way to be already. Problems with tipping points and international dimensions are the important challenges, precisely because they are difficult and because it may suddenly be too late. All other problems will be solved some day, simply because it will never be too late to solve them. Of course, the solutions may come too late for *individuals* to enjoy them, but the most important thing is to ensure that there will still be individuals to enjoy things in the future. In that sense it is never too late, where those other, 'simple,' kinds of problems are concerned. Unfortunately, those seem to be the kinds of issues that get the most attention in the public awareness and our daily lives, even with the world in the state that it is.

In a full world we encounter problems of a materially different nature from the kinds of problems humanity has had to deal with in the past. When the world is full, individual actions and problems that have previously been local have repercussions on the global scale. Recycling abilities have been overwhelmed and spill over onto a grander scale. There are no safe havens for exploited populations. Species go globally extinct, and ever more species are lost in cascading chain reactions of ecological dependence. Overharvested systems do not recover, and harvesting shifts elsewhere with similar effect. In a full world there is nowhere else to go for a fresh start when you have exhausted opportunities where you are. A full world is truly globalized. (Even though some resources have substitutes, truly limiting resources (like water, key elements in biological and agricultural systems, and the atmosphere's capacity to absorb carbon) do not. And even if humans are able to switch to another resource, other species may not. When you are butting up against such critical limits we can say that the world is 'full' even though not all limits are exceeded or all potential resources are fully exploited.) Global problems such as climate change, biodiversity meltdown, fisheries collapse, ocean acidification, interference with key nutrient cycles, like the nitrogen and phosphorous cycles, and so on, are of a scale and complexity hitherto unknown to mankind, and solving such problems may be encapsulated under the notion of 'Saving The World.' 'Saving The World' is, of course, just a shorthand for the implementation of real-world real solutions to large, complicated, 'world-threatening' problems that involve tipping points and international dimensions.

Parts of this book were originally an essay submitted for the Zapffe Prize, a prize announced in the name of Norwegian philosopher and mountaineer Peter Wessel Zapffe. Zapffe was an exponent of biosophy. He articulated severe pessimism with regard to human existence on Earth, and felt that human consciousness was a tragic evolutionary mistake. The Prize is for 'philosophical and ethical musings on human population growth, including analyses of the causes and effects of such growth in relation to other species and nature in general.' While this essay does not dwell on human population issues explicitly, my favorite Zapffe quote is reproduced in the opening pages.

The final chapter of this short work is entitled 'On The Tragic', as a reference to Zapffe's magnum opus, and doctoral dissertation, *Om det tragiske* (On The Tragic[2]), which sadly has never been translated from the original Norwegian. For those of us who care deeply about the natural world, the global challenges we face can feel like profoundly personal tragedies. Many of us are so engaged with the problems facing the world, and the species we love, that our ability to address them effectively becomes pivotal to our own happiness and quality of life as well. Hopefully, we can find means of turning this emotional engagement into a force for good despite the scale and the urgency of the problems that are threatening to overwhelm us. The title of my submission was *Ethics For A Full World*. For a different audience, an alternative title might have been *Can Animal-Lovers Save The World?* Hence the wilfully convoluted and unmodern title of this book, which to my mind harkens back to theses of a past century, when a man like Charles Darwin could publish his revolutionary theory under the full title: *On the Origin of Species by Means of Natural Selection, or the Preservation of Favoured Races in the Struggle for Life*.

The second chapter of this book, 'Why Are We Not Acting To Save The World?', was not part of the original essay, and can to a large extent be read in isolation. It motivates the final chapter ('Afterword: Can We Save the World?') and the project described therein. It also serves to motivate the need for a new ethic, which is elaborated on in the ensuing chapters. It is also rather long and slightly different in style from the others, focusing more on what others have said before me, and on fields where I have no particular expertise and have to rely more on the insights of others. To some it may therefore seem a distraction from the main theme of the book, particularly if you find yourself getting bogged down. If your main interest is in ethics, our relationship to other species and the natural world, and the need for a different ethic to replace our old anthropocentric one, you could decide to skip this chapter altogether, or return to it later, perhaps before reading the Afterword. You may even find that many parts of this book can be read out of order, or piecemeal.

Chapters One, Three, and Four together make the case against the prevailing anthropocentric ethic. Given everything we have learned over the centuries, you would have thought that one of them was that it is not all about humans. While many of us have, as a society it seems that we have not. Humans are just one of the millions of species on this planet. For some of us it is personal, because we love species that are immediately impacted by the desecration of the Earth; many of which are long gone, many that are on the threshold, and many that are simply suffering needlessly at the hands of man. While sadness and depression are natural reactions to this state of affairs, I hope the combination of feelings, knowledge and true understanding may sustain a burning rage that will help channel our energy into doing something about it. Something real. Something more than just window-dressing and busywork.

A new effort I am trying to initiate, explores the vital question 'Can We Save The World?' As a preliminary step to more concerted efforts to come up with the actual, real solutions to the problems facing the world, I should like to get a dedicated group of political scientists and other people with complementary backgrounds and experiences to thoroughly analyze the question of whether we really could save the world (with existing institutions) and what the main structural challenges facing such efforts are. The nature of this more limited project, which I am trying to find partners and supporters for, is outlined in the Afterword, in an effort to reach out and hear from interested readers with a visceral reaction to our plight and a burning need to take effective action.

Not wishing to produce a scholarly treatise for a few academics, this is not a thoroughly referenced work. In the interest of focussing on a few core ideas, and keeping it short and for a more general audience, it does not strive to give an exhaustive history of philosophy or review of intellectual antecedents. Scant attention has been given to the works of others, except where it serves my purposes, nor much attempt given to mapping where one stands on the shoulders of giants. Some are touched on in passing, none given the attention they deserve. Some citations are provided where part of the pedigree was clear to me, or where text appears as a direct quote. Apologies for all sins of omission.

Nor does this book contain an exhaustive description of all the woes facing us, or a litany of facts pertaining to the ecological damages visited upon the world. It is a pet peeve of mine that authors often seem to think all their readers are a *tabula rasa* that need to be filled up with information about the state of affairs, leaving little or no column space to the question of what we are going to do about it, and how. A similar phenomenon pertains to seminars and conferences as they are typically organized, filled to the brim with one-way communication, leaving no time for progressing beyond what is already known and understood by somebody, or to get work done. I will not insult your intelligence by assuming that most of the problems related to our ecological footprint on Earth are not already known to you, and available in the literature to anyone who cares to find it. Nor will I belabor the text by explaining every little thing in terms of first principles, or providing a lot of associated examples. If you run across a concept with which you are unfamiliar, and my account of it does not meet your needs or desires, Google it. Perhaps, at times, the endnotes may help. Nor do I write for the unquestioning, the incurious, or for the easily offended. Sometimes my writing aims to function at a meta-level, and I hope it works at least some of the time.

The tasks involved in 'saving the world,' are so overwhelming, urgent, and so crucial, that we all need a multitude of partners and allies in this great transformation. If we fail to connect with a critical mass of confederates our personal lot will be a bitter and tragic struggle against the futility of action in isolation – forever impotent, hamstrung, dejected, and tragically frustrated in our desire to make a real difference in the only world that we know and love. For the future of life on Earth, and for our own well-being as well, we need to find triggers that can propel humanity into meaningful action, and mechanisms that can actually solve the problems we face, before it is too late.

Ethics For A Full World

'The "control of nature" is a phrase conceived in arrogance, born of the Neanderthal age of biology and philosophy, when it was supposed that nature exists for the convenience of man.'
— Rachel Carson (1962)[3]

Which book has meant the most to you? No matter who you are, and whether or not you have actually read it, the correct answer is arguably *On the Origin of Species* by Charles Darwin.[4] Before the concept of Darwinian evolution by means of natural selection, Western civilization could understand nothing about life on Earth. In the words of Theodosius Dobzhansky: 'Nothing in biology makes sense, save in the light of evolution.' No other body of thought has had such an impact on our view of the world and our place in it, of life, of how the world works and of the processes that shape our lives. Work on 'the new synthesis,' from 1930 onwards, combined Darwin's insight with genetics, and made it possible to understand a host of mechanisms that make all living things the way they are.

Copernicus relegated Earth to simply one of many planets — not the Center of the Universe, but just another rock in orbit around a rather ordinary star. Darwin did the same with humans; not created in God's image after all, but shaped by the same processes as all other animals, and not fundamentally different from them. Humans are a part of nature, not put here by God to rule it. For the first time, it was possible to understand life on Earth. Before Darwin we could not even place humans relative to the rest of creation; we had no basis for phylogenies. The term 'creation' itself, along with 'creator' (in the context of life on Earth) and 'creature,' became an unfortunate misnomer.

The new science of ecology demoted humanity further from the position evolutionary biology and astronomy had relegated it to. In a food chain, the species at the bottom support the entire structure and are paramount for the maintenance of the whole. If organisms are mutually inter-dependent, like organs in a body, or the different stages of embryology, which is more important? Darwin himself made a point of reminding himself, repeatedly, not to describe species as 'higher' or 'lower.' Ecology allows us to understand the interactions in natural communities and how things work on time scales slower than the evolutionary. Ecology made it possible to understand the ebb and flow of population changes and expanded the use of 'community' and 'society' to other organisms and associations of different species in nature.

When a new worldview becomes dominant it is usually the product of a scientific paradigm shift. Ecology will also force a reality-check on traditional liberalism. There can be no individual welfare, or freedom, removed from the ecological matrix upon which the individual life form depends.[5]

> 'To bear children into this world is like carrying firewood into a burning house.'
>
> — Peter Wessel Zapffe[6]

We are beginning to see unmistakable signs that our philosophy, and ethics, our institutions, and the ways we have organized ourselves are not up to the challenges we face in a globalized world. In today's world, a power plant in China and a meat eater in Norway decide the outcome of a polar bear cub's swim in the Canadian Arctic.

Evolutionary biology, and later ecology, placed humans firmly as a part of nature. Man is an animal like any other, created and molded by the same process as all other species. In that sense it is trivially true that *Homo sapiens* is a part of nature. But with our opposable thumbs and our technology Man has placed himself outside of nature — different and apart from it, as in the Bible. Not apart from nature in the sense that we do not have an effect upon it — on the contrary — but in the sense that we are not affected by or regulated by nature on the scales of time and space on which we live our lives.

To be regulated in the ecological sense means to exhibit density dependent dynamics, whereby dense populations have lower growth rates, or decline, while small (sparse) populations tend to grow.[7] No population grows forever. Regulation is the reason population sizes are kept within certain bounds. A population that exceeds the local environment's potential to produce the food it needs will be regulated by the availability of food, and go into local decline. Other species' ranges can be limited by climatic conditions. Humans, on the other hand, have settled every continent, under all sorts of environmental conditions, and are, as a global species, no longer limited by local constraints. Dense populations can continue to grow by drawing on resources from a much greater scale. The time scale that is relevant for regulation of populations of humans has little or no impact on most people's daily lives. By exploiting the accumulation of biomass over geological time scales we have to a certain extent even freed ourselves from having to live off the steady stream of energy from the sun.

We have also put ourselves outside of nature in the sense that we currently are not subjected to much in the way of selection pressure. Nearly everybody lives a long life, and those who die early do so arbitrarily, due to things that have little or nothing to do with their personal traits or genetics. Practically everyone has a chance to reproduce if they want to. Differential reproduction still occurs, but this variation also tends to be unrelated to physical traits, skills, or inherent abilities. Without systematic differences in mortality and reproduction there will be no further evolution (save in the negative sense, that release from selection causes changes in gene frequencies as formerly unfortunate traits are allowed to increase[8]). Our fates are determined more by serendipity, modern medicine, technology, and the social structures surrounding us, than by our own prowess.

Clearly our society and our communities exist within nature and are dependent upon it. But we have removed ourselves from nature, elevated ourselves above it, so that we may live as if it didn't exist. In principle, we too will one day be regulated by the forces of nature, but for the time being we have, by means of our technology, managed to keep nature at arm's length, extricating ourselves from local resource constraints and dependency on individual species. As global omnivores with impressive technologies we have been able to liberate ourselves from the dictates of natural fluctuations, and need not suffer directly when we have destroyed a prey species, or a mutualist, or experience the long-term consequences of eradicating competitors or natural predators. But in the end, and the end *will* come, nature will catch up to us and we too will once again become part of nature — victims of our own avarice, and the impoverishment of nature that we ourselves have precipitated. We too will once again feel resource limitations, but only after we have destroyed nearly everything around us will we reap the repercussions of our own actions.

Nature has, temporarily, been unable to regulate the human population. We must therefore voluntarily submit ourselves to regulation by 'the constraining force of ethics.'[9] As long as our ethics are not up to that task we remain a species 'out of control.' It is small comfort that some day we will once again be part of nature — a species that also feels the brunt of ecosystems collapsing around us — when in the meantime we will have destroyed most of what makes life worth living.

The way humans are behaving, on the time scale that is relevant to our daily lives, the distinction between concepts like 'nature' and 'culture,' 'artificial' and 'natural,' between 'nature,' 'the world' and 'the universe,' become meaningless if we still consider humanity, in today's situation, as a part of 'nature.' In the trivial sense, nature is everything. If there is anything special about humanity, it would have to be our ability to wipe out a profusion of other life forms – because we operate on such large scales and are such omnivores that we don't immediately feel the consequences when we over-exploit other species. In the Anthropocene era,[10] humans are more an environmental condition that other species are constrained by than a part of the same environment.

> 'Woe unto them that join house to house, that lay field to field, till there be no place...'
> — Isaiah 5:8[11]

We will never again experience something 'natural.' In an artificial climate, warmer, wetter and wilder than any humanity has ever encountered, we will not recognize the world. Every day we will wonder what it would be like if we had not altered the climate. A warm winter day, without snow, with rain and slush, foggy; every new day will be compared to what we believe it ought to be, wondering how it would have been had we not converted it to something of our own creation. We will be wondering how the animals and plants are coping out there; wet, cold – frost and moisture in rapid succession, with greater variation, unpredictability, new competitors, altered food availability, the signals for migration, germination and reproduction out of tune with the new reality. Not a day will pass without the feeling that it is, in every way, somehow unnatural, and our fault at that.

Of course we must be aware that this state 'outside of nature' is a relatively new thing. As a species, we have no experience with such a situation prior to the last 100 years or so. It cannot last. Several limits for human activity have already been overshot;[12] it is likely many of us alive today will live to feel some of the consequences, and experience a world entirely different from the one today's society is built upon.

There is not room here to itemize the damage that seven and a half billion humans wreak on our planet and its inhabitants, or even the damage we managed to do while we were still much fewer. Nor, hopefully, is it necessary. A few examples will serve. If we look at the fate of individuals of other species it is hard to imagine the sheer extent of killing we do every year, and the amount of suffering this entails.

Global total catch of wild fish is said to have peaked in the 1990s at about 90 million tonnes per year.[13] Assuming half a kilo per mean-sized fish, that would entail that we kill 180 billion fish every year; 26 times the number of humans on Earth (and that is without counting the discards, which are also largely dead). Since many fisheries are small fish like anchovies, pilchard, etc., the average fish size is actually way below half a kilo.[14] One attempt at estimating the extent of suffering from our global fisheries indicates that the total kill may be at least 1–5 *trillion* individual fish per year. Since this estimate leaves out a diversity of causes for which fish are killed, the total number of fish killed by humans each year may be as great as a thousand times the global human population. While global fish catches supposedly stagnated at 90 million tonnes, we now eat another 70 million tonnes of fish from fish farms, and these fish are in turn fed on a much greater number of wild-caught fish.[15]

Now a recent attempt to reconstruct historic catches has suggested that global fish catches actually peaked at 130 million tonnes in 1996, and has since been declining even more sharply than hitherto believed. So the seas and oceans of the world used to be even richer than we knew, and our catches have been even more unsustainable than previously thought, declining at a rate of 1.2 million tonnes per year.[16] Global statistics are compiled yearly by UN Food and Agricultural Organization, FAO, but they are based on national reporting and hence suffer from highly variable data quality. Because, guess what, nations lie about their catch numbers like they do with logging data and other indicators, and the numbers reported to the FAO have been incomplete, misrepresented and misinterpreted. Catches from small-scale commercial and subsistence fisheries are commonly neglected or unreported. So are fish caught for 'sport,' as well as by-catch, illegal fishing, and certain other categories. Where countries have reported 'no data' these have commonly been replaced by zeros in FAO records, which clearly need not be the case. So a number of false assumptions have led to annual total global catches, from 1950 through 2010, being underestimated by more than 50% (current best estimates). Needless to say, it is hard to responsibly manage fisheries when you don't even know how much is really being caught. There are numerous reasons, including political reasons, why quotas and catches are commonly much higher than what is sustainable. Illegal fishing is commonly reviled, but *legal* catches are the greater problem.

It has been claimed that we kill an estimated 100 million sharks per year (sometimes this number is attributed to the shark fin trade alone); this number is probably on the way down since sharks have been over-harvested all over the world, and so many shark species are now endangered.[17] According to some estimates we reduce the biomass of large fishes by 80% in the first 15 years after opening an industrial fishery on them, and have only *one tenth* left shortly thereafter.[18] We are eating our way down food chains and over-exploiting fish stocks everywhere while we constantly have to seek them out in deeper waters and with more advanced techniques.[19] A recent study concludes that our beloved pet, the domestic cat, kills an estimated 1.4–3.7 billion birds and 6.9–20.7 billion mammals annually.[20] Another one hundred million birds die in collision with buildings, just in the United States.[21] While the number of animals used in research is about 25 million per year, in the US, the number of mammals and birds killed in food production (still just in the US) each year is approximately ten billion,[22] half again the human population on Earth. That number does not include fish or other aquatic animals that we also eat. Globally, three billion mammals and 57 billion birds are killed for food each year according to FAO numbers.[23]

Where animal rights activists focus on the well-being of individuals, ecologists and conservation biologists concentrate on populations, species, ecosystems and habitats. Conservation biology is applied ecology and population genetics, directed at reducing anthropogenic extinctions and loss of biodiversity. Island biogeography describes what is left of nature as residual habitat islands in a sea of human activity, where previously the reverse was the case: islands of human habitation in a sea of wildlands. Ecologists and conservation biologists study the effects on the diversity of nature and how species and populations die out when the areas remaining to them dwindle and the remnants are further fragmented by humans. The natural background rate of extinction, how often species go extinct in the absence of human influence, can be estimated from fossil records. It is on the order of 0.1–1 species per year per million species. Conservative estimates indicate that the current rate of anthropogenic species' loss is greater than the prehistoric background rate by a factor of a thousand or more, and that we can expect it to swell further in years to come.[24] There is no reason to think that speciation has sped up from its background rate in a comparable manner.

The greatest threats to life on Earth are, respectively, human land use (agriculture/forestry, settlements, infrastructure), over-exploitation (fishing, forestry, hunting), introduced species, and climate change.[25] In the years ahead climate change may catch up with over-exploitation as an extinction driver, but mainly in interaction with the other factors: absolute loss of habitats, and the fragmentation of the remains, as well as over-harvesting, makes for small populations that have greater difficulty moving in response to, and adapting to, changes in climate, while competition from a growing number of alien species is set to explode.

When you wipe out a species you have not only killed the last individual of that species, you have blocked the birth of all potential future individuals of that species, for eternity – an endless stream of beings that could have flowed from the last individuals if we had not destroyed them. Extinction is irreversible; the number zero is an absorption point. This is what Michael Soulé and Bruce Wilcox had in mind when they wrote: 'Death is one thing, an end to birth is something else.'[26]

Ecologically, it is not just the continued existence of species that is important, but also their ecologically functional roles that need to be maintained. The US Marine Mammal Protection Act of 1972 affirmed that one could not allow species to 'diminish past the point at which they cease to be a significant functioning element in the ecosystem of which they are a part.' Unfortunately, this and other laws with similar intent have not been enforced to the point where they have become effective in reaching this goal. We lose the thundering herds, the boundless schools, the immense flocks, the overwhelming natural phenomena — and the wealth of emotion they can stir in us — long before we put the species' continued existence at risk. This impoverishment, and the erosion of the species' functional role in the ecosystem, occurs long before the species dies out and is gone forever. According to a WWF report, we lost half the wild animal life on Earth between 1970 and 2010.[27] And a lot more was lost before that. Vaclav Smil has estimated that even in 1900, the total biomass of wild terrestrial mammals was about as large at the anthropomass of the approximately 1.6 billion humans at the time (about 72 Mt live weight or about 11 Mt Carbon), but 100 years later wild animal biomass had fallen to less than 5 Mt C, with human biomass at least ten times that.[28] By now (March 2016), human biomass would have increased to at least 370 Mt live weight and 68 Mt C. By Smil's calculations, humans and their livestock outweighed wild terrestrial mammals by at least 35 to one by the year 2000. Since livestock have also increased since 2000 and wild animals have continued their decline, while humans have gotten heavier and increased from 6 billion to 7.4 billion in number, this ratio has gotten significantly higher since then. (By the time this book is out total global human population will probably be 7.5 billion so the ratio is outdated almost as soon as it is calculated.) It goes without saying, that in such a skewed relationship one could do untold levels of damage.

As a process with absorption points, extinction is an example of a more general phenomenon: processes with thresholds, or tipping points (break points). Systems with positive (self-enhancing) feedback loops[29] are common in nature, in ecology, and in the global climate system.[30] A tipping point is the point where self-reinforcing processes gain the upper hand and spin out of control. In dynamic systems theory, which among other things describes the fluctuations of natural populations and changes in ecological communities, one can speak of 'basins of attraction': widely disparate states where it can be difficult, if not impossible, to return to the state we were used to once you have crossed into a new domain or state space. As individuals, we live in a world, and on a time scale, where things change gradually and slowly, move in cycles, steadily round and round or back and forth. We are not used to dealing with irreparable damage. We all know that when you bend a branch it flexes evenly and gradually, and when we ease off the pressure it curves effortlessly back and eases back into roughly its original shape. We can repeat this process again and again. But when the branch snaps, there is no way back. Like the straw that broke the camel's back. Yet we imagine and act as if more complex systems won't ever break. As a species and as a society we are not good at dealing with such points of no return. Most people are not even aware that these exist, or they refuse to believe it.

In ecological systems, a tipping point might be when, for instance, a forest ecosystem is deforested to the point where it becomes dominated by grasses, and the grassland burns yearly, precluding the regeneration of a forest (without extremely intensive, and costly, fire suppression efforts). Or overfishing may lead to an ecosystem becoming dominated by jellyfish, and other invertebrate taxa, which consume fish eggs and larvae so that fish stocks do not recover. Another tipping point may occur when global warming has reached the point where permafrost areas, like those in the vast Siberian tundra, melt sufficiently to release the immense quantities of methane stored there.[31] At the opposite end of the spectrum, in the physical world, a 'snowball earth' might result if global cooling got to the point where the increased amounts of snow and ice leads to increased albedo, reflecting more energy from the sun back out into space, causing further cooling. An example of negative feedback loops is the hypothetical 'Daisy World,' described as an example in the Gaia hypothesis. In it, the world is covered by two kinds of daisies, black and white. The white daisies do well when the climate is warm, black daisies do well when the climate is cool. If the white daisies should start to take over the world, the increased albedo would lead to cooling of the climate, which in turn would lead to the decline of white daisies and more black daisies. And vice versa, as black daisies increase that would lead to warmer conditions which favor the white daisies. This stabilizing effect is the opposite of the positive feedback loops that are involved in tipping points. When global warming causes forests to die, and their carbon stores are released to the atmosphere, that is a positive feedback loop which is inherent to tipping points and may shift conditions into a completely different basin of attraction.

In population dynamics we typically see stabilizing, negative feedback, such that as a population of a given organism increases, individuals face increased competition for resources or greater risk of disease or predation, such that the population will tend to decline again. At low densities, conditions will be more ideal, and the population will once again start to increase. But in some cases populations may exhibit negative dynamic coefficients even at lower densities. In ecology these are known as *Allee effects*: once a population drops below a certain threshold it may continue to decline. For instance, social animals may have difficulties in finding each other or may fall more easy prey to predators at low densities; those that would otherwise benefit from cooperative behavior may be severely disadvantaged when their numbers are low, individuals in a sparse population may have difficulty finding mates or attaining the conditions to breed successfully. So this also is a positive feedback mechanism: once numbers start falling, they will continue to fall – just like, as at the other end of the spectrum once a quantity has risen above a certain threshold, it will continue to rise. This is the nature of tipping points.

Systems theory and information theory teach us that more complex, more diverse systems often have greater resilience[32] – greater ability to recuperate after an external perturbation. They have more pathways through which to dissipate the impact and to absorb it. Yet they can still break, and become something completely *other*; usually something simpler, something poorer. The enhanced resilience of some complex systems, may lull us into a false confidence, as they remain functional despite the multitude of abuses we hurl at them – up to a point. Nature has many stabilizing mechanisms, but when these are breached all bets are off. In fact, diverse systems like tropical rainforest, cloud forests and coral reefs may be extremely fragile. It may be that the causality is the other way around: that species-rich assemblages like rainforests and coral reefs require a stable environment and freedom from disturbances in order to persist. Furthermore, the tendency to focus our attention on the most diverse biomes has some unfortunate side-effects. It would be most unfair to disregard the plight of individuals and species that carve out a life for themselves in low diversity ecosystems simply because the species count per unit area is lower.

Few sciences have reached a point where they have become truly predictive. Ecology can still not predict the ultimate consequences of losing a species, or the aftermath of an introduced species, or a degree of climate change. What we are doing to nature is like the old Chinese torture method 'death by a thousand cuts' – a piece gone here and a piece there until the entire entity has perished. When we atomize the threats to ecosystems we can of course not describe the long-term repercussions of cumulative stresses in a straight-forward manner.

> *'An Ecologist lives in a world of wounds.'*
> — Aldo Leopold[33]

It is a common ploy to point out that extinction is a natural phenomenon. The implication is that whatever is going on happens 'naturally,' and is therefore nothing to worry about. If you see humanity as part of 'nature,' then everything humans do is 'natural,' and thus need not overly concern us. If it is our nature, then in a way it is not our responsibility. It is not something we can do anything about, nor is it even certain that we *should* do anything about it... Using the terms 'nature' and 'natural' in this manner undermines the concepts themselves.

It is trivial that extinction is a natural process, that has been going on as long as life has existed. Without extinction the world would look entirely different. 'The tree of life' would be more like 'the bush of life,' or the moss, and most of the 'innovations' that are part of life as we know it, would not exist. The interaction between extinction and speciation gives us the biological diversity that exists at any given time. There have been times in the past, during the succession of life on Earth, where extinction has out-paced speciation, and rapid radiation (the formation and spread of new species) has followed five previous mass extinction episodes.

The difference is that this time we have a choice. This time it is our fault and our responsibility. This time, it is we who constitute the external force that is wiping out our fellow travellers on this planet. If we are as highly evolved as we like to think, then surely we have a choice in the matter. Otherwise, we are simply slaves of our own 'nature.' Then we are just like the meteorite that extinguished the dinosaurs — provided the mass extinction we are now causing proves as 'reversible' as the earlier ones. Then all our purported intelligence and our vaunted culture are to no avail. Perhaps they are plain evils. At least to those among us who care about the species of the here and now, the (for now) result of four billion years of evolution on this Earth.

We cannot freeze the state of the world at any particular moment in time. Natural extinctions must take their course. But we don't have to add to it, and certainly we should not be the drivers of an extinction rate thousands of times higher than the prehistoric background rate. At least, we would not want to be responsible for the very unravelling of the web of life. At this point in time, humanity has a choice to make. Ethics are about such choices.

> *'The thing that differentiates man from animals is money.'*
> – Gertrude Stein (1936)[34]

Economics is sometimes referred to as 'the science of choice.' Students of conventional economics are told that there are two basic means of production: labor and capital. But no, the foundation of our economy is not labor. The basis for our economy is nature, where we fetch raw materials and food stuffs, which provides water, sunlight, energy, and a stable climate, recycling of wastes and nutrients, creates the conditions for growing our food, maintains atmospheric gas balances and the pH of the oceans, and, not least, habitats for all other species – without whom we could not live, and life would not be worth living.

In the standard model of the macroeconomy, nothing exists outside the economy. The world is just money, goods and services circulating between companies and households. There is no environment, so there are no costs associated with the use of natural resources or the waste products that necessarily follow from such use. Our economic system lives off irreplaceable natural capital, which we unthinkingly treat as if it were income.[35]

There are no mechanisms in mainstream economics to relate to the overall scale of human activity. Once, that might have been rational, when there was still a lot of open space left on Earth; new land was there for the taking, and humanity's ability to influence the relative enormity of nature was thought to be insignificant. But now we face a new situation: the world is full, and the frontier is no more. It is a different thing entirely to live in a full world than to live in an empty world, or a world half full. Humanity has never before experienced a full world, and our economic system and our monetary system are not designed for such a situation. If you think of the world as infinitely large, there is nothing wrong with ignoring the availability of resources or the flow of pollutants. But when the economy is getting large relative to the planet on which it resides, then costs will start to make themselves felt. This is what we mean when we compare a 'frontier economy' with a 'spaceship economy.' When the world was empty, man-made capital was a limiting factor. In a full world, natural resources and recycling capacity set the real limits on our activities. Now it is the number of fish in the sea that determines how much fish we can harvest, not the number of fishing vessels or fishermen.

Our technology and our omnivory have enabled us, at least for a while, to bypass local resource limitations. In a full world, limitations, whatever they are, are global. In the past, substitutions allowed us to proceed, but not all resources are substitutable, and in a full world there is no other place to obtain more of our irreplaceable natural resources and no place to receive our overflow. In a full world, the consequences of our actions are global.

When the world is full, it would seem a good idea to have an economic system that can cope with the absence of (continued) growth. It is time we had an economy that was compatible with the laws of thermodynamics and ecology. For too long now we have had *uneconomic* growth[36] — growth that does not yield increased welfare, but creates more problems than it is worth; makes us poorer rather than richer.

There is much waste still in the system, perhaps because our current economic system has focused efficiency gains on returns to labor and capital, rather than on long-term sustainability and on minimizing environmental damage and harm to other species. Imagine a bottom trawler scraping the ocean floor, breaking, pounding, grinding, destroying everything in its path, killing indiscriminately to harvest a few select species of fish or shellfish, while the rest is thrown overboard, usually dead or dying. It is like hunting moose with bulldozers, and would probably be illegal if it didn't happen out of sight under the sea. It may surprise some to learn that a sixteenth century French law imposed the death penalty for bottom trawling.[37]

*

Without science we don't know when we have a problem. All the same, the union of science and technology that took place during the last 150 years has brought extraordinary problems. Any technology is benign when first introduced. It is only as it matures and expands that the repercussions begin to manifest themselves and become clear to us. Take the automobile, for instance. When the first cars rolled into our lives, they were so slow that no one was killed in traffic. There was no traffic to speak of. Many early automobiles were electric. But pollution from petrol driven cars was not a problem, because there were so few of them. There were hardly any roads, compared to our predicament today, and they were modest by today's standards. Today, we have covered vast stretches of the land under asphalt, replanned our lives around the automobile, and made all the places we might have liked to visit just like the place we came from: buried under asphalt and marred by noise, pollution, traffic jams, stress, etc. Cars, run on fossil fuels, were seen as a solution to the pollution problems from an earlier means of transport, the horse. Not until a technology has matured to the point of ubiquity do the consequences become clear to us. By then we are so dependent upon it, that it is hard to liberate ourselves from it again. Often, this does not happen before it is replaced by another innovation.

Even a technology like agriculture was innocuous when it was a new phenomenon on Earth. Agriculture led to overpopulation, and the greatest destruction ever of the natural world. Agriculture and forestry account for the greatest part of our land use, which in turn is the dominant factor driving our mass extinction of other species. When the world is full, when the system has been pushed too far, that is when a multitude of tipping points with large scale repercussions will start to converge on us. With tipping points, you can't simply extrapolate from current trends. If there are underlying ecological mechanisms set to be triggered, present day and historical statistics may tell us nothing about what is just ahead of us. Even though there are copious signs that things are not going well in the natural world, some people still claim that certain socioeconomic indicators show that things are going quite nicely for humans, and in certain cases even moving in the 'right' direction. Yet, if they don't take into account the underlying ecology and whether or not critical tipping points are approaching, they don't tell us anything meaningful about the state of the world. For all we know, we may have already crossed some invisible threshold, and may be, inexorably, on a path to a state that most people don't even want to think about. We have choices to make, more important, more all-encompassing, than any humanity has ever had to make in the past. Despite its moniker as 'the science of choice,' economics has tended to shy away from dealing with what constitutes real progress and remains reticent about what it means to live a good life, preferring instead to leave such weighty matters to 'the consumer.' Yet to be human is to be more than just a consumer, and humanity has to be more than just the sum of our parts. How do we price a devastated world, and the aftermath of exceeding a critical tipping point? Can we use our knowledge and our technology to get humans to think long term and act rationally, but still anchored in feelings for all life?

To be sustainable, society must stop behaving as though it is not a subset of nature, and our economy has to learn to coexist within nature's ecology. A sustainable world will probably not result before we expand the domain of our ethics once again, and build new institutions and covenants to ensure that we live within ecological limits. Culture, technology, and ethics change more rapidly than evolution. We need a sustainable ethic, adequate for a globalized world — a world where our actions have global consequences. In a full world, everything is political.

Why Are We Not Acting To Save The World?

> *'Hope has two beautiful daughters. Their names are anger and courage; anger at the way things are, and courage to see that they do not remain the way they are.'*
> — St Augustine[38]

In *A Sand County Almanac*, published posthumously in 1949, Aldo Leopold pointed out that 'individual thinkers since the days of Ezekiel and Isaiah have asserted that the despoliation of land is not only expedient but wrong.' So why have we not fixed the problem since Isaiah, let alone since Leopold?

Good solutions may be hard to find. If I had the solution I wouldn't be writing this book. I would be out doing it. Or perhaps I *would* be writing a book, if the solution required other people knowing what it was.

The fact remains, none of us can do it alone. So the question is not how could we save the world, but how do we get humanity to save the world? It doesn't help that 'we all know how *not* to cut down a tree.'[39] The critical question is how do we get other people to not cut down trees? One thing to our advantage, we generally know the kinds of things that need to be done. What we don't know is how to get these things done in the kind of world that we have created. Or how do we change our current system so that we will be able to deal with the problems that we face and implement the necessary changes, *in time*? How to make the necessary possible? The social sciences have not become operational to the point where they can give us straight-forward answers to these sorts of questions.

'Why We Are Not Acting to Save the World' was the title of a chapter in a 1987 book by famed behaviorist B. F. Skinner. Rather than paraphrasing, I will quote Skinner directly on this conundrum:

Traditional explanations of why we are doing so little are familiar. It is said that we lack responsibility for those who will follow us, that we do not have a clear perception of the problem, that we are not using our intelligence, that we are suffering from a failure of will, that we lack moral strength, and so on. Unfortunately, explanations of that sort simply replace one question with another. Why are we not more responsible or more intelligent? Why are we suffering from a failure of will?[40]

Skinner's answer pointed to psychological and game theory mechanisms that are by-products of our evolutionary history as short term utility maximizers, selection for 'fight or flight' responses in crisis situations rather than facing long term challenges, and so on. To save the world is to do something about the future. But the future doesn't exist yet. According to Skinner, 'the environment shapes people's actions,' so how can a future which is not yet our environment, affect our behavior today? Hence warning labels on cigarette packages are no more effective than warnings about exacerbated droughts and heat waves. We cannot know what the future will bring, other than as a prediction laden with uncertainties. In the same way that we don't know that we will get cancer if we keep smoking. We know the risks of smoking only 'statistically,' as an average effect on well-being and longevity, not in terms of the particular effect it will have on a particular individual in a particular time and place.

Nothing in our evolutionary history could prepare us for what is about to come. Skinner distinguishes between 'knowledge by description' and 'knowledge by acquaintance,' which is more apt to get us to take action. We cannot know the future by acquaintance, only as an uncertain prediction. 'In general, the more remote the predicted consequence, the less likely we are to follow advice.' Warning of an uncertain death at some future date is not effective in getting addicted smokers to abstain from that one cigarette today. Evolution acts on the here and now, it does not prepare us for the future. Instead we have been selected for high reproduction in a high-mortality world, very unlike the one we have lived in since the advent of modern medicine and the sessile and predictable agricultural lifestyle. Knowledge by description is not a good motivator for action, and neither is any description of a devastated future.

But Skinner leaves something to be desired. We need institutions with real power at the global level to deal with crises that require collaboration between nations. The kinds of problems of cooperation that made nation states necessary are now global, and nation states are not up to the task. Game theory comes into play. It is hard to get people to sacrifice something for future benefits many of our generation won't be around to experience. We get free-rider problems and cheaters. The connection between the state of the world and any single action by an individual is remote. Individuals are hamstrung and pacified, because meaningful change requires that everyone cooperates. Except for a few token actions that you yourself can derive direct benefit from: taking the bus to work beats sitting in endless traffic jams; there are direct personal benefits to riding a bike, provided there aren't too many cars on the road. Much of our inertia is probably derived from lack of empowerment, not knowing what we can do that would make a difference.

I am not a social scientist, so I don't know how to get the things done that we know need to be done. But the social scientists are not much help either. The fact is that we've constructed such a diffuse system, with checks and balances and counter-balances everywhere, canceling each other out, that no one knows how to bring change when we need it. No one knows how to translate knowledge into action in the face of large scale crises such as this. Our models of democracy were developed 200–100 years ago, in a time when people couldn't conceive of humans threatening global ecosystems. We are all hamstrung in this system we have created. Heroism is dead.

We know what needs to be done, we just don't know how — how to get humanity to act. We need more than business as usual to save the world. We have to get our economy, fisheries, agriculture, our transportation needs and our lifestyle choices subordinated to ecological tolerance and consideration of the other species with which we share the planet, now and in the future. But we still lack a mechanistic, operational, understanding of society: we don't know how to change the world, even when we know that we must. We only make things worse by pretending that we do. Politicians are not good at going beyond business as usual. Extreme pressure is needed from the rest of us. If we're to have a chance, we need to take a no-holds-barred look at the factors that keep us from taking action.

It is not that the world is devoid of people who have been trying to do something, hard-working people with good intentions. It is of course possible that things could have been even worse without the efforts of many people over past decades – and centuries. The point is, what are we doing that can actually help, that addresses the challenges at the appropriate level and intensity, that has a chance to be sufficient? As with all historical processes, we don't have a control to compare with. Unfortunately, it is still the case when tipping points are decisive, that too little and too late is equivalent to doing nothing. We can still act to benefit individuals, but if we want to have larger effects on populations, species, ecosystems, or even the biosphere as a whole, we should not be naïve. Certain point-improvements may be noted in governments as well, but as long as they continue to do more that contributes in negative directions than in positive directions, this can hardly be construed as success. Indeed, one is left to wonder if some efforts don't do more harm than good, by creating in some quarters an impression that something is being done and that someone is on the job, undermining the impetus for getting involved ourselves.

If we know how to solve life-threatening problems in a globalized world, then why haven't we done so a long time ago? The challenges are interwoven and interact in complex ways; coordinated action is vital and overdue.[41] The difficulty lies not in finding the solutions, but in how to get them implemented. We know much about what needs to be done, but not how to get humanity to do it. Certainly we know some things about what works and what doesn't, but this knowledge has not been compiled in an accessible form for interested parties to peruse.

Nor is it true that absolutely nothing has happened in the international arena. A couple of notable agreements, like the Montreal Protocol, which regulates substances that deplete the ozone layer, have been widely hailed as successful. A few political scientists, like economist Scott Barrett,[42] have studied why some international treaties work and others do not. National sovereignty and the lack of enforcement at international levels means treaties should be designed to be self-enforcing, otherwise nations will only sign up to treaties that are so unambitious that the signatories expect to attain the targets in any case. 'If they are to succeed, treaties must strategically manipulate the incentives states have to exploit the environment.'[43] Nations must have the necessary incentives to participate in a treaty, and signatories must have the necessary incentives to comply with its requirements. Taking lessons from game theory and the study of past treaties, Barrett stresses incentives for participation and incentives for compliance as a form of self-enforcement, the discouragement of free riders, side payments (whereby winners can compensate the losers to make it more attractive for the latter to participate, and enabling all parties to become winners), learning from experience, and gradually ratcheting up the demands on participants. As in 'Prisoner's Dilemma,' nation states would like to have a treaty because they see that the consequences of not having an agreement to cooperate may be bad all around. Compliance, reciprocity and cost-benefit analyses are central to such games. The same approach will not work on all problems, so the design of and the success of a given treaty will depend on the nature of the underlying problems, as well as the acumen of the negotiators. 'I have been amazed to discover how little many treaty negotiators know of the experiences of earlier negotiations, and of the lessons that could and should be drawn from them. It is not just the lack of a theory that explains why negotiations so often fall short of potential. Ignorance of history is also to blame.'[44] There are a number of trade-offs in the dynamics of negotiations, for instance between the stringency of requirements and the broadness of participation. 'First best outcomes are not always attainable. There are good reasons why Montreal is an exception.'[45] The major failing of the Kyoto accord and subsequent climate negotiations, as well as the biodiversity convention and others, was to ignore enforcement – precisely the wrong thing to do. They did not have self-enforcement built in from the beginning, so did not deal with participation and compliance up front, unlike Montreal.

An alternative to a broad international consensus agreement, as has been attempted in the process of climate negotiations, has been proposed by James Hansen.[46] In this alternative scenario, a smallish group of countries could form a climate pact to greatly reduce their carbon emissions internally (for instance by instituting a carbon tax at the source – e.g. the well head or the mine site, because there are relatively few such sources and policies related to them are therefore simpler to implement – and distributing the proceeds of such a tax as a dividend among the populace). Subsequently, this small in-group would levy import duties on products from countries that did not have similar taxes on emissions. This would encourage other nations to join the pact, in order to harvest such tax revenues for themselves rather than face the cost of import duties when trading with members of the pact. One of the difficulties is of course that these sorts of agreements quickly run afoul of existing international trade rules, like the WTO rules – such as they are. Many would probably agree that some of these ought to be renegotiated anyway.

Treaty negotiations are themselves social systems that may exhibit tipping points (and other vagaries of social interactions and dependencies): 'If the instrument is a strategic compliment [...] then there is likely to exist a threshold or tipping point, and provided the treaty gets countries over this threshold, participation is likely to tip.'[47] Montreal appears to have been a success[48] for a number of reasons that cannot be expected to hold in other cases. The consequences of not passing an agreement was directly linked to increased illness and death from cancer, an illness with particularly high, and directly measurable, social and monetary costs. The costs related to taking action were tiny compared to the estimated benefits. In fact, for the United States (and other rich countries), the benefit of acceding to the Montreal Protocol exceeded the costs by a wide margin, irrespective of the behavior of other countries.[49] Consequently, it also made monetary sense for rich countries to offer payments to poorer countries to participate in the agreement. A technical solution existed[50] and a number of the large producers of CFCs (like the Du Pont corporation) were poised to make good money on the production of substitutes, and improvements were continually and rapidly being made in both the production of substitutes and in driving down costs. The changes made sense in economic terms for some of the largest producers, like the US. Perhaps the Montreal negotiations were helped also by the fact that they occurred at a time when our societies were less impacted by neoliberalist *laissez faire* ideology and had more respect for science.

Barrett also identifies The North Pacific Fur Seal Treaty of 1911 as a positive example of a treaty which worked for a while, until it didn't... But this was a pact with a very limited number of players, and it managed what could be treated as a common property resource – which is easier to handle – rather than a global public good, such as the global climate and the atmosphere's ability to absorb and recycle excess gases from human activity. Barrett seeks not only a history of international negotiations, but a theory for understanding how and why they fail, improving our ability to deal with collective action problems.

Although following the glacial pace of the International Whaling Commission (the IWC), most countries eventually also stopped whaling, but perhaps not until populations of the great whales were too low to be economically important and products from whales had become largely obsolete. But while attitudes towards whales have changed for the better in most countries, it would be premature to say that the whales have been saved. Even while we are failing to take decisive action on global warming, we are letting climate change overshadow other problems, like the biodiversity crisis, which is at least as important and has been recognized longer.

Negotiators should learn from past experiences, but understanding pertinent mechanisms is crucial since solutions have to be fine-tuned to the particulars of each case. Biodiversity, for instance, is a difficult challenge because threats include factors like habitat destruction and fragmentation and invasive species, the abatement of which it is difficult to make money off of, and many of the costs of which are not priced in our current economic system. Nor are consequences always easily linked to particular actions, due to a number of mechanisms like the 'death by a thousand cuts' effect. When Rachel Carson wrote *Silent Spring* in the early '60s, the emphasis was on environmental pollutants. There has been some progress with regard to the release of toxins in our immediate surroundings, but cleaning up some effluents before we dump them in fjords and rivers, scrubbing chimney plumes, or getting CFCs out of spray cans, is seemingly much more doable than allowing other species space to roam, freedom from persecution, or a predictable climate.

Any witness to the ongoing debacle of trying to strike an effective international climate deal (or not, as the case may be) would conclude that this process is chaotic and ludicrously flawed. There seems to be little rhyme or reason at this level. Instead of a mash-up of a multitude of rather haphazard proceedings in a fairly diffuse and arbitrary landscape, it would have been nice to see a more sanely structured process with more consciously and rationally made decisions. It's a wonder to me that anything works at all in our society. I suspect the things that do, only do so because they have grown organically from something rudimentary and evolved slowly over time, and the arrangements that simply crashed and burned are no longer with us. Though some systems may take longer than others before they crash.

> *'Sometimes doing your best is not good enough. Sometimes, you must do what is required.'*
> — Winston Churchill

The political world today is made up of so many nation states, and some federations, with different structures, different challenges, different levels of human capital, and different foci, many of them deeply dysfunctional. Within 'democratic' systems we observe a range of dysfunctionality, fairness and representation, as well as great variation in the level of public participation and awareness. They differ in the role of money and private influence in politics, in the balance between bureaucratic autonomy and professionalism, and in the extent to which the task of challenging executive action and administrative practice is left to the courts. Some are plagued by polarization, and may find that actions that would obviously serve the public good are politically impossible. Different institutions often have contradictory mandates, and find themselves at cross purposes both between different departments internally and with other agencies externally. Bureaucracies need a workable balance between technocratic competence and democratic oversight. So many of our 'leaders' are buffoons. One wonders about the kinds of people who go into politics, their suitability and preparedness for the job. Nations manage to allocate vast resources to 'national security' issues and finance, but virtually none when it comes to more important issues, like those that aren't just about humans. Lobbying and influence for sale hamstring the democratic process. Business interests, like fisheries, agriculture and forestry interests, can allocate much more effort to swaying an issue, because they have money riding on the outcome, while few others are directly involved. Other people may have concerns about what is happening in fisheries, for instance, but it is not their full-time job. Collective will may be hindered by misdirection, or by excessive fragmentation, or lack of focus. We have perverse subsidies, clientelism, pork barrels, and revolving doors. Readers interested in some of the political decline causing issue like these may, for instance, want to read Francis Fukuyama's *Political Order And Political Decay*.[51]

And it is not just in governance. Getting the right people for a given job is always challenging, but you would think we would be able to do better. People tend to hire people like themselves. Administrators hire more administrators, usually people with a similar background as themselves, and so on. Pretty soon you may have an overweight of administrators, and a dearth of qualified professionals to do the real work. Frequently, the people making hiring decisions do not seem particularly qualified, or prepared, for the job. In words attributed to Steve Jobs: A people hire A people, B people hire Cs... We have market failures and tragedy of the commons effects: any time an actor does not pay the full cost of his actions, but manages to pass some of that cost on to others, so that benefits accrue to the individual in question but costs are spread among the many, irrational outcomes ensue. This happens in politics, in matters that are supposed to be under democratic control.[52] It happens when special interests interfere in politics and produce outcomes that are not in the greater interest. It happens in particular because only humans participate in these processes, and what is good for other species only enters into the equation indirectly, if they have a group of humans to represent their interests and fight for their cause. When a single issue is much more important than any other, political deadlock, balkanization, and incoherence is not to be taken lightly. One could hope that all the noise and dysfunctionality in the system canceled each other out and led to good outcomes in spite of everything, or that trial and error may still get us there in time, but that seems a cavalier attitude to take, and at odds with actual developments.

Our evolutionary history has ill equipped us to (intuitively) grasp dynamic systems theory, probability theory, and statistics. We are notoriously bad at prognostication and prediction. Few sciences have taken the leap to becoming predictive, and the ones that are closest to advancing to that stage people have a singular ability to ignore. People live in a political world, not a scientific world. As a society we neglect to use the knowledge that we already have. Few of those that have training in communication also have scientific training. To a first approximation, *no* politician has training in natural sciences. On the other hand, since we all have a greater or lesser degree of influence, we are all politicians. In a globalized world, everything is politics.

Knowledge and understanding is of course key to effectively running a society. In our current democratic system the ultimate power and responsibility rests, nominally, with the general populace, those who vote or have the right to vote. You can claim that this ignores existing power structures, and mechanisms that make democratic control difficult, but in a 'democracy' these too are the responsibility of the people. If such factors are pivotal, that just means that our 'democracy' is weak, or perhaps even non-existent. It appears that issues colored by probability estimation, statistics, or even simple mathematics, present particular challenges to the general public and their ability to govern responsibly. Of course, the people select politicians to represent them, and in turn run the systems that deal with such matters, but a certain understanding is clearly needed in order to select good representatives, even as a crowd. In a sense you can't have it both ways. You cannot say on the one hand, that the general public can be trusted with important decisions, and on the other hand, that the general voting public can be easily duped by the machinations of the mainstream media, corporations, or by underhanded politicians.

*

Nassim Nicholas Taleb has popularized the notion of the Black Swan, *Cygnus atratus* – a bird that was not known to the Western world until their exploration of Oceania, more particularly the Australasian ecozone – as epitomizing the unanticipated, the unknown unknown, events beyond our experience, expectation, and ability to imagine or predict.[53] Reference to black swans as an extremely unlikely phenomenon appears to go back at least to the Roman poet Juvenal (first or second century AD), with the expression 'a good person is as rare as a black swan'[54] (the same expression seems to have been used about the likelihood of finding 'a perfect wife'). Until black swans were shown to exist at all, they were a phenomenon outside all past experience, representative of something that could hardly be imagined to occur before it does. Taleb links the occurrence of what we think are rare or unlikely, even 'impossible,' events, with large impacts, to the poor performance of people, even so-called experts, in playing the stock markets, predicting political events, or generally estimating likelihoods and distributions. Stock markets are notorious for our inability to pick winners and our difficulty with timing, and they are subject to unforeseen events with disproportionate effects, despite having spawned a vast and lucrative industry of analysts. According to Taleb, just ten days in the market accounted for half the return over the past 50 years.[55] A widespread tendency to overlook linkages (that is, statistical dependence) between events, which in turn means that exceptional events are not as uncommon as we tend to think, has a large impact on our ability to predict, or estimate the likelihood of occurrences, and in turn even to think in an informed way.

Physical phenomena (height, weight, etc. of some being) are commonly expected to follow a Normal (or Gaussian, or 'bell-shaped') statistical distribution.[56] Indeed the central limit theorem posits that a phenomenon derived as an arithmetic mean ('average') of a sufficiently large series of independent events will tend to be normally distributed. However, there is a widespread tendency for people, in many different walks of life, to overlook the actual dependence of discrete events, notably in social systems, which in turn leads to distributions very different from the Normal. Taleb includes those involved in the stock markets prior to the financial crisis of 2008 and the banking crisis of the 1980s, where large American banks lost nearly all the money they had earned (cumulatively) in all previous history combined.[57] Such exceptional events are not visible in past samples, and sometimes our most egregious errors are due to extrapolation from inadequate samples. 'His claim is that almost all consequential events in history come from the unexpected – yet humans later convince themselves that these events are explainable in hindsight.'[58] This is a known cognitive bias, the narrative fallacy in history, and professional historians are as susceptible as anyone to spinning seemingly plausible narratives after the fact. We convince ourselves that we 'understand' historical events once we have a story that seems to make sense. We extrapolate from past experience, even severely circumscribed ones, and thus our ability to imagine future events are equally limited. 'No one' could predict the occurrence or the consequence of events like World War I, those of September 11 2001, the dissolution of the Soviet Union, or the rise of Google (or the internet itself). Accidents of history, particularly the occurrence of events from the long tail, those with disproportionate and disruptive effect, limit our ability to predict. The narrative fallacy may cause us to learn the wrong lessons from history.

In social systems, where events are commonly not independent, we get distributions very different from the Normal. Random events, or happenstance, have cumulative effects. Winners keep winning, and minute, arbitrary effects early on can have huge effects over the long term. Cross a threshold and authors, actors, sports stars, etc. will just get more and more and more attention, to the point where the nature of their measured success is quite beyond anything seen among the rest of the sample population. These are systems where a single observation (person, fortune, fame, professional career) can throw off the entire distribution, and may give very different properties. This extends to the realm of the super-rich and the super-successful, where for instance, one Bill Gates or one J. K. Rowling can experience success on a whole other order of magnitude and dwarf the performances of all others, in some instances of all others *combined* (for instance in a sample of the net worth of one thousand people, or the book sales of a thousand randomly selected authors). Certain professions and certain cultural phenomena are like this, where it does not involve any more effort on the part of a successful player to attract one more reader, software user, or sports aficionado. Social cohesion, and other forms of statistical dependence, lead to phenomena with statistical distributions having very long, or 'fat' tails, which means that supposedly 'rare' or 'improbable' events will occur much more frequently than we would think, if we were inclined to expect a Normal distribution. Our ability to estimate, say, the average wealth in a sample of a thousand, or ten thousand, randomly selected people, depends entirely on the presence or absence of a Bill Gates. Nothing like this occurs were the task, say, to estimate the average height or weight in a sample of a thousand humans. Taleb links such oversights to events in financial markets, with ensuing financial crises, broken bubbles, the Long Term Capital Management (LTCM) debacle, and so on, where it becomes quite impossible to predict, and, consequently, to plan. The unexpected happens more often than we expect and carries disproportionate weight when it does.

Without the ability to forecast, our ability to plan is limited. Epistemic arrogance makes us predict and plan even in systems vulnerable to black swan effects, without due consideration of our ability to do so. Because extreme events do happen, and have extreme consequences when they do, even when they were previously widely held to be impossible or extraordinarily unlikely, our ability to plan for them is very limited. This is likely to have consequences for society's ability to plan and carry out political interventions as well, even – or perhaps *especially* – the very important ones. Taleb notes a history of extreme budget and planning overruns, such as costs and completions dates of such public projects as the Sydney Opera House. Once a project has become delayed, further delays tend to accumulate, and estimates of completion times and final budgets will be increasingly off if we don't account for this effect. Underestimating how long something takes is common. Most of us can nod appreciatively when confronted with our own inadequacies on this score. What is less appreciated is how vast the overruns can get once they get started. One of our greatest failings when dealing with such processes is false confidence. Often this is due to reliance on models with hugely inapplicable assumptions, and it is worst when we don't even recognize that that is what we are doing. If processes are subject to a high degree of randomness (or determinism in a dynamic system so complex it is indistinguishable from true randomness) and social contagion, we cannot know in advance which efforts will succeed.

Indeed, it may be impossible to plan for saving the world. If so, we should have that knowledge, because it will be critical to how we approach the task. Knowledge is still power. We just need better knowledge, including knowledge of our limitations and biases. We could incorporate the existence of black swan events and our inability to plan, and merely try to make the most of opportunities as they arise. One approach could be to rely on opportunity and luck, or a diffuse/unguided approach, as a study of political processes, nationally and internationally, might suggest is what our ruling classes are indeed hitching their hopes on. One could take advantage of some tricks, such as attempting to limit errors rather than trying to predict. The precautionary principle ought to include aiming for robustness to extreme deviations, as well as limiting the consequences of our errors.

Perhaps history does not move in orderly or gradual ways, but makes sudden and unpredictable leaps, like punctuated equilibrium in evolutionary theory: long periods of stasis punctuated by seemingly sudden and unpredictable, or at least *unpredicted*, spurts. In evolutionary biology, the Red Queen hypothesis, named for the Red Queen in Alice in Wonderland,[59] famous for her saying 'You have to run faster than that to stay in the same place,' and moving so fast that it was all Alice could do to keep up with her (yet they did not appear to be moving relative to their surroundings), relates to the kind of rapid change you need when interacting with a diversity of populations and other species that are all changing in response to each other and changing environmental factors. Social systems are also characterized by a multitude of interactions like this, a web of interactions in all directions and components responding to changes all over the place, and bi-directional feedbacks. With regard to future events, such as consequences of our environmental impacts, we should try to hedge against that *other* anthropocentric effect: because we are still here, it may be likely that past historical, and prehistorical, perturbations may have been relatively mild, and that more severe outcomes might be relegated to the future. History should not be a pacifier.

All this is not to say that nothing, or no one, has ever succeeded in the history of the world. Rather, when something does succeed we tend to overlook the role played by pure, dumb luck. And we often do not see all those efforts that did not succeed. Contrariwise, if someone has taken preventive measures a success would usually not be observed either. You can't really plan for success. But you may have to try anyway... If so, at least one ought to practice adaptive management, not stick to rigid plans, but readjust as one goes along based on experiences with what has been tried, and proceed with constant monitoring and re-evaluation.

History has given us a few lessons concerning the difficulties of central planning. The great philosopher of science, Karl Popper, was also critical of our ability to predict and plan for the future. In his *The Poverty of Historicism* he emphasizes 'the human factor' in social events, our inability to completely understand the human factor, and the dependence of the future upon scientific knowledge and innovation, which by their very nature are unknowable in advance.[60] In this sense also, large changes are unpredictable. Popper argued that if we try to make major changes, like revolutions, some things will not always work as people expect them to do, and this will backfire on us and jeopardize all our efforts. Hence, he felt that the best we can do is make small, gradual changes. Popper was perhaps constitutionally disinclined towards major revolutions, and advocated piecemeal social engineering rather than Utopian social engineering, which he denigrated: 'The piecemeal engineer will, accordingly, adopt the method of searching for, and fighting against, the greatest and most urgent evils of society, rather than searching for, and fighting for, its greatest ultimate good.'[61] Piecemeal social engineering is akin to adaptive management. Hegel also did work on this: every intervention is a leap into the unknown, where the result always thwarts expectations.[62] Perhaps politicians and bureaucrats have internalized the notion that major change is difficult to get right, risky and even dangerous to them, and that is why we never see any dramatic changes in how things are done. Certainly not *planned* dramatic changes. And perhaps that is why politics seems to be completely stalled, both domestically and internationally.

In social systems, luck, and contagion, play an important part. It is important to get lucky. One can endeavor to exploit this inherent unpredictability by being exposed to unplanned rare or unlikely events that can be taken advantage of (while playing it safe with what we cannot afford to lose – limiting our exposure to that rare event with consequences on a different scale entirely from what we are used to). One can endeavor to be as well prepared and as well placed as possible to take advantage of serendipity when it occurs.

But perhaps for the concerned citizen this seems a mind-bogglingly inadequate, even irresponsibly passive, approach to dealing with world-threatening events. Of course, if we are to proceed with a string of smallish sociological experiments, and gain experimentally based social sciences along the way, as Popper advocates, then we have even less time.

Or has the world become so complex that we cannot plan any real interventions? If it is true that we cannot plan things, then we should acknowledge that limitation and try to find ways to move around it.

Thomas Homer-Dixon has explored the notion that our world has become too complex for us to control in his book, *The Ingenuity Gap*.

> Most of us occasionally suspect that the world we've created is too complex and too fast-paced for us to understand, let alone control. Most of us sometimes guess that even the 'experts' don't really know what's going on, and that as individuals and as a species we've unleashed forces that we cannot manage. [...] The complexity, unpredictability, and pace of events in our world, and the severity of global environmental stress, are soaring.[63]

We may have ever better tools at our disposal, but a concomitant increase in complexity leads inexorably to an arms race: the race between the complexity of our situation and our ability to cope with it. As speed and complexity of the human world continues to escalate, even if we were not completely overwhelmed at the moment, we soon will be as complexity begets ever more complexity, the world spins faster and faster, and more decisions, requiring a higher level of sophistication, need to be made at an ever quickening pace. This is the ingenuity gap: the gap between the growing complexity of the systems we are part of, and the ingenuity required to wield the total set of tools at our disposal in order to solve emergent problems. Those who need to make decisions suffer from information squeeze, as well as time squeeze, and our cleverness and understanding would eventually be limiting factors even if they weren't already. For a while we may see a widening gap also between societies, communities — even individuals — that manage to keep pace and those that do not. As a shortfall of sophistication needed to tackle new challenges threatens the social fabric of many less resourceful countries, some may descend into downward spirals. But in the end we are all in the same boat.

> Human beings have been smart enough to turn nature to their ends, generate vast wealth for themselves, and double their average life span. But are they smart enough to solve the problems of the 21st century?

This is perhaps particularly tricky as the big problems of the twenty-first century stem from humanity's great successes, namely turning nature to its own ends, generating vast wealth for itself, and doubling average life spans. Changes in population, technologies, and our way of life have interacted to create a qualitatively new world which we are now struggling to keep up with. And once again, the past is not a good guide to the future.

> The West certainly has every reason to be proud of its successes; its capitalism, science, liberal democracy and marvelous institutions that have made extraordinary contributions to human prosperity and freedom. And certainly Western societies, and again the United States in particular, have seen a remarkable string of economic and political achievements in recent years. But Western triumphalism is partly based on a selective reading of the evidence. Problems and issues that don't fit into this optimistic worldview tend to be downplayed or ignored. Moreover, a significant part of the West's current success is the result of a confluence of events and processes that its elites neither control nor really understand. Western triumphalism is dangerously self-indulgent, and even delusional; it assumes agency where there may be mainly good luck.

There is nothing very new about this insight. In his 1978 book, *The Arrogance of Humanism*, David Ehrenfeld writes:

> Also among the mechanisms that make a mockery of progress is *inertia*. The humanists often speak of overcoming inertia, not realizing that inertia increases in proportion to the complexity of our invented institutions. The more specialized, compartmented, and intricate we make our society, the more difficult it is to make any fundamental or sweeping changes of a humanist sort. Even changes about which there is little disagreement among thoughtful people – such as the need to stop subsidizing truck and air transportation at the expense of railroads – have become impossible to implement. Too much of 'the system' would have to be uprooted, too many errors of planning and failures of control would have to be exposed. Thus even if all the humanist managerial decisions were as simple as the transportation choice appears to be, the humanists would still be prisoners within their own structure. And most of the decisions are infinitely more problematic.[64]

As our 'leaders' are rarely the best among us, it is not to be supposed that they are any more on top of things than most of us. As Raymond Dasmann entitled a chapter in his 1975 book, 'Nobody Is at the Wheel.'[65]

But even though our lives and societies, and the challenges facing us, are ever more complex, the solutions need not be. Leaving large areas of land and habitat alone for the continued use by other species is not in itself a complex idea. Nor is the notion of not fucking up the climate. 'Thou shalt not make the oceans acid' is not a complicated edict. The only complicated aspect here, is how do we get complex human societies, and billions of people, to abide by such simple rules – or to establish such rules and social norms in the first place. Protecting vast expanses of land from human encroachment and development is a simple idea, but how to get it done is not. Perhaps especially once we have already taken too much for ourselves. If the areas ceded to other species are vast, and we err on the side of caution, we do not need to go into the complexity of deciding just how much is enough. And the traditional approach, which has been to estimate what is the absolute minimum we must leave unto others, gets very complicated indeed. In fact, ascertaining the very minimum is ultimately impossible, even in theory. On the other hand, if we decided to be generous, things would get very simple. In fisheries, for instance, determining maximum sustainable yields has eluded people for generations. Currently, 90% of the world's fisheries are thought to be overexploited or fished to capacity.[66] The richest fishery ever known, the cod fishery on the Grand Banks off the eastern coast of Canada, has been closed since 1992 and shows no sign of recovery. Such practices do not leave much room to grow. Yet if we had not been so set on pushing the envelope to the maximum, and had sought to use less harmful fishing techniques, the issues would have been really quite simple. Nature is a complex system, with complicated feedback-mechanisms and hidden trigger points. Fortunately we don't need to run it ourselves — we just have to stop pushing it. Provided we stop in time. If we don't, we will have to try to run some kind of mockup version of it. And we will fail.

One of the reasons improvements in technological efficiency does not always lead to better environmental outcomes is known as Jevons' paradox: increases in the efficiency of resource use tend to lead to higher resource consumption. When fuel efficiency in automobiles improves, people respond by driving further, because driving is now cheaper. If roads get bigger, to relieve congestion, more people drive more and further, until the roads are as clogged as they were before the expansion. On the global scale, efficiency gains are eaten up by the continued expansion of the economy.[67] This, although unrelated, reminds me of a finding in Britain, where all the UK's efforts to reduce carbon emissions were wiped out by an increase in soil bacteria activity, breaking down soil carbon at a higher rate, due to the warming that had already occurred.

Something similar happens with technology and our domestic appliances. As communication tools proliferate we are expected to communicate with more people in more ways.

Thus the technologies that save us time and labor individually — that empower each of us — bind us collectively into a frenetic, mad race in which we often feel more caged by obligations and demands than before. The tools of our liberation often seem to imprison us. Harvard economist Juliet Schor, author of *The Overworked American*, makes a similar point. 'Technology,' she says, 'reduces the amount of time it takes to do any one task, but it also leads to the expansion of tasks that people are *expected* to do. This is what happened to American housewives over the twentieth century as they got new appliances. They didn't actually do less work — they did more things. It is what happens to people when they get computers and faxes and cellular phones and all the new technologies and all of the new technologies that are coming out today.'[68]

Politicians, planners, and bureaucrats frequently forget that when changes are instituted, people *respond* to the new conditions in ways that may undermine the intended changes and short circuit the hoped-for improvements in unanticipated ways. The history of development aid and poverty alleviation, in particular, is fraught with these kinds of lessons.

Our democracy is ill equipped to handle problems with tipping points and breaking points, issues where it may suddenly be too late, or no way back. It is hard to get a majority of voters to internalize knowledge in time. The social 'sciences' are not operationalized to the point where we know how to change the world when we need to, and we are still lousy at drafting effective international agreements. In our complex world, it is hard for nations to act unilaterally. Many of the challenges we face are global in scope and ramification, and require solutions at the global scale, but we lack strong institutions at the global level and have no democracy at that scale.[69]

Society's advances seem to have given many of us an impression that things are under control, which Thomas Homer-Dixon calls the 'delusion of control.'

> ... science's rate of advance depends on the characteristics of the natural phenomena it investigates, simply because some phenomena are intrinsically harder to understand than others, so the production of useful new knowledge in these areas can be very slow. Consequently, there is often a critical time lag between the recognition of a problem and the delivery of sufficient ingenuity, in the form of technologies, to solve that problem. Progress in the social sciences is especially slow, for reasons we don't yet fully understand; but we desperately need better social scientific knowledge to build the sophisticated institutions today's world demands.
>
> Our species' scientific and technological prowess is nevertheless extraordinary. We create miracles from raw nature, and we have revolutionized our existence in a few lifetimes. These accomplishments are to be celebrated. Unfortunately, they have also made us overconfident of our ability to solve the problems we face. Today, a disturbingly large proportion of people in rich countries seem to believe that our ingenuity is practically boundless and that our technical experts have all the authority and knowledge they need to deftly manage our ever more complex world. These beliefs and the complacency they produce are often completely unwarranted: in fact, we often have only superficial control over the complex systems we've made and critically depend on.[70]

If even experts can have difficulty keeping up, then what hope for the average voter, who has to integrate across a wide span of specialised fields, and on whom, in turn, our democratic system pins its hopes?

> In many cases, the complexity and speed of operation of today's vital economic, social, and ecological systems exceed the human brain's grasp. Very few of us have more than a rudimentary understanding of how these systems work.[71]

And this in a society that doesn't even respect knowledge... The dysfunctionality of the American political landscape at the moment should serve as a powerful indictment against the anti-rational and anti-intellectualism. And let us not kid ourselves that things are markedly better elsewhere, although the US may seem extreme. Somehow it just doesn't seem adequate to trust in the wisdom of crowds, and emergent properties of a messy process.

You get three people in a room together, and typically they can't agree on anything. And the smarter, and the better informed, they are, the greater the tendency towards discord over minutiae, unless they are specially trained to disregard the irrelevant and look for common ground. Others, in turn, will argue that the world doesn't need saving at all.

In a democracy every citizen has a duty to obtain the knowledge and understanding needed for him or her to make responsible decisions. Perhaps this is a responsibility that many could quite happily do without. Most people don't see the difference between a forest and a spruce plantation. They see trees everywhere, along the road, when they whiz past in their SUVs on their way to their second homes, or their cabins, and think it is forest they see, even though row upon row of trees planted for fiber production provide few of the qualities maintained by a living forest. They see these tree farms and believe we have heaps of 'nature.' In many places around the world this confusion is the result of deliberate acts, leaving thin strips of 'gallery forest' along roads to create the illusion of forest, a kind of Potemkin forest if you like. A mere 1–2% of the American populace are deemed 'environmentally literate,'[72] and the situation may not be much better other places; it is just that the Americans have had the wherewithal to investigate the question.

*

Our chosen monetary system has greater implications for world developments than our conscious decisions about politics and philosophy. While we allegedly live in a democracy where everyone should participate in our governance, hardly anyone is aware how our elected monetary system holds sway over our decisions, knows much at all about the monetary system, or reflects upon alternatives to this system or its ramifications. And while most of the important challenges ahead of us are discovered through the scientific process, and argued in scientific terms, concerning mechanisms and data from the world of science, most people do not really understand the scientific process or its subject matter.

Yet it is not lack of knowledge so much as our unwillingness to use the knowledge that we *do* have that is keeping us from relating to our environment in a more responsible manner. Our environmental problems and conservation issues are not caused by not knowing what needs to be done to avoid them or solve them, but by the shortage of political will to actually do so. The term political will may even not be very well applied here. There may be many good people in politics with the will to do something; with structures and strictures the way they are it may not be so much a question of the will to do something, but the *ability* to get something – anything – done.

Ecology tells us which species have low productivity and can ill afford our exploitation. But in spite of advanced models to calculate how much populations can stand, we still manage to over-exploit almost all the world's fisheries populations, almost as soon as we start 'harvesting' them. Problems like these, with tipping points and international dimensions, are related to super wicked problems,[73] and share some of the characteristics of wicked problems.[74] The existence of tipping points means that it may become too late; time may be running out to solve the problem, if it hasn't already. International dimensions means that the institutions ('central authority') to solve them are weak or non-existence, and consequently policy responses discount the future irrationally. Super wicked problems, in addition, are also characterized by those who have to solve them being the same people who cause them in the first place. Climate change (global warming, global weirding,...), biodiversity loss, ocean acidification, over-exploitation of natural resources (land, fisheries, natural recycling and regeneration capacity, etc.), and so on are all such crises where we (humans) are all part of the problem, some of us, perhaps, more — or less so — than others. Super wicked problems are not only mathematically intractable, but, more importantly, *socially* intractable. When I refer to super wicked problems in the following, these are the kinds of issues to have in mind. They are also the problems the solution to which I refer to using the shorthand of 'saving the world.'

Levin et al. seem to echo Popper on super wicked problems:

> Unlike Webster (2008) and Lazarus (2009), we argue that one-shot 'big bang' policies for super wicked problems, which require behavioral change by all relevant populations immediately, either fail to garner adequate support or, in those rare cases where such policies are adopted, are likely to produce societal 'shocks' that hamper implementation and compliance, derailing a policy no matter how well designed. Even if such a policy survives, rarely do decision makers assess how the policy might be designed to ratchet up over time to become more ambitious.[75]

Our evolutionary history has ill prepared us for estimating probabilities, intuiting probability theory or dynamic systems theory, predicting and understanding statistical phenomena. It stands to reason that we are bad at a lot of things in this new world we have created, as we evolved to cope with the challenges of an older and different world; in this sense we evolutionary products are like military theorists who are always 'fighting the last war.' Dieticians struggle with this constantly, as modern-day humans still have a hankering for salt, sugar and fat, items that could be hard to obtain in a past life, but which today are overabundant and cheap — and major contributors to mortality rates.

> *'If they can get you asking the wrong question, they don't have to worry about the answers.'*
>
> — Thomas Pynchon[76]

There is a cottage industry among psychologists, neuroscientists and experimental economists in exploring the flora of logical fallacies that humans are prone to, many of which are sadly relevant to our current predicament. The narrative fallacy: we are prone to creating narratives that fool us into thinking we understand events. Confirmation bias: we absorb facts and accept hypotheses much more readily when they conform to the beliefs and ideologies we already hold than when they do not. Humans are pattern-seeking animals, and when we find one that seems to fit we have a tendency to latch on to it as *the* explanation, as long as it aligns with our already held ideology and beliefs. Hyperbolic discounting: we discount the remote future less than the near future, which leads us to make choices that our future selves, using the same logic, would prefer that we hadn't made. Anchoring: this cognitive bias causes us to focus (anchor) on a particular piece of information, relevant or not, and allowing this to color how we deal with subsequent tasks and decisions.[77] Framing effect: drawing different conclusions from the same information, depending on how that information is presented. We are very vulnerable to the incompleteness of knowledge. There is a critical asymmetry here: we are much more aware of what we know than what we don't know. Anchoring on what we (think we) know introduces an interaction between two cognitive errors. Then there is what Nassim Taleb calls, 'Scorn of the abstract: favoring contextualized thinking over more abstract, though more relevant matters. "The death of one child is a tragedy; the death of a million is a statistic."'[78] This is somewhat reminiscent of the old adage 'Out of sight, out of mind,' which seemingly allows a lot of people to ignore environmental issues unless they are right under their noses. We have neglect of probability — the tendency to completely disregard the likelihood of particular events when making a decision under uncertainty – and normalcy bias – the refusal to plan for, or react to, a disaster which has never happened before. We suffer from an overemphasis on what we know, and subsequent failure to take into account what we don't know, particularly the unknown unknowns, made infamous by former U.S. Secretary of Defense Donald Rumsfeld.

Wishful thinking is another cognitive error we humans are susceptible to. It may lull us into thinking things will be all right, even if we don't get personally involved. It seems related to the ostrich effect. Although the notion of ostriches sticking their heads in the sand to hide from threats is clearly apocryphal, the way people manage to ignore an obvious negative threat while going about their daily lives is, sadly, super-pertinent in the case of the super-wicked problems looming over us. Thomas Aquinas called it *ignorantia affectata*, or a cultivated ignorance, and it may be akin to the compartmentalizing that most people use to allow them to go about their lives as if their everyday actions, or lack thereof, do not constitute a threat, in aggregate, to everything they hold dear.

The list of our cognitive biases is too long to go into here (interested parties should read the works of Daniel Kahneman, Amos Tversky and others).[79] Furthermore, people are unaware of the logical fallacies they are prone to.[80] We are bad at recognizing our cognitive errors, fallacies, and predilections. We rationalize. This is somewhat akin to the Dunning-Kruger effect: the incompetent are incompetent to know their own incompetence.[81] People don't know what they don't know, or even that there is something to know that they ought to know. They also do not understand the consequences of their ignorance. And the less people know the less they seem to question their own lack of knowledge or understanding. The skill-set required to determine how well you do something is strongly linked to the skill-set needed to do them well in the first place. Which is why such a huge majority believe they are better than average drivers, or whatever. Sometimes called the Lake

Wobegone effect... In a field we don't know we don't know what there is to know. Or as Charles Darwin noted in *The Descent of Man*: 'Ignorance more frequently begets confidence than does knowledge.' The self-esteem movement likely has exacerbated this effect. People who truly are good at something are not so prone to overestimating themselves, because, Dunning says, if they find something easy they assume others do too. So, in effect, they overestimate other people instead. Depressed people are also not so likely to overestimate their own abilities.

Building on some of these fallacies, George Marshall, in his book *Don't Even Think About It: Why Our Brains Are Wired To Ignore Climate Change*, asks: 'Why do victims of flooding, drought, and severe storms become *less* willing to talk about climate change or even accept that it is real?' and 'Why does having children make people less concerned about climate change?'[82] Of course, it could be the other way around: the kind of people who would have children in this day and age are more inclined to not worry about climate change, or if you *were* worried about climate change, or other pending or ongoing disasters, perhaps you would choose not to have children. Though perhaps having made the decision to have kids, people also have to make the effort to convince themselves that they are not monsters, or at fault in their own misfortune – or, rather, that of their descendants. We have arrived at the peculiar situation where people who have children should be environmentalists, and environmentalists should not have children.

Given the error of our ways, we should strive to take advantage of some of the tricks of the trades – those trades that need to respond rationally to uncertainty and the depths of our ineptitude. We should be constantly on the alert for cognitive biases and logical fallacies, and try to use them for good whenever possible and acceptable. When you cannot predict, try instead to limit error and to get in position to profit from serendipity without incurring too much risk. This is reminiscent of the precautionary principle so widely accepted and practiced in conservation and law. When applying the precautionary principle, we should perhaps be aware of that *other* anthropocentric principle: the risks (for, and from, the environment) in the future are likely much greater than what we can gauge from the past — because we are still here, we know past extremes were relatively limited.

We can postulate a number of reasons for why we are not acting to Save The World. Not enough people understand the situation. People don't know enough to understand when someone tries to explain it to them. Nobody tries to explain it to them because they see they will never understand. People don't have the background or the intellect to understand the situation, and they don't know that they don't understand. Anecdotes do not make a science. The general public has too poor an understanding of the scientific process. It is too easy to obfuscate, and thereby confuse large segments of the population, and divide humanity against itself. People are easily manipulated by false dichotomies and other logical or rhetorical breaches. People fall victim to a flora of logical fallacies such as *post hoc, ergo propter hoc* (correlation does not equal causation), tautology, hasty generalization, irrational extrapolation, oversimplification, or *ad ignorantiam* arguments, because they do not have logical, statistical or scientific training. Some even believe that God, or Jesus, will save us, or that whatever happens it is all part of a divine plan, or that what is meant to be is meant to be (which of course it is, but nothing is meant to be; this is a tautology). Many humans are subject to magical thinking (and there may be evolutionary reasons for this, including evolutionary artifacts).[83] People are too busy to gain the background needed or to try to understand. Policy makers need to prioritize growth over environment to keep our financial system from collapsing, due to the way our financial and monetary system is designed. By the time people come into a position of influence they are more beholden to stability than to the future. People need the money, as well as the economic growth, to meet their loan payments and to assure their retirement savings. Businesses will commonly not produce a new environmental technology before there is a critical demand, and the demand may not be present until after an ecological tipping point has been surpassed.

People have kids, so they have mortgages and need to keep working and saving. Much of the time most of us are just trying to do the best of a bad job. Once people have property and kids they are effectively pacified and co-opted. There is a logical progression that people gradually become more preoccupied with protecting what they have rather than building a better world, where such things could be preserved in the long term. Insidious hope: hope keeps us from taking action. The frog in hot water parable. Game theory: the tragedy of the commons, 'Prisoner's Dilemma', collective action problems, and a host of cognitive errors. We are evolutionarily attuned to urgent fight-or-flight responses rather than long-term threats and challenges. Nation states are not up to the challenges of a modern-day globalized world. People are in a state of continuous anxiety with regard to their relative situation in the social hierarchy. The 'powers that be' would never allow certain changes to be made. Our enemies are too powerful. Self-preservation mechanisms kick in: people cannot afford to let certain information sink in, or to allow certain views of the world to take hold in their minds. We cannot act alone, and we need others to act along with us. If we don't have critical mass we will not succeed, and people will not join unless they feel we have critical mass. First-mover disadvantage: it is extremely hard, personally costly, and at times even dangerous, to be among the first to take action. People aren't willing to do anything for the environment. Partially because they've lost hope of improvements on the large important issues – so why make personal sacrifices for minor causes that won't be enough? Every improvement is nullified by continued growth in population and consumption. Acting to save the world entails taking a cost up front, for an uncertain benefit some time in the future. Possibly a benefit you yourself may not get to experience. Taking up-front costs is also difficult to do in a market economy.

What we are willing to do depends on what others are willing to do. In an economy that sets us all to competing against each other, a sacrifice is much more costly if no one else is sacrificing. A globalized world makes it hard to act unilaterally. We need mechanisms to induce us to front-load costs. We need to find out what exactly are the limitations and barriers keeping us from solving these kinds of problems.

As Henrik Ibsen wrote, if you take the basic lie of his life, the 'life-lie,' his pet illusion, away from the average person, you take his joy of life as well.[84] We want to feel important, even when we're not. And useful... In his book, *Requiem For A Species: Why We Resist The Truth About Climate Change*, Clive Hamilton outlines the many forms of denial and coping strategies that keep us from collectively taking action on climate change, as well as the insidious mechanisms inherent in the politically and philosophically enshrined growth machine.

> ...the growth machine, which we thought we had built to enhance our own ends, has taken on a life of its own, and resists fiercely the slow awakening to its perils of the humans it is supposed to serve. The growth machine has, over time, created the types of people who are perfectly suited to its own perpetuation – docile, seduced by its promises and unable to think beyond the boundaries it sets. The closer some get to the levers of the machine the more they must be committed to its goals. It is hard to imagine that anyone who believes that economic growth is part of the problem would ever be allowed near those levers. More likely they would be ridiculed in the newspapers and denounced in the parliaments. Ordinary people may at times question the wisdom of relentless growth and conclude that it cannot go on forever, yet they are soon bounced out of their subversive reverie by the inducements to go shopping. The system has created the type of people who are perfectly suited to what it needs, unending expansion.
>
> In this way the growth system governs itself. We think we have power, but the growth system awards power only to those who will

advance its objective. We internalise the discourse (as Michel Foucault would say) so that we begin to articulate the interests of the system and govern ourselves to its rules. So in our consumption behaviour we conduct ourselves in ways that perpetuate the system, and in our public behaviour we are implicated in political structures that also serve the needs of the growth machine. Our political leaders tend to be those who have internalised the goals of the system most faithfully and are therefore most immune to arguments and evidence that might challenge it. The state itself, which once represented the interests of the people, even if those interests were often thwarted by the power of business, has been reshaped since the 1970s to serve the interests of the Economy.[85]

In our ostensibly secular society, economic theories and cost-benefit analyses may seem to have taken the place of religion.

> *'The ideas of economists and political philosophers, both when they are right and when they are wrong, are more powerful than is commonly understood. Indeed the world is ruled by little else. Practical men who believe themselves to be quite exempt from any intellectual influences are usually the slaves of some defunct economist.'*
>
> *— John Maynard Keynes*

Psychologists, neuroscientists and political scientists have discovered that humans also commonly suffer from *motivated reasoning*.[86] Emotions are more primal than reasoning, so people shy away from facts they don't like. Facts and novel points of view can threaten people's sense of self, their in-group loyalties, their very identities. Feelings trump reason, and it is very hard for people to revise their opinions based on contradictory evidence.

> Reasoning is actually suffused with emotion (or what researchers often call 'affect'). Not only are the two inseparable, but our positive or negative feelings about people, things, and ideas arise much more

rapidly than our conscious thoughts, in a matter of milliseconds — fast enough to detect with an EEG device, but long before we're aware of it. That shouldn't be surprising: Evolution required us to react very quickly to stimuli in our environment. It's a 'basic human survival skill,' explains political scientist Arthur Lupia of the University of Michigan. We push threatening information away; we pull friendly information close. We apply fight-or-flight reflexes not only to predators, but to data itself.

We're not driven only by emotions, of course — we also reason, deliberate. But reasoning comes later, works slower — and even then, it doesn't take place in an emotional vacuum. Rather, our quick-fire emotions can set us on a course of thinking that's highly biased, especially on topics we care a great deal about.[87]

This goes a long way towards explaining why zealots don't believe science, at least not science that threatens their identity. Ideology cements viewpoints. Who you trust depends on your ideology. Humans cherry-pick facts that fit their preconceived notions and deeply held beliefs. Or as Upton Sinclair noted already in 1935: 'It is difficult to get a man to understand something, when his salary depends upon his not understanding it!'[88]

Information that counters people's strongly held beliefs tends to cement those beliefs rather than lead to a re-evaluation and a change of heart. Thus, information can actually have the opposite effect of what the disseminator intended. If your political viewpoints or emotions have you too invested in a particular issue, or the stance of your particular in-group, you will struggle mightily against ugly facts that challenge these notions. Information that threatens a person's firmly held beliefs not only gets rejected, it further cements those beliefs that are contradicted by it. People commonly cling to their ideology even more strongly when it is contradicted by science or other facts that they don't like.[89]

And that undercuts the standard notion that the way to persuade people is via evidence and argument. In fact, head-on attempts to persuade can sometimes trigger a backfire effect, where people not only fail to change their minds when confronted with the facts – they may hold their wrong views more tenaciously than ever.[90]

Our minds create these kinds of mental shortcuts, because in some circumstances the ability to make quick, intuitive decisions on the fly is adaptive. But in a different set of circumstances, such as a world very different from the one in which we evolved, it can be disastrous. Simple rules of thumb and automatic behaviors can stand us in good stead in a fight-or-flight situation, yet backfire when long-term survival – for ourselves, our offspring, the species, or the ecosystem – is at stake. Smart people may also be seriously misinformed or lack comprehension of a particular, but, moreover, they may be better than most people at constructing arguments to confirm their most cherished notions. Or as Michael Shermer puts it, smart people believe weird things because they are skilled at defending beliefs they arrived at for non-smart reasons.[91] (Though perhaps that is not so smart...) Motivated reasoning may be a defense strategy against cognitive dissonance, related to the ostrich effect, confirmation bias and disconfirmation bias. Another way of illustrating this doctrinaire resistance to changing one's ingrained belief system, even among trained scientists, was expressed by Max Planck in 1936: 'An important scientific innovation rarely makes its way by gradually winning over and converting its opponents: it rarely happens that Saul becomes Paul. What does happen is that its opponents gradually die out and that the growing generation is familiarized with the idea from the beginning.'[92] Thinking is hard work for some people, and they apparently go to extreme lengths to avoid it. There is now a rich body of work identifying such biases and cognitive mechanisms that make people respond in weird ways to information. Coupled with well-funded disinformation campaigns and the political and financial might of opposing forces, the existence of cognitive mechanisms like these go a fair way towards explaining why the dissemination of evidence has not gotten us further towards meaningful outcomes.

For decades, activists, scholars, and NGOs have made the mistake of assuming that once the facts were known and people and politicians truly *understood*, they would take action. But, as we have seen, there are numerous mechanisms that make it so that things don't happen even when the facts are available and widely understood. Furthermore, if you take it upon yourself to enlighten others, all your opponents have to do is pretend that they still aren't enlightened.

> 'We now face the prospect of a kind of global civil war between those who refuse to consider the consequences of civilization's relentless advance and those who refuse to be silent partners in the destruction. More and more people of conscience are joining the effort to resist, but the time has come to make this struggle the central organizing principle of world civilizations.'
>
> — Al Gore[93]

Our technology, worldview, our morals and ethics, our common knowledge, our ability to act, individually and collectively, our power structures, they have all played a part in shaping the world we live in. Of course there are also powerful forces aligned against us, and much has been written about this recently.[94] We must understand the power structures if we are to wrest from them the rights we want. Reform is never given voluntarily from those who reap the benefits of power and privilege.

We need some hope lest we turn despondent. We need to be able to entertain some hope of success if we are to stay motivated for a long, difficult struggle, and that in turn demands that we can muster a critical mass to bring meaningful change. Acting unilaterally is hard, even if the single lateral is an entire nation. The best of us can be hamstrung by isolation. Or hopelessness.

But hope may also be pacifying. Hope keeps us from taking action. Hope can keep prisoners in a death camp from rising up against captors that they vastly outnumber. What circumstances made the difference between those involved in the Warsaw Ghetto Uprising and those that did not rise up in a similar or related situation? I expect it was largely the happenstance of opportunity, who you are with and their skill-sets, or simply desperation. The hope of individual survival if one just keeps one's head down can interact with the fear of dying if one leads a charge, so no one leads a charge. Such hopes and fears interact with our inability to predict outcomes, and we can easily lull ourselves into believing that things will be less severe for us than what a dispassionate and rational observer would conclude. Some held up as paragons of courage might protest such a designation. Courage, they say, is just doing what has to be done; there is no other choice.

Hope is a dual edged sword. Hope is what keeps us from fighting to the death until we have nothing more to lose. At the same time, in the drudgery of everyday tasks it is hard to engage to the max unless we can sustain some hope that our efforts may be crowned with success. Hope leads people to believe weird things. 'Our critical faculties break down under the onslaught of promises and hopes offered to assuage life's great anxieties.'[95]

Derrick Jensen points out that we 'hope' in matters where we have given up agency and given ourselves over to fate, or whomever will have their way with us, as when we get on a plane and hope it does not crash. 'Hope is a longing for a future condition over which you have no agency; it means you are essentially powerless':

> When we realize the degree of agency we actually do have, we no longer have to 'hope' at all. We simply do the work. We make sure salmon survive. We make sure prairie dogs survive. We make sure grizzlies survive. We do whatever it takes.[96]

'Hope is what keeps us chained to the system, the conglomerate of people and ideas and ideals that is causing the destruction of the Earth.' The boundaries between hope, wishful thinking, and the ostrich effect are unclear.

On the flip side, it has been argued that fear is a poor motivator for action, and that 'environmentalists' have made a major tactical error by playing on people's fears for the future.[97] Psychologic threat (fear) has been shown to trigger more focus on extrinsic goals and values (financial success, personal appearance, and social standing) at the expense of intrinsic goals/values,[98] such as kindness, affiliation, community feeling, independent thought and action — the exact opposite of the focus that might lead to taking better care of the natural world. Fear is a limbic system response intricately linked to fight-or-flight reflexes, intense focus on self and one's own immediate survival, and behaviors such as running and hiding, or freezing, in response to outside threats. Other studies have shown that appeals to fear are most likely to change people's behavior if a) they are aware of clear steps they can take to protect themselves, and b) if these steps are conveniently available[99] — not traits we associate with super-wicked problems. Threats that people feel are uncontrollable or unavoidable are more likely to lead to the closely related response anxiety, a state that rarely promotes good outcomes. People need to know what they can do differently. One needs to know what one can do before one can act. And if people don't see what they can do, they try not to think about it, they engage in displacement activities, or they tell themselves that the issue is not really important.

Clearly fear can get us off our asses in extreme situations — but if you take your clues from horror movies, it can also lead to some very irrational behaviors (highly annoying ones, too, when you observe it in others). Fear will likely only motivate us when it is acute. Fear of something further away is more likely to make us risk averse and make us cling to the familiar, or even turn away from the information that might otherwise have instilled fear. In an uncertain world, we seek reassurance in familiarity and hope, and consistency by getting our established worldview reaffirmed. Yet while pundits grouse about fearmongering, most of us are still not as worried as we should be.

> 'A thing is right when it tends to preserve the integrity, stability, and beauty of the biotic community. It is wrong when it tends otherwise.'
> — Aldo Leopold[99a]

It is logically inconsistent to be willing to fight to defeat Hitler, but not for a livable planet. Or a planet worth living on...

What would Gandhi do to solve today's environmental problems? We need creativity and political savvy, and Gandhi had both in spades. He would probably set a good example. But the power of the good example is limited, and today's challenges require that everyone makes an effort and that we collaborate at national and international levels. We need systems that make everyone behave responsibly, not just a few idealists. Shifting the onus onto individual action, without also setting up structures to enable it, is to set us all up for failure. Even Gandhi would probably fail because it is hard to rouse people to action around anything but their immediate personal interests, and it is hard to get people to risk life and freedom before they are absolutely desperate. The ecology is such that by the time we humans are desperate it is probably too late. Besides, every campaign needs an easily identified enemy; it is much harder to act when we are all part of the problem. Too many of us are invested in the status quo. We can't even regulate the banks, why would we be able to regulate our collective behavior, globally, and save the world? In any case, we are hamstrung and don't know what we can do in a system dominated by a passive majority.

Many of my friends in the 'conservation business' say right out, at least in private or in unguarded moments, that we are not doing what is required, that we are losing the war, but that they keep doing what they are doing in the hope that if they can slow down the slide towards complete biodiversity meltdown just a tiny bit, then perhaps there will be enough left to build a recovery on. Even if such a recovery would take millennia, or even millions of years.

Unfortunately, in a system with tipping points, there is no benefit in delaying the inevitable. If you don't attain a complete success, the end result is the same whether you work hard or not. It is a little bit like driving off a cliff. Even if you manage to slow down a little before going over the cliff, you are still going over the cliff, and when the cliff is a high one it matters not at all how fast you were going at the time. For those who dare to think about it, this is an important reason why it is hard to keep your motivation up if you just keep plodding along, doing what little you can do, hoping for the best, and why it is so critical to take a hard and honest look at whether what we are doing, as a society, is sufficient.

Much of what is being done seems to be just placating people, justifying the status quo, giving perhaps an impression that someone is on the job, and that we don't really need to get involved ourselves. Someone is on it. Except that no one really is. Lots of people are putting on a brave face, but it is nowhere near adequate, and our concerted efforts need to be taken to a whole other level. From people in the NGO sector you can't even get an honest answer about how we are doing, because they have to put a positive spin on their own ability to bring real solutions in order to maintain their funding. I've even known people in the social sciences too sanguine about what has been achieved, because if they don't really have good answers for us at this point, then someone might start asking what they have been doing with the money they received in the past. It is a sad day when many of the players ostensibly trying to save the world cannot even be forthright about how well we are addressing these issues, because of their need to please and attract donors or funding agencies.

Somewhere along the line many big NGOs (BINGOs) shifted towards working in collaboration with the corporate sector, and allowing this to color their approach on a number of issues. Corporate relations became a big part of the job. In other cases, the NGO sector's funding depends on the very government that their watchdog function mandates them to monitor. Around the world, good people run around like hamsters on a treadmill, checking the boxes required by the terms of their paychecks, their job description, and their deliverables for the year, unable to stop and think of what is really needed, or to respond should any promising new initiative come along. Another hazard of organizational life can be that sometimes the organization's own long-term survival and fundraising ability is accorded too much weight in strategic and tactical decisions. Given the choice between going through the motions, continuing play-acting at doing a job, or becoming unemployed, most will choose the former. Some people make good money going through the motions and keeping their head down and their mouth shut, not asking any tough questions of themselves or others. Good people spend their lives fundraising while Rome burns. Or perhaps it is the Alexandria Library that's burning. Really it is much bigger than all that. Oftentimes, in our hectic reality, people simply don't have time to do a good job. The rapidly changing pace of life means that everybody is busy playing catch-up, leaving no time to even think about saving the world.

Part of the problem is what I like to call 'Nobody remembers what the place used to be like.' Mammoth trees, deep woods, vast shoals of fish, flocks of birds to darken the skies or blanket a lake... Nobody alive today really remembers these magnificent manifestations of the past (though by excavating what historical information has survived we may attain at least a modicum of 'knowledge by description' – it is largely too late for 'knowledge by acquaintance'). In fisheries science the phenomenon is known as a 'shifting baseline.'[100] Succeeding generations of fisheries scientists adopt frames of reference that cover only what they themselves have seen during the course of their careers. Their personal basis for comparison becomes the new normal. People are almost infinitely adaptable; we get used to *anything,* and then we think this is the way things are supposed to be; we don't miss what we do not know. We are born into a world that is already a faint shadow of its former glory, perhaps unrecognizably so — what we are used to from our growing up becomes our standard for how we want things to be. We don't even realize what we have lost, or know what it is, deep inside, that we are longing for. When the land and the sea and the air are so impoverished that we have few or no happy memories of nature, and visiting it gives hardly a glimmer of what it used to be, a vague and unsatisfying experience, then we have nothing left but to shop, consume, watch movies or television, and, if we are lucky enough, to seek out the company of a few friends whom we enjoy. Or we pour out all our love towards our pets: they being the nearest we come to nature and as close as we can get to an experience of wildness, to something real. Our ability to live in the present, in both time and space, is eroded by not having a place where we belong.

Edward Abbey wrote that our suicidal poets (Plath, Berryman, Lowell, Jarell, etc.) did not go outside enough and that the indoor life is the second best thing to a premature death. But what do we do when the outdoors is no longer worth going outside for? Without a connection to nature, it may be hard for coming generations to feel empathy with or love for the species impacted by our way of life. Perhaps the shame and the guilt would be overwhelming if we allowed ourselves to think about it. We have been torn away from nature, and perhaps the trauma is something humanity has had to live with ever since the first humans started tilling the land and had to settle in one place, which they subsequently were obliged to defend with violence and then ended up degrading.

We are easily bought. By material things and conveniences. Collectively, we sacrifice the earth for a few pieces of silver and some trinkets. People get older, they make more money. They have families and get dependent upon a steady income; their families depend on it. They get over-comfortable, staid. Insularized to where they don't feel the truth so viscerally. With mortgages, children and future pensions to worry about, perhaps they can no longer afford to see the truth. We forget, or suppress, what is really worth caring about. Few of us can remember more than about 30 years back in time. Without this memory we lack a sound basis for comparison, and we see relatively slight changes over this time horizon.

In part, we are paying the price already. We live without the majestic natural phenomena. Many options are already lost to us. Nature is but a shadow of its former wealth, and we have forgotten how to live in it. It is difficult to find nature rich enough to withstand our exploitation. Most of us in the Western world have even forgotten how to grow the food that we need. We have lost the closeness to other species, and to the diversity of nature. We have isolated ourselves in a bubble which is all we know.

> *'If you don't change direction, you end up where you are headed.'*
> — John H. Gibbons[101]

We live in the era of the old Chinese curse: 'May you live in interesting times!' Although you might not know it to look at it. The daily 'news,' as it is presented to us, is a humdrum affair. The same thing ... every ... single ... day ... It has all happened before, somewhere. It may be in a different place this time, it may have happened to different people, but so what? How many interesting news' days do you remember in your life? For me, it is perhaps two, maybe three. I'm too young for the Cuban missile crisis. When the Wall came down, that was certainly a newsworthy event. September 11 2001, that was interesting. I was captivated by the images for about a week. And here in Norway, the day Anders Behring Breivik bombed government buildings in downtown Oslo, and went on a shooting spree in a Labor Party youth camp, that was different. Nothing like that had ever happened here before. Though, again, these events were primarily new because of where they happened, not for what they were. (Except of course for the people affected directly and personally, but they all knew about it already and didn't need to read about it in the news or watch it on TV.) Horrible as these events were, they pale into insignificance beside the horrors we visit upon other species every single day. And of course, they set off a whole lot of ridiculous aftermath, which was a long drawn out bore and a tragic waste. People get to where they are more concerned about 'terrorism' than about climate change or biodiversity meltdown, or other more direct sources of mortality. And the media and politicians give terrorists attention even though that is precisely what they seek; that and our overreaction. Fears are irrationally enhanced when it involves fear of the unknown, the new, the unfamiliar, the unseen, where the risk factors seem uncontrollable, and result in a large number of fatalities at once (rather than many more deaths spread out more in time or space). Politicians need to be seen to be doing something. Newsworthy events as currently construed by our news media are hardly the important issues that are needed to keep up on what is going on in the world. In retrospect certain days in history were interesting days, although very few people realized it at the time. Meanwhile, the sheer volume of everything that is wrong in the world is overwhelming, for anyone who dares to look at it. But, largely, you won't find it in the mainstream media.

It has been customary to blame the media for all manner of societal woes. But this is a chicken and egg problem. Since most media are commercial, or at the very least in competition with a multitude of commercial outlets, the media tend to reflect the populace. The media try to give people what people think they want. So we get what people in the media outlets think we want. Like politicians, or the corporations, they cannot stray far ahead of what the general populace appears to want. Ultimately, the responsibility rests with the consumer, with the voter, but alas not with the individual consumer and voter; it is with the non-existent *average* consumer and voter that the ultimate responsibility resides. Once again, the atomization of responsibility at work. Media, politicians, corporations, they are all just people. Mere humans.

Mostly, the 'news' is just social pornography. The regular 'news' doesn't do much in the way of analysis. In a way, you cannot blame the newspapers etc. too much, because it is not events that are interesting or meaningful that make a difference to the world we live in, but long term trends. Most 'news' would be more useful, and more intelligible to us if it were reported once a year as a statistic, and compared to previous years. Without an explanatory hypothesis, mere information itself is meaningless, and gives the false impression that we know more than we do. While 'the news' is caught up in an endless string of events, important matters go virtually unreported and our focus is misdirected. Politicians have become reactive, caught up in the news' cycle and unable to concentrate on important matters or deal effectively with serious long term trends.

In the information age, most people still do not know about the rewilding movement, efforts to make ecocide an international crime prosecutable in an international court, efforts to advance a steady state economy as an alternative to our current perpetual growth economy, or about activist organizations like Sea Shepherd and 350.org. Perhaps this is because of the sheer volume of information out there, perhaps it is because of the misdirection of the news industry, or simply the fickleness of the public. Sadly, reporters, politicians, bureaucrats, and those who work for corporations are no better than most of us, and like most of us, they don't do a particularly good job. Nor are they any better prepared to do a good job than most of us.

Many of the battles do-gooders have been fighting for decades are a distraction from what is really threatening the future of life on Earth. The media keep most people endlessly distracted from what is really important. The more we follow the 'news' the less we know. Our judgement is impaired by the noise and our tendency to narrative, anchoring, framing and other fallacies. For most of what is reported as 'news' (deaths, fires, 'terrorism,' crime, finance) I would rather read an annual statistic with trend comparisons, and for analysis (especially on conflicts and controversies that have lasted for a decade or more) I would rather read an essay in a monthly journal than day-to-day (blow by blow) updates. In many cases I can happily wait to read about events in history books, or I can enjoy the elucidation of the *mechanisms* in play in books and other literature. Any news worthy of our attention should have a shelf-life of at least a month, and the news' cycle is so frazzled that I would rather get my information from someone who has put care, time and effort into it.

Information is a far cry from knowledge, or understanding. Most information is mere noise, blurring the signal to noise ratio to the point where we understand less rather than more, all the while our narrative tendencies making us believe we understand things better even when veering from one explanation to another. Not only does the cornucopia of data bits thrown at us from all sides make it harder to detect patterns in the noise and foil our understanding, it also makes it harder for us to find the important stuff. And nobody is reading, or watching, the same things, so it is hard to get critical mass behind any given idea any more. Coupled with the state of the average person's education, these mechanisms explain how we can live in the age of information, yet have so little knowledge, understanding, insight, and power. This is also a relative phenomenon. There has probably never been a time in history when it was important for us to know and understand and comprehend, and to be empowered, like right this moment, today.

*

Unfortunately, as Moisés Naím, columnist and former Venezuelan minister of development, has pointed out in his book *The End of Power*,[102] we face a severe lack of real power in the world — precisely when we would have needed it to get things done. According to Naím, there has been a decay of power itself, and politicians everywhere have noted a huge disconnect between the amount of power people think they have and the amount of power they actually have. Power isn't what it used to be, and not just in politics. People perceived to be 'in power' today, politicians, religious figures, bankers, generals, media moguls, CEOs, etc., tend overwhelmingly to have less power than their predecessors — if they have predecessors. Many of the entities they head are too new for them to even have predecessors (nimble startups have made major inroads into the domains of old corporate giants, and so on). There are more constraints on the use of power today and power is easier to lose. It may seem counterintuitive in the context of the increasing concentration of capital, but Naím points to greater turnover among top-ranking companies and among CEOs, more wars being won by the weaker side, the decline of party bosses and autocratic rulers, small hedge funds managing more money than the large banks, etc. The last few decades have seen the rise of a flora of micro-powers. Revolutions in media and telecommunications have shifted the ground under the powerful media moguls of yore, and politicians have to be more responsive to a greater variety of immediate pressures and feed-backs. Improvised explosive devises (IEDs), drones, cheap and ubiquitous telecommunications and so on enable smaller, non-traditional forces to inflict greater casualties on larger opponents at an asymmetrically low cost. Traditional forms of authority and influence have been undermined. Politicians are increasingly trapped in a system, and kept scurrying from one sound bite opportunity to the next.

Barriers which previously served to prop up powers, have been falling. Naím explains this shift by what he calls the 'More revolution', the 'Mobility revolution' and the 'Mentality revolution.' Today there is more of *everything*: a greater number of nation states (according to Naím the number of sovereign nations has quadrupled since 1940), more people (especially more people globally in the politically important middle class), more computers and smartphones, more universities, more books and magazines, more media outlets, more cars and more airplanes, more 'educated' people, more NGOs and social institutions, more lobbyists with more money behind them, more, more, more... We've had revolutions in media, finance, technology (broadly available and at low cost), the rise of emerging economies, etc. People — and everything else in our society — move around more; they have higher expectations, and demand more in practically all of life's arenas. Obviously, there is still a lot of power out there, but we've seen a broad transformation and decentralization of power.

Power is relative. When everyone has power, no one has power. Powers cancel each other out, unless one party can forge larger alliances than others. Such alliances can be unwieldy and flighty. By one definition, power is the ability to get someone to do something they wouldn't ordinarily do. With an increasing number of checks and balances, and a growing number of micro-powers, paralysis and inaction may easily result.

> A world where players have enough power to block everyone else's initiative but no one has the power to impose its preferred course of action is a world where decisions are not taken, taken too late, or watered down to the point of ineffectiveness.[103]

'Although the aforementioned risks fall short of outright anarchy, they are clearly already interfering with our ability to address some of the great issues of our time.' Couple this with decades of neo-liberal ideology that stated that politicians shouldn't really do much beyond getting out of the way of economic forces, and we are left with a severe deficit in our ability to take charge of our predicament. 'The more slippery power becomes, the more our lives become governed by short-term incentives and fears, and the less we can chart our actions and plan for the future.' Naím calls for political innovation, to respond to this new condition. He cites historian Henry Steele Commager to the effect that, since the introduction of Greek democracy, there was the French Revolution and a surge of political innovation in the eighteenth century, but virtually none since. All political institutions (with the possible exception of the

United Nations) stem from the eighteenth century, which seems truly odd when compared to all the other changes we have seen since then. Humanity has done extraordinary things in physics, biology and electronics, and harnessing technology for power, but in the social arena we are enormous bunglers. While many aspects of the decentralization of power may be seen as social improvements, they do tend to make it harder to get things done. Where once the game was about getting those in power to use it for something good, now we can hardly do real good because nobody has that power. To save the world, we need new social contracts in order for power to be wielded for the public good. And when I say 'public,' I include members of other species...

*

In their controversial 2004 paper[104], *The Death of Environmentalism*, Michael Shellenberger and Ted Nordhaus argued that 'environmentalists' have been shooting themselves in the foot by becoming technocrats and policy wonks rather than talking about values, a compelling, positive, vision, and actions that people can connect with on an emotional level. They should take a leaf from the playbook of conservative strategists and focus more on values. 'The environmental movement's failure to craft inspiring and powerful proposals to deal with global warming is directly related to the movement's reductive logic about the supposedly root causes (e.g. "too much carbon in the atmosphere") of any given environmental problem.' Environmentalists miss opportunities for alliance building by focussing on too narrow a framing of the problem, and being perceived as just another special interest group, locked in their little single-issue boxes... Which is odd, when 'the environment' is everything, and at this point, frankly, the 'only' 'thing' that matters. Though some would have it that even using the term 'the environment' is an emotional disconnect and a strategic error of world-ending proportions...

I keep getting pitches from WWF, the conservation group formerly known as the World Wildlife Fund, to support them in the battle to stop the poaching of elephants. I am, of course, in support of this most admirable goal. But all I can think of when I see their material, is: WWF is a big organization, and it has been around for a long time, so why haven't they stopped the ivory trade by now? And if they haven't, after all this time, why should anyone believe that they will succeed in killing it now? Only a very few, select organizations still get my donations money, even though we are ostensibly on the same side. What is wrong with this picture?

Perhaps if we are so inept at begetting real change, technofixes will become our last hope. Politicians like technofixes because they obviate the need for behavioral change in the general populace and the need for more costly interventions. Furthermore, technofixes can involve the creation of new industries and employment opportunities for the people. Part of the problem with techofixes in the past, has been that we tend to focus on the wrong problems, and choose methods that can be commercially lucrative for particular operators. We genetically modify crops so that they can tolerate more of the pesticides and herbicides that particular producers sell. We chose a particular design of large, centralized nuclear power plants because, unlike smaller and safer alternatives, they produced enriched uranium and other by-products for bomb making, and partial monopolies for large corporations. We have to be vigilant against the new problems that the 'solution' creates. Some have contemplated adding sulphur to jet fuels in order to create a thicker layer of particles in the high atmosphere to block out more of the incoming sunlight. Of course this would also increase the acidity of rainfall and contribute to the acidification of the world oceans. And you have to solve *all* threatening aspects of a particular problem. Measures for reducing global warming, for instance, also have to take into account the acidification of the oceans, which is also caused by high CO_2 concentrations in the atmosphere. But when things get really desperate we may prove more imaginative, and take steps that we wouldn't dream of today. Virtual reality may become the solution if we let things go too far before we take significant steps.[105] Perhaps one day the real world will be only for the super-rich, while everybody else will be at home on the couch getting all their sensory stimulus and all their experiences piped in from a VR-machine. No need to travel, no need for good food, only enough energy and nutrients, like *Soylent Green*, piped in to keep one at a minimum level of awareness... On the other hand, VR may soon be better than real life. Coral reefs, for instance, may soon only be available on VR.

Many of the challenges we face are structural, and changing some of these structures may be hard and difficult work. Maybe even impossible. Especially if the fact that we are severely pressed for time is taken into consideration. Of course, it is possible that things could be worse. Perhaps somebody, somewhere, has done something good along the way, without which the state of the world today would have been even worse. But it is hard to tell. In the political world, there is little direct incentive to fix a problem before it occurs. No credit to be gained, because few will notice. An ounce of prevention is worth a pound of cure; but not for the practitioner. There is no recognition for the preventer; no recognizable success, so no recognizable payoff. In theory, we could save the world and not be aware of it (notably from unknown threats). Sometimes environmentalists are accused of being alarmist, and claims abound that they have been proven wrong when a disaster doesn't occur within a certain time frame. The repeated mantra that 'Malthus was wrong' springs to mind. Of course, it is just conceivable that some of the worst scenarios may have been avoided, or at least delayed, because someone did speak out. Nevertheless, we obviously still have our work cut out for us.

> *'The greater part of what my neighbors call good I believe in my soul to be bad, and if I repent of anything, it is very likely to be my good behavior. What demon possessed me that I behaved so well?'*
> — Henry David Thoreau[106]

According to Skinner there are a number of reasons why we don't heed advice, even when the consequences can be extremely dire. It can be easier to escape in other ways: by ignoring or forgetting the advice or finding a way to escape that does not require solving the problem.

> It is true that advice about a personal future may be effective. Many people have stopped smoking, for example, and perhaps some of them have done so because they were told that it causes lung cancer. That is all the more significant because smoking is strongly reinforced, because the effects of stopping do not follow immediately, and because the advice can be dismissed as merely statistical ('Smoking doesn't cause cancer in everyone, and it won't in me'). But except for a few people who, like physicians, are accustomed to taking that kind of advice and seeing the consequences close at hand, most people have probably stopped for more immediate reasons – a rough throat or a cigarette cough, the annoying constraints of no-smoking signs, the protests of strangers, the condescending tolerance of friends who have stopped, the inflated cost of cigarettes, and so on.
>
> That very fact may be helpful, however. Can something of the sort be done to solve our problem? Why not arrange immediate consequences that will have the effect that remote consequences would have if they were acting now? There is nothing very new in that suggestion. Ethics is mainly a matter of the conflict between immediate and remote consequences. How can we forgo a reward in order to avoid a later punishment or take punishment for the sake of a later reward? Cultures have helped to solve the problem by supplying immediate consequences that have the same effect as the remote ones. They shame their members who fail to forego immediate rewards or refuse to take immediate punishment, and

commend those who do. If eating too much salt and sugar were more serious, it would be called shameful.

It might also be called illegal or sinful, because in advanced cultures sanctions of that sort are taken over by the government and religions. Those institutions outlive people, and those who respond to their sanctions can therefore be said to be working for a future beyond their own.[107]

Our ethics set the standard for how we treat others in the here and now, but also reflect the relationship we have to the future and those that will live in it; those of our own species as well as those of other species.

Obviously, what we have been doing isn't enough, or much of what we've been doing hasn't been working. Not saving the world is the cognitive failure to end them all — we worry excessively about minor issues, yet seemingly hardly at all about the issue that would make all the others irrelevant.

We Need A New Ethic

'Conservation is getting nowhere, because it is incompatible with our Abrahamic concept of land.'
— Aldo Leopold (1948)[108]

So far an anthropocentric ethic has not been adequate to get us to take control of those parts of our collective behavior that are threatening the natural services that we and all other species rely on to sustain life.

The last few centuries, since the occupation of the Americas with the aid of smallpox and other diseases, have been dominated by Western culture. Western culture has in turn been Judeo-Christian culture. Christianity is the most anthropocentric religion the world has ever seen.[109] Various traditions have portrayed humans in a realm of their own, halfway between beasts and angels. Materially different and separate from the rest of creation. Animal rights and the rights of nature were both on a firmer footing in ancient Greece and even ancient Rome, despite a bestiary of atrocities visited upon the Animal Kingdom, than after the coming of Christianity, whereupon the standing of other species, and of nature itself, was greatly diminished.[110]

In Christian tradition wilderness is the very antithesis of Paradise — Paradise was a garden. Christians did not run the risk of being reincarnated as a bear or a tree... By eradicating heathen animism, Christianity made it possible for us to exploit nature without feelings for other 'things.'[111] Early Christians destroyed the holy groves where northern European heathens worshiped a plethora of (natural) deities. To kill off this nature worship, they recast nature as a dark and scary place, filled with voracious beasts. Satan came to embody this animal nature, depicted with horns and hooves and tail,[112] or claws and fangs, or wings... In any case, Christians did not expect the Earth to last long – a vengeful God was set to destroy it.[113] Christian people's focus was on Heaven, not on Earth. Animals were soulless entities, which we would never have to meet in Heaven.

It is probably not a coincidence that Judeo-Christian tradition arose in the corner of the world where organized agriculture first arose, in what was once known as 'the fertile crescent' and where our practice of laying waste to the land has gone on the longest and where its manifestations are therefore the most severe. The Judeo-Christian worldview is hierarchical and dualistic in a way that nature is not. The land in which it arose is now largely desert and wreckage.

Scripture is both better and worse than what has since become Christian doctrine. There are passages in the Old Testament (Hosea and Isaiah, for instance, exhort humans to greater consideration of other species) that appear not to be heeded by more modern practitioners. I generally find it hard to make sense of the Bible, but then I have that problem with all poetry. And the shifting interpretations and fashions in most religions are even harder to keep track of.

Provided we are not purely selfish utility maximizers, philosophy becomes important. Our culture could have chosen to follow St Francis of Assisi, Spinoza and Leibniz, rather than Descartes and Thomas Aquinas. St Francis is said to have calmed a man-eating wolf by reminding it of its membership in the Christian community.[114] His world had no hierachies, no *scala naturae*, no dualism. St Francis believed in humility as a virtue, not only for us as individuals but for humans as a species.[115] Many animistic and pantheistic philosophers had a completely different worldview from Descartes'. For Spinoza, a tree or a stone had just as much worth and right to exist as a human.[116] The idea that the whole world, all of nature, should exist solely for the sake of Man was seen by many as the ultimate hubris.

Christianity has not shown much concern for other species. According to Ryder, Christianity's poor rap on other species is in some sizeable part due to a single passage by St Paul,[117] perhaps because other species were not deemed important enough to merit much mention at all. Commenting on Deuteronomy 25:4, which reads: 'Thou shalt not muzzle the ox when he treadeth out the corn,' St Paul writes: 'Does God take care for oxen? Or saith he it altogether for our sakes? For our sakes, no doubt this is written: that he that ploweth shall plow in hope.' Most theologians have taken this to mean that God most decidedly does not care for oxen.[118]

Ryder writes about Thomas Aquinas:

> Aquinas was born in Sicily in 1225, only a few months before St Francis died, into a world riven by religious dispute. Throughout the south of France and northern Italy at that time the Cathars had replaced Catholicism as the dominant religious influence, teaching that nonhuman animals as well as humans had immortal souls and forbidding the consumption of meat. At the age of nineteen Aquinas joined the austere Order of St Dominic, recently founded to suppress such heresy by the instigator of the Spanish Inquisition. Aquinas was very much influenced by Aristotle,[119] many of whose works had only recently become available to European scholars, and it seems he absorbed from Aristotle the idea that less rational beings, such as slaves and animals, exist to serve the interests of the more rational.[120]

Renaissance humanism did not make things much better – with occasional exceptions such as Leonardo da Vinci, Michel de Montaigne and Giordano Bruno. The latter was influenced by Copernicus' heliocentric astronomy, and argued that there are numberless earths circling around other suns beyond our solar system, that Man is like an ant next to eternity, and that 'Nature is God in all things.' He rejected the concept of an hierarchical universe; Earth, like the Sun, was just one of many celestial bodies, and God was no more tied to any particular part of the infinite universe than any other. He was burnt at the stake in the year 1600 when he refused to recant his heretical pantheism.

After Descartes' mechanical philosophy, with its dualism and animals as mindless automata, somewhat more considerate attitudes were awakened during the Enlightenment, with Voltaire and Rousseau, but Kant could still claim that animals existed merely for our use — that they were 'things,' merely means to an end, and that end was Man. Jeremy Bentham, on the other hand, in his *Introduction to the Principles of Morals and Legislation* in 1780, compared the fate of animals to that of black slaves, and envisioned a time 'when the rest of animal creation may acquire those rights which never could have been withholden from them but by the hand of tyranny.'[121] Much later, John Muir would write: 'I have never happened upon a trace of evidence that seemed to show that any one animal was ever made for another as much as it was made for itself.'[122] Later still, John Cobb, in his book *Is It Too Late? A Theology of Ecology*, proposed a 'new Christianity' based on an expansion of morals to include the rights of nature.[123]

Humanism would seem to have descended from Christianity, due to their shared belief in the superiority of humans. David Ehrenfeld describes humanism as 'a religion without God.'[124]

Nature is not here for our sake. There is no goal or purpose in nature, nature just *is*. A chickadee or a spider crab is a small miracle, and even more so for coming about without divine intervention, but via an unguided, natural, process without intent or purpose.[125]

If the sun is set, in five billion years, to expand and engulf the Earth, what does it matter what happens here in the meantime? Worth, or value, is necessarily subjective. It has to be a value for *someone*. Consequently, ethics also becomes a personal choice. Each of us has to *choose* what will be important to us, knowing full well that we cannot objectively defend that choice.

But what if my values do not coincide with yours, what if they are entirely incompatible? You may value humans, while I value cats, tigers, orcas, sharks and snow leopards, trogons, tuataras, squid and corals. Can we make your values reconcilable with mine? Or will it always be Might Makes Right?

Kant avoided subjectivity by appeal to his categorical imperative.[126] You should act in such a way that you can wish for such behavior to be a common rule.[127] This is not a statement about the *value* of an action, simply its logic. Logic becomes the ultimate arbiter. If the remote consequences of your actions, if adopted by everyone, do not make sense, but result in logical contradictions, then that is not a proper manner in which to behave. Yet, I contend, we still need a *reason* to submit to the dictates of logic...

> 'In their behavior towards creatures, all men [are] Nazis.'
> — Isaac Bashevis Singer (1972)[128]

Liberalism quickly finds itself face-to-face with a phenomenon, the essence of which is encapsulated in the title of the old Paul Simon tune: *One man's ceiling is another man's floor*. Your exercise of your freedoms soon constrains the kind of world I can live in. Conflicts always arise when we take advantage of the liberties granted to us, whether they be interpersonal or between species. Because of such conflicts, we can envision circumstances whereby things that were previously considered rights might no longer be compatible with greater goals or values, and might therefore cease to be rights (the 'right' to free reproduction, for instance). This is analogous to rules that caused us no longer to have the 'right' to unlimited speed on our highways, and so on. The decisive factors determining our environmental impact are: how many of us there are, how we behave, and what technologies we use to do it. The 'right' to populate the planet with humans and take resources away from other species is finite. Sooner or later we must draw a line, and say: so far, but no further. The resolution of such conflicts cannot be reduced to Might Makes Right.

We have organized ourselves into societies to get away from the practice of Might Makes Right: to manage those things that are not emergent properties of natural phenomena, like our genetics, or Adam Smith's 'invisible hand' – those things that require cooperation and consideration of others to whom we are not closely related or who do not belong to our little in-group. Evolution cannot get us to limit our population size. It would appear that our current anthropocentric ethic is not up to the task either... Of course we can do something about 'the laws of nature'; not in nature itself, but in our societies. Society's *raison d'être* is to enable arrangements that require cooperation, norms, rules and regulations, protection of weaker groups, or correction of historical injustices.

Our language makes a taxonomically erroneous distinction between humans and animals. How we treat both those of our own species and those of other species is a matter of ethics, and like other aspects of culture our ethics change over time.

In the struggle against slavery, one did not argue that it should merely be done more humanely.[129] Slavery was not a category of problem open to compromise. If ownership of slaves and the exploitation of black people was wrong, as the abolitionists believed, it was wrong always, everywhere, and in every form, regardless of how humanely it might be practiced.[130]

To put the rights of other species into perspective, it may be instructive to compare with human rights. Do we have human rights simply for being born human? Can we really say with certainty that we humans have intrinsic value? If so, whence is this value derived, and in what way does this value depend on what species we belong to? If someone is in charge of ascribing value to things, individuals, or species, is he free to ascribe value to whatever, and in whatever manner, he wants? Do I have to do anything to deserve or acquire this value, or right, or do I have it regardless of how I behave? If the latter, why do not individuals of other species have the same value or rights by default?

We humans have legal and ethical rights. Our legal rights exist to the extent that they are recorded in laws. Human rights are something we allegedly have simply by being born human. Despite this claim, in the absence of a deity to create purpose and intent in the universe, it should be obvious that human rights are merely a social convention. For instance, the US and the USSR recognized different sets of human rights. To this day, the UN deals in 'civil and political rights' and 'economic, social and cultural rights,' with separate treaties, each of which used to be backed by its own superpower.

But if you are the last person on Earth, it will not avail you much to occupy a street corner, demanding your rights. Who grants us these rights? Human rights are said to be inalienable, in the sense that you don't lose your rights even if you live in a society that does not acknowledge those rights, or denies them to you. The right, the moral prerogative, is supposedly something you have simply because you are human.[131] Yet, since there is nothing in nature that has created this right, this institution, it must be society that has created it, *ergo* a social convention. To speak of something as a 'right,' or a 'human right,' therefore makes no objective sense. They are rights merely within the context of a certain society at a certain time.[132]

'Rights' and 'duties' are said to be two sides of the same coin. Thus, as a holder of rights, you must respect and uphold the rights of others. It is commonly argued, however, that people who do not have the ability to recognize the rights of others (these might be, for instance, young children, the psychologically ill, or the mentally handicapped) still retain those rights. That same argument ought to apply to other species as well, if these are deemed unable to uphold 'duties' vis-à-vis the rights of others.

The fact that people can disagree over what 'rights' are 'human rights' accentuates that these are social conventions. If we are the ones who have established these conventions, then we are also free to extend them to whomever we wish. The set of rights holders has been made more inclusive over the years, and not for the last time. Historically, various groups of people have always retained certain advantages for themselves by denying the extension of rights to new groups. Few of these expansions have been achieved without the use of violence, even wars.[133] Universal human rights, which today most of us take nearly for granted, are a fairly recent construct.[134]

> *'Men have never loved one another much, for reasons we can readily understand: Man is not a lovable animal.'*
> — Edward Abbey[135]

That humans have intrinsic value is simply assumed. Possibly because it is a difficult case to make. The intrinsic value of other species is also difficult to uphold. One should not be so quick to assume intrinsic value in one yet reject it in the other. If one despairs at making the case for intrinsic value in non-human species, one should apply the same rigor in attempting to prove it in humans. Whether failing both, or succeeding in both, one might resign to granting both equal consideration; alternatively one might resort to utilitarian arguments, or accept that all value judgements are ultimately subjective.

In some quarters we might hear the query: 'What do we need wolves for?' In a different region, or a different time, they could ask: 'What are rattlesnakes good for?'[136] For someone who does not hold with an anthropocentric worldview, such a question is not only stupid, but offensive. You might as well ask: 'What use are we to wolves?' or 'What does the cod need us for?' For that matter: 'What do I need you for?'

All species are different. That is why we recognize them as different species. If we are going to accord other species different levels of consideration we should be able to identify the relevant distinctions that justify any difference in how we treat them. That is, we should not only be able to point to differences in traits, but also be able to explain why it is that these particular characteristics justify a difference in treatment.

Soul, Consciousness, Self-Consciousness or Self Image. Intelligence, Sentience. Feelings and emotions; knowledge of death; a sense of time, past and future; the use of tools or technology; reflection. Language. Culture. Free Will. Empathy. Rationality. Moral Actions. Those who like to issue proclamations to the effect that such traits are unique to humans have been repeatedly driven from one defensive rampart to the next as science has gotten around to examining their truth content. It is not long ago that well-regarded people could claim that humans are the only species that plays, and still expect to be taken seriously. Even invertebrates are now known to use tools.[137]

Here is another example: Vincent Dethier[138] writes: 'One of the characteristics that sets man apart from all other animals (and animal he indubitably is) is a need for knowledge for its own sake. Many animals are curious, but in them curiosity is a facet of adaptation. Man has a hunger to know. And to many a man, being endowed with the capacity to know, he has a duty to know.' In this short text, closer scrutiny reveals *every single claim* to be unsubstantiated. We do not know that the need for knowledge for its own sake sets man apart from 'all other animals.' Nor that the nature of curiosity in other animals is different from that in humans. Do we really know that all 'men' have a hunger to know? Indeed it would not seem to hold up even to the casual observation of humanity. Furthermore, not long ago many would have claimed that women, for instance, or perhaps some other races of man, lacked these traits. So, may we speculate that only some 'men' are different from animals? Does this indeed apply to all other animal species, or just some? How would you even investigate a claim like 'no other animal has a need for knowledge for its own sake'? It seems obvious that this claim has not been tested, and is therefore just a prejudice. As an outside observer I might have to observe you for a very long time before I could speak confidently about whether or not you feel a need for knowledge for its own sake. Prejudice is never pretty.

Humans also used to believe that we live to a greater age than other animals. This is patently untrue. Bowhead whales are now known to live more than 250 years, the oldest known mammal. But certain species of mussels can grow to 500 years of age, while some sea urchins, tube worms, tortoises, carp, sturgeon, and some deep sea fishes, and the ancient tuatara grow substantially older than humans. Some sponges and corals may live to be thousands of years old, and scientists have found Greenland sharks up to 400 years of age, that only reach sexual maturity at around 150 years old. It might appear that if humans have a unique trait it is the innate desire to think that there is something unique about them. That has more to do with perceived needs than with any physical reality.[139] Nobody has ever been able to detect a 'soul,' whether in humans or in any other 'creatures.' If you could find one – in humans or others – you would still need a good reason to make its presence or absence the distinguishing trait upon which to base our treatment of others. As David Ehrenfeld writes: 'It is no coincidence that the word "rationalization" is derived from "rational."'[140]

Our views of other species' cognitive abilities, consciousness and awareness are still largely based on assumption. Historically, we have relied on circular arguments, and received wisdom today is still not free of such lapses. Humans have a large brain, and a large, convoluted cerebral cortex; consequently we chose to believe that these traits are critical determinants of our mental abilities, and that we have them to a greater degree than others... In the nineteenth century, craniometrists even defined intelligence as brain size and designed instruments to measure it as such.[141] When dolphins and sperm whales were found to have larger brains than humans, bad-loser humans decided that it was in fact the brain-to-body size ratio that was important for intelligence. Why it should be so, rather than the absolute size of the brain, is not entirely clear. Now it turns out that certain fish (e.g. *Gnathonemus petersii*, 3.1%) have a higher brain-to-body weight ratio than humans (2.3%)[142]. Yet we have the temerity to question whether fish have feelings. The parsimonious hypothesis, the differences between humans and fish not withstanding, is to assume that they are like us. *Of course* fish feel pain. Pain is an important survival mechanism, without which any organism would face a severe selective disadvantage, not knowing when to get out of harm's way. Assuming that we humans are somehow special seems contrived, and certainly not the parsimonious default hypothesis. Much has been made of other species' instincts over the years, under the assumption that their brains are too small to house much in the way of intelligence. But could it not be that intelligence is a more efficient and more compact tool to enable beings to adapt to their environment and respond correctly in a diversity of situations, rather than a bestiary of instincts for every imaginable event? Could it be that such a vast set of instincts might require *more* brain capacity than a versatile intelligence? There is still a lot we do not know about brains and how they work.

While there is still much we do not know about the functioning of different brains, there have been notable recent advances such as the discovery of spindle cells, specialized neurons that in humans are associated with higher cognitive functions such as abstract reasoning, and the presence of spindle cells in the brains of cetaceans. Meanwhile, as we have seen, the documentation of the inadequacies and failures of our own brains is also an active field of inquiry.

Much of our culture's view of other species has been shaped by argument from analogy, which in many cases amounts to false analogy. I can't even be sure that *you* experience suffering the same way that I do, but the null hypothesis is that since we resemble each other, you probably experience things in much the same way that I do and not in the way that, say, an elephant does. But it is not clear that this reasoning places the boundary for similarity where it belongs. Why believe that the relevant difference lies not between two humans, but between humans and other species? Mammals and other species? Or between vertebrates and other animals? What is the significant factor on which to base any difference in treatment, and where is the demarcation line between those that have trait x and those that do not? Since we are related by descent it is probable that many of the traits that are difficult to observe are traits that we may still have in common.

There are probably traits that *Homo sapiens* exhibits to a greater or lesser degree than other species. Any species will be extreme in some direction, some dimension – in a continuum. But these are matters of degree, not essential qualitative differences.

> *'What is the purpose of the giant sequoia tree? The purpose of the giant sequoia tree is to provide shade for the tiny titmouse.'*
> – Edward Abbey[143]

For every right and consideration granted to *Homo sapiens* one should take a hard look at the extent to which it is defensible to restrict these exclusively to humans. What traits are so uniquely human that they can be used to separate those individuals that should be accorded such 'rights' and those that do not qualify? Does the dividing line for whether someone or something should be treated not just as a means to some other end, but also as an end in itself, pass incontrovertibly between humans and other species? And if so, why?

Humans still commonly claim to be the sole moral agents in the biosphere. This view should not be taken for granted either, but be subjected to rigorous hypothesis testing – or you could tentatively accept the antithesis until the claim has been exhaustively tested (though it is hard to prove a negative). Several researchers think they have shown that corvids have a 'theory of mind,'[144] something that some humans lack or have only to a limited degree. But it is generally difficult to say something definitive about others' mental state,[145] including that of other humans.

According to Peter Singer, consciousness (but not necessarily self-consciousness) and sentience (feeling) are the proper basis for ethical consideration.[146] The ability to feel pain and to suffer is critical in Singers' ethics, as it was for Bentham. If an organism has the ability to feel pain and to suffer, then we have to be mindful of this. Social organisms will suffer more than non-social ones, because they also suffer indirectly when those closest to them suffer or disappear. It also seems likely that highly social species have a more highly developed sense of compassion (empathy) and a greater ability to imagine the mental state of others. For Bentham the question was 'not Can they reason? nor, Can they talk? but, Can they suffer?'[147] Singer draws the line 'somewhere between a shrimp and an oyster,' but science may shift such a boundary again and again.

As children on a fishing trip we are brainwashed into believing that fish do not feel pain. And if they do feel pain, we are told, they don't 'experience pain the way we do.' Evolutionarily, pain has an essential survival function. The ability to feel pain is a sense that allows us to move away from environmental factors that would otherwise prove harmful: an individual that could not feel pain would have severely reduced fitness, and one should expect evolution to promote organisms with a sensory apparatus that registers impressions in sufficient agreement with reality to allow individuals to flourish and leave descendants with similar abilities. A more parsimonious null hypothesis would be that anyone with the ability to move away from a harmful influence, or in some other way act to handle it, has the ability to feel pain. At least if they have a nervous system.

Since the ability to feel pain is such a key survival trait, it is reasonable to assume *a priori* that all organisms with a nervous system and ability to move, feel pain. Whether the ability to suffer has survival value is not equally obvious. To the extent that plants lack the ability to move, and lack a central nervous system, one could be tempted to assume that they do not feel pain. Our moral obligations to plants, and comparable taxonomic kingdoms, should perhaps be taken up in a separate discussion.[148] Other ethical systems, such as Taylor's focus on inherent worth,[149] do not rest on this distinction. Aristotle thought that happiness was the only intrinsically valuable thing, as happiness is the only thing pursued for itself. One can also discuss what it means to 'feel' pain, or 'to suffer,' but these are empirical questions — that it may be hard to obtain satisfactory answers to.

With regard to consciousness, self-awareness, rationality, and how a measure of pain is *experienced*, one might think, rather, that the strain must be even worse for a species that does not understand what is happening to it and is perhaps more easily gripped by panic. One should be extremely careful not to trivialize the suffering of a tiger or a lynx stuck in a box trap, a wolf or a fox in a leg-hold trap, a fish pulled from the depths by a hook in its mouth and perhaps unable to equalize the pressure on the way up, a predator that has to live its entire life in a cage, or anyone drowning in a net. Of course, not everyone dies from the same poison, and not all poisonings are equally painful, but these are empirical questions that cannot be answered *a priori*. Prejudices have no place in such issues. Preconceptions are particularly problematic where they coincide with economic interests, convenience, or desires.

If any of the statements about the supposed uniqueness of humans should turn out to hold true, that is just an historical accident. In evolutionary time it won't stay true for long. If humans alone have a particular trait now, it is only a matter of time before other species acquire the same skills, or some degree of the same characteristics. Of course, such a development is conditional upon us not driving them extinct first, or reducing genetic diversity to such an extent that evolution has little raw material left upon which to act.

WE NEED A NEW ETHIC | 93

> '... to any one for whom wild things are something more than a pleasant diversion, [conservation] constitutes one of the milestones in moral evolution.'
>
> — Aldo Leopold[150]

Skinner suggested we find ways to create immediate rewards for actions that yield benefits in the long term, and arrange for future costs of our behavior to be felt in the present. Ethics is all about setting up such rules, and society sets up mechanisms whereby the violation of a shared ethic makes costs that would otherwise only be felt in the future, immediate. Ethics is part of the machinery required to make not only idealists behave well. Religion can do this too, and indeed can play a central role in shaping people's ethics, and thereby their behavior. A shared ethic eventually trickles into law, education, religion and social sanction — all, in turn, aspects of culture and social mores.

An ethic should go beyond what can just as easily result from amoral mechanisms like evolution, game theory, or Adam Smith's 'invisible hand.' Through our intellect and our culture/technology, we have the opportunity to look ahead at long-range consequences, while evolution merely acts on the here and now, on what has immediate utility. Whether or not we manage to organize ourselves in such a way as to take the necessary steps (with existing institutions, in their present state), even where our own survival as a species is at stake — or the survival of life on Earth — remains to be seen.

Our view of the world is not static, even though it may seem so to us on the time scales we are used to considering. Our views and beliefs are a product of historical accidents that shaped the history of philosophy. And history need not be one-way. We may end up taking a step 'back' to worldviews that were more common before Descartes and in cultures more removed from our own Judeo-Christian tradition.

Of course one could use religion to do good. You could argue, despite the overwhelming trend towards the opposite in Judeo-Christian tradition, and probably most other organized religions, that the belief in a creator can justify consideration for other species, and indeed could affirm an intrinsic value for them. After all, Noah saved two of each species, presumably so they, as God's creations, would survive and persist on Earth. Presumably both God and Noah had a good reason. Or, as John Muir urged, all creatures 'are part of God's family, unfallen, undepraved, and cared for with the same species of tenderness and love as is bestowed on angels in heaven or saints on earth.'[151] Christians inspired by such views to be good stewards of the land, might make good allies in the struggle for our fellow inhabitants of this planet. David Ehrenfeld has called this the 'Noah Principle.'[152]

But one of the problems with organized religions is that they are so easily misdirected. You could try to turn religion to do good, for instance to convince the faithful that we have been tasked to look after God's creation; to tell them that God created all animals and that, therefore, to abuse them or eradicate them from the Earth would be not only imprudent, but sacrilegious. But, because organized religions are dogmatic and authoritarian, if they can be used to do good, others can just as easily turn them against you for opposite effect. One can easily lose control of an argument that does not stem from rational thought with a basis in evidence and hypothesis testing, and, as in other disciplines that lack clear mechanisms for determining who 'is right,' theological arguments can quickly degenerate into interminable quarrels with no prospect of resolution. Therein lies the danger of allowing religion too much influence on our worldview; and subsequently our ethics and, thereby, our laws. Dogmatic or axiomatic systems evolve too slowly and are far too vulnerable to manipulation. They have no built-in mechanism for self-correction relative to observable reality and therefore no means of emerging from potentially endless disagreement and fruitless wrangling.

But one can learn from religions, and the tools they have used over the centuries to build a sense of commonality of cause, values, and the feeling of belonging to an in-group.

> *'For this world that men have made, none of us is bad enough. For the world that made us, none is good enough.'*
> — Edward Abbey

Adam Smith-quoting neoconservatives no doubt will tell you that self-interest is the most powerful force on earth. Sociologists and evolutionary biologists will tell you that we will sacrifice more for those closest to us, in time, in space, even by descent. Humanists expect us to solve the problems of poverty, societal injustice, economic inequity, and inter-generational conflict of interest. But the vaunted concern we are supposed to feel for our fellow man has shown itself to be woefully inadequate in getting humanity to organize to solve these problems that our culture makes such a big deal out of. Perhaps other sensitivities are required to fight, and win, the battles that really need to be fought.

How we behave towards other species is symptomatic of how we treat nature as a whole, the world in which we live. If possible, humanity is even worse at behaving properly towards other species than we are towards people that are far away from us in time or space.

We need a new ethic, as the old one has not given us enough of an impetus to do what is needed. With an ethic that extends consideration to other species — species that many of us love more than we love humanity — we may perhaps finally embark on dealing seriously with the problems that are threatening life as we know it. We live in a time when corporations are said to have rights, or legal 'personhood,' so why not other species (or individuals of other species)? As animal-lovers are at the forefront of the push to expand the domain of ethical consideration, do they hold the key to Saving the World?

A Different Ethic

'Man in his arrogance thinks himself a great work, worthy the interposition of a deity. More humble and, I believe, true to consider him created from animals.'

— Charles Darwin[153]

In 2004 it was reported that researchers at a dig on Flores, Indonesia, had discovered the remains of a new species in the genus *Homo*. *Homo floresiensis* looked a lot like tiny *Homo erectus*, and was given the nickname the 'Hobbit.' Subsequent finds indicated that they may have lived as late as 12,000 years ago.[154] It is a prehistoric accident that we in the current era are the lone species of the genus *Homo*. Similarly, it is mere coincidence that we exist in a time and place where most people can maintain, without too obvious a self-deception, that we are the most intelligent species. What if evolutionary history had proceeded slightly differently, such that we at the present time shared the planet with one or more species that were similar to us, or incontrovertibly surpassed us, socially, intellectually, emotionally, or technologically? Where would we be if we were irrefutably number two, or three, in intelligence, consciousness, linguistic ability, self-awareness, and power? Would we still extol these particular traits as the very measure of worth or the basis for ethical consideration? Would we still be so quick to base our ethics in relation to other species on the precept that Might Makes Right?

If we had present-day species that were more similar to us, more people would have difficulty defending that *Homo sapiens* is the only species worthy of being treated as an ethical/moral object, or *subject*, with rights and full protection under the law, and so on. If you are of the opinion that Man has no contemporaries of equal worth, then this would still be a transient state. If life on Earth is allowed to continue long enough, new species will sooner or later surpass all human abilities that are not already exceeded by species alive today. Any species currently extant may in time give rise to descendants sufficiently similar to us that we would consider them worthy of ethical consideration (or 'rights'). If we wipe out the progenitors of these future species, we would preclude such a progression and take 'rights' from potential successors that could have had standing as beings with rights, moral *objects* as well as *subjects*. It is even possible that *Homo sapiens* could give rise to new species by descent, that we today would *not* grant such standing, or 'rights.'

Ethics, like probability theory, can be difficult and not always intuitive. Most of us would not do ourselves what we let the butcher do on our behalf. The same person who finds it ethically permissible to pull a railroad switch to save five people on the track from a runaway train, knowing full well that the train will instead run over another person on the track you have just diverted it onto — under the conviction that this is the lesser of two evils — is unwilling to push a passer-by in front of the train to stop it.[155] Wars have been fought over ethical ideas. Yet we behave as if our own intuition is up to the task of tackling the ethical problems we encounter in everyday life. Current ethics for many of us seem to be unaffected by the last 500 years of developments in philosophy and the sciences; it is enough to make one wonder at the relevance of ethics as a discipline, or at our own rationality...

We could imagine a different ethic, one which to a greater degree takes account of things we have learned over the 500 years since Copernicus, than what the mainstream ethic does today. Perhaps in that way we might return to something more akin to worldviews that Western tradition has displaced. Culture, like nature, is not linear.

We destroy nature, wipe out other species, and impose untold suffering and death on individuals of other species, because we *can*.

In our relationship to other species we still subscribe to the tenet that 'Might Makes Right.' We need an expanded social contract that encompasses communities and individuals of species beyond our own. Such pacts were once common in cultures that 'we' for one reason or another labelled as 'primitive.' Darwin himself felt that a more advanced or civilized society would have a broader ethical vision. Indeed, he promoted such expanded sympathies, or an expanded ethic, as a criteria for a more fully civilized person.[156]

We are in fact much worse off than a focus on actual numbers of species lost would indicate. Apart from the irreversibility of extinction, and the interests of the individuals (of that species) themselves, the loss of a species' ecological function is perhaps a greater tragedy than the loss of the species per se. Most of the repercussions of a species' loss are felt already when it ceases to be an ecologically significant component of the ecosystem. And as previously noted, we lose the species' ecological function long before the last individuals are gone and the species is lost forever. And the vast majority of people are precluded from experiencing the species in question, long before it is irretrievably extinct. The loss of an ecosystem service is felt by many species in the community, which in turn can set off a cascading chain of causal links.

Discerning folk no longer think that God created humans in his own image, but rather that humans created God in our image. Darwin showed that all creatures are shaped by the same process: a value-neutral process without goals or meaning. Man is but one species among many million. When one species, be it *Homo sapiens* or *Campephilus imperialis*, dies out, we will never again have individuals of that species. All future and potential individuals die with the last specimen.

It has become a common-place point of view that we must not only show consideration for those close to us, but also extend such consideration to people further away, and to an increasing extent, to those further away *in time* – to future generations. Those not yet born have a right to a world that is not depauperate. A sustainable future requires that we not take degrees of freedom, or 'rights,' away from those that will come after us.

> *'If the earth must lose that great portion of its pleasantness which it owes to things that the unlimited increase of wealth and population would extirpate from it, for the mere purpose of enabling it to support a larger, but not a happier or a better population, I sincerely hope, for the sake of posterity, that they will be content to be stationary, long before necessity compels them to it.'*
> — John Stuart Mill, 1871[157]

Consideration only of individuals in our own in-group has long since been acknowledged as inadequate. A new ethic could be based on the fact that all species have come about through the same value-neutral process, and are therefore of equal value. Such an ethic could be made practicable enough to live with, albeit not as convenient and self-aggrandizing for us, even if it would involve certain transpositions of value-rankings of individuals between species. Living organisms survive, reproduce, and evolve over generations, in competition with others, because they *can*, not because they are more valuable than others.

Nor is it the case that more recent species are more valuable than older species. All species have an equally long line of descent, and even if some species are more conservative in their evolution while others have changed more rapidly, that does not mean that they are better or worse adaptations. All species are as adapted as they need to be, in competition with others; no more, no less.[158]

Deep Ecologists like Arne Næss or George Sessions would accept a certain amount of (human) environmental impact, even killing other species, as long as it is necessary for the satisfaction of vital or basic needs. One may, for instance, eat others, when it is necessary (for survival). Utilitarians are of course correct that we have to eat; all animals need to eat (with the exception of a few particular invertebrates that have incorporated an adequate concentration of photosynthetic algae in their own tissues). And if we don't dress in animal skins we dress in cotton, which may be equally damaging to the planet.[159] The only way to have an ecological footprint of zero is not to be born. If we expect people to commit suicide to reduce their ecological footprint, we are bound to be disappointed a lot.

Arguments for caring more about humans than about individuals of other species must be primarily utilitarian: based on what is convenient for us. It is hard to keep a functioning society going if members constantly have to watch their backs for fear of being killed, eaten, etc. People are reluctant to concede individuals of other species value or rights because that would make our daily lives more cumbersome. That would entail making changes, including changes with economic consequences. While true, such utilitarian arguments are severely limited, ethically speaking.

Life would become complicated if stepping on an ant carried penalties similar to those imposed for the act of killing a human being. But stepping on an ant is most likely an accident, and the accidental killing of humans isn't punished either (except in cases of extreme negligence).

The origin and reach of altruism is a scientific field unto itself — notably in evolutionary biology where it has been a challenge ever since Darwin's day — and not something I can go into here.[160] Suffice it to say that much focus has been on the extent of the in-group that might benefit from such behavior, the extent of its relatedness to the altruistic party and potential payoffs, at various levels, and the economics of different strategies (strategies like 'tit for tat' and games like 'Prisoner's Dilemma'). Sometimes it is a matter of reciprocity, rather than true altruism. To make sense evolutionarily, altruism would have to pay off somehow. The particular path that the evolution of altruism has followed might partially explain where our sympathies and our affections lie, but if such feelings extend beyond what evolution and game theory can account for one might look to cultural 'evolution' to explain the remainder. Much of the discussion seems to assume that we are inherently selfish, but this need not be true. Humans are a highly social species, after all. Our ethics should, over time, reflect both our innate abilities/dispositions and our culture, such as it may be.

We all have to eat, and most of what we eat is parts of other species. There are lots of things we can eat without killing the individual from which the food is derived: many vegetables and grains, mushrooms, milk, cheese, fruit, etc. Some people even eat only non-reproductive parts of other species, reasoning that nuts, seeds, etc. could have become new individuals. But frequently we eat parts of individuals that are killed for our nourishment. That may, of course, become hard to justify if the individual we are eating is equal to or greater than ourselves in value.

One way out of this bind, without having to become a vegan (although that would undoubtedly be a good thing in today's world), is to confer value at the species level. It is species that survive over time; individuals are doomed to die soon anyway. It is species that evolve, become progenitors for new taxa, and adapt to changing conditions so that life can persist in the future. The survival of the species is necessary for the future existence of all potential future individuals of the species – and those of other species that may descend from it.

Since the survival of the species is paramount, it becomes increasingly important to look after individuals of a species the closer it gets to extinction. Consequently, we might justify the eating of an individual of another species (if required for our survival) as long as that species is more numerous than our own. This is in accordance with what we usually see in nature: predators eat mainly prey that is more abundant and productive than themselves. This is a result of the structure and thermodynamics of food chains, and behaviorally it is more efficient to establish a search image for, and specializing on, common prey.

Such an ethic is congruent with established norms of behavior:

we might strike a mosquito, because mosquitoes are enormously plentiful and the loss of an individual is accorded scant importance. We could defend our eating herring, shrimp, chicken, etc., as long as these species exist in greater numbers than we do. (Note, however, that common names such as 'mosquito' and 'shrimp' denote higher taxonomic units than species; some species of mosquitoes and shrimp do not exist in great numbers, and if we are to equate species we must be judicious about not treating several species as one or combining them numerically.) Individuals of rare and endangered species become extremely valuable, and one would attach great importance to ensuring that these are not harmed in any way. Furthermore, it would be a matter of great moment to maintain large and vigorous populations of edible species such as cod, herring, a variety of arthropods and molluscs, etc., if we wish to continue consuming animal protein. If *Homo sapiens* itself should become threatened with extinction, that might justify taking greater steps to ensure our survival.

The value of an individual of a species, such as *Homo sapiens* or *Panthera tigris*, might then be seen as inversely proportional to how many of them there were — i.e. how far the species is away from absorption at zero. This, in turn, could introduce a stabilizing frequency dependent regime, whereby species' populations increase when rare and decrease when overly abundant.

Alternatively, or supplementally, individuals of a given species might simply be something one respects, likes, feels compassion for, commonality with, or loves, *for, in and of itself*. Categories such as 'things one eats,' 'things one admires or loves,' 'things it is permissible to kill,' 'things one can own,' 'things one feels a connection to,' 'things one is devoted to,' or 'things towards which we have duties,' are also socio-culturally constructed in a way that can change over time as we develop as individuals, or as our culture evolves. (The term 'thing' is used here in a broad sense that may encompass individuals, species, populations, social groupings, etc.) Clearly, there can be a diversity of 'good,' albeit ultimately subjective, ethical reasons to avoid harm to individuals of other species, as well as the loss of species and natural ecosystems. Many of us, though, feel — somehow — that the ethos of Might Makes Right is simply *wrong*.

Every instance of dereliction of duty towards a being with inherent value is an injustice. Hence, it is worse to harm a population or an entire species, and even worse to harm an ecological community or an ecosystem. This way of looking at things does not require a holistic or organicist view of environmental ethics such as Aldo Leopold's 'Land Ethic' or Holmes Rolston's 'Ecological Ethic.'[161] Tom Regan urged moral consideration for all beings that are 'a subject of a life.'[162]

The problem of subjectivity may interfere: from my point of view a harm done to me is a greater worry than a harm done to you. Kant's categorical imperative[163] can aid us in resolving issues like that. Another powerful tool in ethics is John Rawls' 'veil of ignorance,' from his book *A Theory of Justice*.[164] We could expand upon Rawls: imagine if you did not know what species you would be born as, where, or at what time you would be born. If not only our rank among humans but our own place among all life forms is shrouded behind such a dearth of information, we might think differently about what we consider to be justice. The veil of ignorance commonly yields results akin to the Golden Rule, expounded by Jesus and most religions: you should treat others the way you would like to be treated yourself. Expanding these to include other species hinges in part on our ability to imagine what it is like to be of a different species, though in most questions we are likely to face, fine distinctions probably do not need to be made.

In Taylor's system respect for nature is paramount, and this is not compatible with seeing other species as having merely instrumental value. For Kant, however, animals did not belong to the category of things one has duties to; animals were things, not persons or rational agents, and respect is always directed solely towards persons, never things.[165]

'... a man hath no preeminence above a beast: for all is vanity.'
— Ecclesiastes 3:19[166]

Schopenhauer took powerful issue with Kant, and a number of other aspects of European culture. Although in accordance with his times, he does claim that 'as the animal totally lacks abstracts and rational knowledge, it is quite incapable of resolutions, to say nothing of principles; it is consequently incapable of self-control and is helplessly abandoned to impression and emotion.'[167] But then science at the time had not come very far (he wrote before Charles Darwin, and died ten months after the publication of *On the Origin of Species*), and Schopenhauer was wrong about many things, including women, Jews, Jesuits, and other races.

Upon researching the exact references for the quotes in this book I was surprised to uncover in the writings of Arthur Schopenhauer sections of close correspondence to many of my own points here. It just goes to show, once again, that most everything worth writing has already been written, somewhere, by someone, if one can only find it.[168] As illustration of this, I repeat some passages from Schopenhauer's *On The Basis Of Morality* here.[169] Schopenhauer is recommended reading both for his uncommon clarity and the amusing contrast to modern writing and its penchant for political correctness.

> The moral incentive [compassion] advanced by me as the genuine, is further confirmed by the fact that *the animals* are also taken under its protection. In other European systems of morality they are badly provided for, which is most inexcusable. They are said to have no rights, and there is the erroneous idea that our behavior to them is without moral significance, or, as it is said in the language of that morality, there are no duties to animals. All this is revoltingly crude, a barbarism of the West, the source of which is to be found in Judaism.[170] In philosophy it rests, despite all evidence to the contrary, on the assumed total difference between man and animal. We all know

that such difference was expressed most definitely and strikingly by Descartes as a necessary consequence of his errors. Thus when the philosophy of Descartes, Leibniz, and Wolff built up rational psychology out of abstract concepts and constructed an immortal *anima rationalis*, the natural claims of the animal world obviously stood up against this exclusive privilege, this patent of immortality of the human species, and nature, as always on such occasions, entered her silent protest. With an uneasy intellectual conscience, the philosophers then had to try to support rational psychology by means of the empirical. They were therefore concerned to open up a vast chasm, an immeasurable gulf between man and animal in order to represent them as fundamentally different, in spite of all evidence to the contrary.

Hard as it may be for us today to see past his anti-semitism, Schopenhauer was prescient in equating the essential nature of species, including Man, even before Darwin gave this a scientific basis (Schopenhauer wrote in 1839 and published in 1840, while Darwin's *On the Origin of Species* was not published until 1859).

If any Cartesian were to find himself clawed by a tiger, he would become aware in the clearest possible manner of the sharp distinction such a beast draws between its ego and the non-ego. In keeping with such sophisms of philosophers, we find a popular peculiarity in many languages, especially German, of giving animals special words of their own for eating, drinking, pregnancy, parturition, dying, and their bodies, so that we need not use the same words which describe those acts among human beings: and thus we conceal under a diversity or words the perfect and complete identity of the thing. Since the ancient languages did not recognize any such duplication, but rather frankly and openly denoted the same thing by the same word, that miserable artifice is undoubtedly the work of European priests and parsons. In their profanity these men think they cannot go far enough in disavowing and reviling the eternal essence that lives in all animals, and thus have laid the foundation of that harshness and cruelty to animals which is customary in Europe, but which no native of the Asiatic uplands can look at without righteous horror. In the English language we do not meet with this contemptible trick, doubtless because the Saxons, when they conquered England, were not yet Christians. On the other hand, we do find an analogy to it in the strange fact that in English all animals are of the neuter gender and so are represented by the pronoun *it*, just as if they were inanimate things. The effect of this artifice is quite revolting, especially in the case of primates, such as dogs, monkeys, and the like; it is unmistakably a priestly trick for the purpose of reducing animals to the level of things. The ancient Egyptians, whose whole life was dedicated to religious purposes, put the mummies of the ibis, crocodile, and so on, in the same vault with those of human beings. In Europe, however, it is an abomination and a crime for a faithful dog to be buried beside the resting place of his master, though at times, from a faithfulness and attachment not to be found among the human race, he there awaited his own death. *Nothing leads more definitely to a recognition of the identity of the essential nature in animal and human phenomena than a study of zoology and anatomy.*[171] What, then, are we to say when in these days (1839) a bigoted and canting zootomist[172] has the audacity to emphasize an absolute and radical difference between man and animal, and goes so far as to attack and disparage honest zoologists who keep aloof from all priestly guile, toadyism, and hypocrisy, and pursue their course under the guidance of nature and truth?

One must be really quite blind or totally chloroformed not to recognize that the essential and principal thing in the animal and man is the same, and that what distinguishes the one from the other is not to be found in the primary and original principle, in the archaeus, in the inner nature, in the kernel of the two phenomena, such kernel being in both alike the *will* of the individual; but only in the secondary, in the intellect, in the degree of the cognitive faculty. In man this degree is incomparably higher through the addition of the faculty of *abstract* knowledge, called *reason*. Yet this superiority is traceable only to a greater cerebral development, and hence to the somatic difference of a single part, the brain, and in particular, its quantity. On the other hand, the similarity between animal and man is incomparably greater, both psychically and somatically. And so we must remind the Western, Judaized despiser of animals and idolater of the faculty of reason that, just as he was suckled by *his* mother, so too was the dog by *his*. Even Kant fell into this mistake of his contemporaries and countrymen; this I have already censured. The morality of Christianity has no consideration for animals, a defect that is better admitted than perpetuated.[173]

Readers interested in an historical treatment on man's attitudes towards 'animals' should read Roderick Nash's *The Rights of Nature: A History of Environmental Ethics* or Richard Ryder's *Animal Revolution: Changing Attitudes Towards Speciesism*.[174]

Schopenhauer felt that Kant's focus on reason as the prerequisite for moral consideration was misplaced. He argued instead that the 'will to live' was the key requirement, and that this was exhibited by all animals, as well as plants.

> He [the good man] recognizes immediately, and without reasons or arguments, that the in-itself of his own phenomenon is also that of others, namely, that will-to-live that constitutes the inner nature of everything, and lives in all; in fact, he recognizes that this extends even to the animals and to the whole of nature; he will therefore not cause suffering even to an animal.[175]

As opposed to Kant, David Hume emphasized sentience (feeling) as the basis for having interests (self-interest), and he grounded ethics in 'moral sentiments': sympathy (affection, empathy), beneficence, loyalty and patriotism.[176] Schopenhauer reduces this list, in essence, to compassion. Following Schopenhauer, a better ethic for us would be to extend compassion, as he did, to other species. For Schopenhauer compassion was the true and ultimate measure of morality, the moral principle/incentive underlying a true ethic. Religion, duty, oaths, obedience, utilitarianism and Kant's categorical imperative, like fear of punishment or one's good name and honor, were all false reasons for good behavior, and he writes that 'the effect of all religions on morality is really very small.'[177]

But the deed is the hard touchstone of all our convictions: when it comes to the point, and faith is now to be tested by great renunciations and heavy sacrifices, faith's feebleness is then revealed. If a man is seriously meditating a crime, he has already broken bounds of genuine and pure morality. Thereafter, the first thing that stops him is always the thought of justice and the police. If he banishes this by hoping to escape detection, then the second barrier that opposes him is a regard to his honor. If he now surmounts this rampart, then after those two strong resistances have been overcome, the odds are very great against any religious dogma's having sufficient power to keep him back from the deed. For whoever is not deterred by near and certain dangers will hardly be kept in check by those that are remote and rest merely on faith. Moreover, to every good action that results solely from religious conviction, it may still be objected that it was not disinterested but done out of regard for reward and punishment, and consequently had no purely moral worth.[178]

Schopenhauer wrote that 'Boundless compassion for all living beings is the firmest and surest guarantee of pure moral conduct, and needs no casuistry.'[179]

Again, the Gospel story of Peter's draft of fishes, which the Savior blesses by a miracle to such an extent that the boats are overloaded with fish to the point of sinking (Luke 5:1–10), affords a similar characteristic contrast to the story of Pythagoras. Initiated as he was in the wisdom of the Egyptians, he [Pythagoras] bought up the draft from the fishermen while the net was still under water, in order to give all the captured fish their freedom (Apuleius, *De magia*, p. 36 Bip.). Since compassion for animals is so intimately associated with goodness of character, it may be confidently asserted that whoever is cruel to animals cannot be a good man. This compassion also appears to have sprung from the same source as the virtue that is shown to human beings has. Thus, for example, persons of delicate feelings, on realizing that in a bad mood, in anger, or under the influence of wine, they unnecessarily or excessively, or beyond propriety, ill-treated their dog, horse, or monkey — these people will feel

> the same remorse, the same dissatisfaction with themselves as is felt when they recall a wrong done to human beings, where it is called the voice of reproving conscience.[180]

He goes on to say (although as so commonly among older and more verbose philosophers, the basis for such a claim is unclear), that: 'This is precisely why the animal has no conscious morality, although the species show great differences of goodness and badness of character, and in the highest genera, even great individuality.' For Schopenhauer, and, subsequently, for Albert Schweitzer with his 'reverence for life,' it was the fact that animals exhibited a strong 'will-to-live' that made them the proper subject for compassion, and the enlightened conscience. And, as we recall, compassion was to Schopenhauer the only true foundation of ethics (or 'the basis of morality'). Again, our feelings and our emotions become the ultimate arbiter, and the ultimate spur to making changes in the world. 'All the virtues flow from justice and lovingkindness; these are therefore the cardinal virtues, and with their derivation, the cornerstone of ethics is laid,' and 'compassion, as the sole non-egoistic motive, is also the only genuinely moral one.'[181] A few pages later, he writes: 'Compassion is the basis of lovingkindness even more obviously than of justice.'[182]

Schopenhauer quotes Rousseau in support of his views, who cites Bernard Mandeville: 'Mandeville has rightly recognized that, with all their morality, men would never have been anything but hideous monsters, had not nature given them compassion as a support for their faculty of reason.'[183] On the faulty distinction of reason as the basis for consideration Schopenhauer is more scathing than most, both before and after.

> As I have said, no authorities from the schools support my case; yet I state that the *Chinese* accept five cardinal virtues (*Chang*) headed by compassion (*Sin*), the other four being justice, politeness, wisdom and sincerity. Similarly, we see also with the Hindus that on the commemorative tablets, erected to the memory of deceased princes,

compassion for human beings and animals occupies first place among the virtues with which they were credited. In Athens, compassion had an altar in the marketplace: *The Athenians have in the marketplace an altar to compassion. They are the only Greeks who worship this god, because of all the gods he is the most influential in human life and its vicissitudes.*[184] Lucian also mentions this altar in the *Timon*, section 99. A saying of Phocion, preserved by Stobaeus, describes compassion as the most sacred thing in man: *We must not tear the altar from a temple, or compassion from the human heart.*[185] In the *Sapientia Indorum*, which is the Greek translation of the *Panchatantra*, it says (section 3, p. 220): *For it says that compassion is the first of all the virtues.*[186] We see that all ages and countries have clearly recognized the source of morality; Europe alone has not, and for this only the *foetor Judaicus* is to blame, for it pervades everything.[187]

Of course Schopenhauer was no more an anthropologist than a natural scientist, as cruelty to other species and desecration of nature is no doubt found in all human cultures, and not least in many historical and present-day Asiatic cultures.

*

Following Joel Feinberg and Kenneth Goodpaster[188] one might posit that having 'interests' is the proper requisite for moral consideration, more than rationality, sentience, or even awareness:

> Now, if a person agrees with the conclusion of the argument thus far, that animals are the sorts of beings that can have rights, and further, if he accepts the moral judgment that we ought to be kind to animals, only one further premise is needed to yield the conclusion that some animals do in fact have rights. We must now ask ourselves for whose sake ought we to treat (some) animals with consideration and humaneness? If we conceive our duty to be one of obedience to authority, or to one's own conscience merely, or one of consideration for tender human sensibilities only, then we might still deny that animals have rights, even though we admit that they are the kinds of

beings that can have rights. But if we hold not only that we ought to treat animals humanely but also that we should do so for the animal's own sake, that such treatment is something we owe animals as their due, something that can be claimed for them, something the withholding of which would be an injustice and a wrong, and not merely a cause of damage, then it follows that we do ascribe rights to animals. I suspect that the moral judgments most of us make about animals do pass these phenomenological tests, so that most of us do believe that animals have rights, but are reluctant to say so because of the conceptual confusions about the notion of a right that I have attempted to dispel above.[189]

Goodpaster wisely makes the distinction between moral rights and moral considerability.[190]

> Neither rationality nor the capacity to experience pleasure and pain seem to me necessary (even though they may be sufficient) conditions on moral considerability. And only our hedonistic and concentric forms of ethical reflection keep us from acknowledging this fact. Nothing short of the condition of being alive seems to me to be a plausible and nonarbitrary criterion. What is more, this criterion, if taken seriously, could admit of application to entities and systems of entities heretofore unimagined as claimants on our moral attention (such as the biosystem itself).[191]

You don't need to have moral agency in order to have moral considerability, or 'standing' in Christopher Stone's more legalistic framing.[192] While reason may not be the best criteria for moral considerability, nor is it necessarily the best predictor for success in this world. Eminent biologist Edward O. Wilson maintains that the most important reason for human success is that we are one of the highly social species, along with ants, termites and bees. Eusociality is a better predictor of success than rationality: social insects like bees and ants represent only two percent of the insect species, but they make up three quarters of the total biomass of insects, which in turn is the taxonomic group which constitutes most of the total animal biomass on Earth.[193] For humans, real 'success' came when we clustered in larger societies and learned to aggregate knowledge and experience over time by means of the printed word. Oral tradition did not carry the same potency as widespread copying and dissemination. Unfortunately, these days there is so much in print and digital circulation that it can be difficult to find the good bits in oceans of dross, or to separate the wheat from the chaff. In that sense we are left a little bit like a moose trying to sustain itself on low-nutrient aquatic vegetation, running the risk of starving to death in a sea of food: we can't process enough to get what we need.

'There is one thing stronger than all the armies of the world, and that is an idea whose time has come.'
— Victor Hugo[194]

To infer from the fact that other species kill and eat each other, and induce suffering in others, to then it is OK for us to do so, too, is to commit 'The Naturalist Fallacy.' You cannot extrapolate from what is to what ought to be.[195] Even if such things occur in nature, that does not mean that that is the way we want things to be in our society. The whole point of organizing ourselves into societies is to get away from the rule of Might Makes Right. To some extent, it is understandable that many commit this breach of logic, because we have no other external guide than that of Nature. Without a God to hand us down rules of conduct, we are forced to figure out for ourselves the difference between right and wrong. What moral feeling has not emerged in us through evolution has to be created culturally. The next step in our moral development should be to abolish Might Makes Right in our relationships to other species.

We cannot conclude from *is* to *ought*. The knowledge accrued to us about Nature, through science, has nothing to do with how we want our society to be. But it may have everything to do with how we get there.

People have engaged for the environment and other species for decades, and while some battles have been won yet we have been losing the war. Generations of conservationists (and 'environmentalists') have become pragmatists in the attempt to win a political struggle — convinced that to get people to save wilderness they have to gain an understanding of how important nature is *to themselves*. 'What's in it for me?' is the time-honored core of any pitch in sales and marketing, where business is involved, but is it really our key motivation in more important matters? Behavioral economists have shown that when people received a financial reward for recycling, participation declined. With the assumption that we are primarily motivated by money, a cottage industry has sprung up involved in calculating the dollar value of nature, other species, and the ecological services they provide *to us*. While it is true that economists, politicians and bureaucrats have a way of overlooking those costs and benefits that are not measured on the same scale as the others — usually the dollars and cents scale — it is not clear that the appeal to the selfish side of our nature, and mundane pecuniary matters, has been a good strategy for those concerned with saving the world.

For some of us it is personal. We who love animals, plants, wildness and wilderness, the beautiful places, unbridled nature, feel in our bones, in our stomachs, in our hearts, every tragedy visited upon our loved ones. Perhaps part of a better strategy is to truly speak our minds, rather than settling for arguments believed to appeal to the concerns of the mainstream. Social systems being what they are, today's lunatic fringe may be tomorrow's mainstream. And a key role for 'extremists' is to make moderate claims seem more reasonable, even when they are not yet widely accepted. Above all, saving the world will involve organizing at a meaningful level and not being afraid to propose measures that are on an appropriate scale if you really want to do some good. Nothing undermines one's position as much as proposing 'solutions' that are obviously inadequate for the task at hand. Nothing loses a battle as inexorably as self-censorship, which causes us to not even fight for what we really believe. We must fight for what we love, not engage indirectly by assuming that humans are stirred primarily by reference to some perceived secondary impact on humans themselves. We must organize in the interest of those who cannot fight for themselves, and hope that truth itself is a powerful tool.

Rachel Carson knew that she would lose adherents if she skipped too far ahead of public opinion. Sensible, perhaps, in its time, but this kind of restraint may have in turn delayed advances in a sustainable direction by many decades. Such pragmatism leads to self-censorship. Will it really make sense to refrain from saying what we really think, for fear that our honest opinions may be used against us, ridiculed, or otherwise harm our own cause? It is perfectly legitimate to love other species more than our own. Those of us who do should not be forced to keep our true convictions hidden for strategic purposes. And perhaps now the world is ready, when we see the reality of a full world. Animal-lovers and nature-lovers should be *more* vocal, and *more* activist, not less. So tell it like it is. As Skinner points out, a sure-fire way to ensure that advice is not heeded is when it is not given, for fear that it is unwanted. In any case, it is clear that good politics is not necessarily good philosophy — and patently obvious that it is not good ethics. Our endless wars, exploitation of others, and our feeble attempts at development aid remind us of the limitations of strictly inter-human ethics. There is little point in sacrificing for someone who is worth as much as oneself. But for someone *more* worthy than ourselves, perhaps.

How often have you heard some bureaucrat or technocrat proclaim that we have to increase food production to feed so many billions of people some time in the future? What if we instead took steps to ensure that there wouldn't *be* that many humans in future? The power of definition is half the battle, and it is contingent upon us to closely scrutinize all premises, spoken or unspoken.

George Marshall, in his book *Don't Even Think About It: Why Our Brains Are Wired To Ignore Climate Change*, says right out that we should not use cute animals and drowning polar bears as arguments for solving the climate crisis, but I disagree. Cute animals already *rulez teh interwebz*, and this may indicate an underlying force that extends beyond entertainment. Saving the world for humans holds no motivational power for me. My quest has always been to save the world *from* humans. For me, the reason to care about climate change is precisely those cute animals, the polar bears, the coral reefs and the calcareous algae and all the non-human life they support — the natural world, not the world that humans have created. Could animal-lovers and nature-lovers, at the forefront of extending the domain of ethical consideration, hold the key to saving the world?

For me, the most important reason to care about environmental destruction and anthropogenic climate change is the terrible effects these will have on other species. Humans have only themselves to blame, and I care more for the victims than the perpetrators. Besides, I don't think our much-vaunted concern for other people is all that it is made out to be. If it were, wouldn't we have solved the poverty issue long ago?

I think there are many of us who care more for other species than we care for mankind, and we shouldn't be afraid to admit it. Perhaps our sympathy for other species can act as an inducement to change where concern for other people has failed? Those who care only about humans need to find tricks to enable them to bear up-front costs today for a possible future reward. Animal-lovers and nature-lovers are less susceptible to the problem of irrationally discounting the future, because both nature and other species, as a whole and as individuals, are getting an extremely raw deal in the here and now. For those who care about other species, the future is already here.

'The great fault of all ethics hitherto has been that they believed themselves to have to deal only with the relation of man to man.'
— Albert Schweitzer, 1931[196]

It should be patently obvious by now that we won't save the world through business as usual approaches. While many of us are involved with making marginal improvement here and there, as a society we are ignoring the all-encompassing trends and dominant mechanisms that inexorably pull society, and thereby the world, in the same direction as before. We put more concerted effort into making a movie than we do almost any human endeavor. Certainly more than we do into making policy and negotiating international treaties. Just think about how many people it takes to produce and distribute a modern block buster like *Avatar* or *The Hunger Games*, and the coordination, project management and fund raising that goes into its planning and execution. Now compare that to national or international governance, which is a haphazard and disorganized affair. Or to the efforts of a well-intentioned NGO... Though maybe those particular movies can do as much good as the NGOs.

Animal-lovers and nature-lovers may have to make common cause with those stirred by the inequity inherent to the growth economy (and its consequent power structure) that is also overexploiting and destroying the natural world. Revolutions, when they come, tend to catch us unaware; no matter what the warning signals might have been, they are sudden and unexpected. Prediction in social systems is hard. And timing is as hard when it comes to social revolutions, 'new' ideas and new language, as it is in the stock markets. So perhaps we are not as far away from doing something as we think.

Man is a species it is hard to love. Perhaps those of us who care about other species are more likely to care what happens to the Earth. If more of us could remember further back, and knew how rich the world once was, then maybe there would be an outcry leading people to rise up to do something about it. Perhaps we are the last generations that can.

Skinner urged society to arrange immediate consequences of our actions in order to promote the common good. Taking action for the future does not come naturally, so we have to invent mechanisms to artificially induce us to simulate long-term thinking. These same mechanisms must 'fool us' into taking the necessary steps before necessity compels us to it. The steps have to be taken sooner or later, and will be much harder if we wait, but we need help to make us take our medicine before it is too late. Ethics, and their translation over time into laws and societal norms of conduct, are among the tools we have to help us substitute long-term thinking for short-term thinking. A broadly biocentric ethic should be easily more effective in this regard than an anthropocentric ethic has been. Animal-lovers and nature-lovers are already seeing, and internalizing, immediate consequences for their loved ones. Of course, for some, the future can get even worse, but we can already see the writing on the wall.

Some say our societies should be on a more human scale. A branch of the 'environmental movement,' if there is such a thing, has given rise to *bioregionalism*, where people learn to live within a bioregion, by getting to know it, understand it, and develop the skills to coexist within it. But such bioregions are also components of a global world, impacting and impacted by the larger world beyond their borders. One way to a better life may be to revert to a simpler life. To live our lives on a scale we can comprehend and make our own. But that demands that there are not emergent properties at a greater scale than the ones we have chosen to concern ourselves with. There are so many of us, that what we do has global repercussions in the aggregate. Most people's ethic does not stretch to life on such a scale. In a full world, ethical concerns are global. It is no longer enough to live in the here and now. This causes a cognitive dissonance that can be hard to live with for anyone unable to completely repress such facts, or unable to stop caring entirely.

On The Tragic

'Thousands of tired, nerve-shaken, overcivilized people are beginning to find out that going to the mountains is going home; that wilderness is a necessity...'

— John Muir[197]

What does it do to us, when we have lost the wilderness, when the patches that remain are pitiful, invisible on a map, so small that we can walk through them in minutes? We are doomed to live in a world that is a pale imitation of its former splendour, a world that is self-inflicted. What does it mean for us to live a life where we never feel life in the raw? What is a life without surprises, where we never experience danger or an adrenaline rush, the feeling of holding life in our own hands, never leaving the tame, padded and thoroughly domesticated cocoon of 'civilized' society?

What the current state of affairs does to us is not part of my argument for a new ethic, as that would embody the kind of self-serving instrumental ethic we should get away from. (Yet some may find it relevant to our predicament.) That might signal that the reason we should refrain from misdeeds towards nature and other species is the harm we do to ourselves, thereby, not the harm done to others — that the suffering of others is only significant for the indirect effect it has on our own well-being.

Kant derived a prohibition against the mistreatment of animals from the notion that it was in violation of a duty to ourselves. According to Kant, Man has a conditional duty to bolster his capacity for compassion and empathy, because enhanced compassion furthers morals in relation to other *people*. Since brutality towards animals kills our compassion and our ability to empathize, we have a duty to abstain from animal abuse.[198] In this,

Kant, for all his rationality, is just channeling Thomas Aquinas, who wrote:

> If in Holy Scripture there are found some injunctions forbidding the infliction of some cruelty towards brute animals [...] this is either for removing a man's mind from exercising cruelty towards other men, lest anyone, from exercising cruelty upon brutes, should go on hence to human beings; or because the injury inflicted on animals turns to a temporal loss for some man, either the person who inflicts the injury or some other; or for some other meaning, as the Apostle expounds in Deuteronomy 25:4.[199]

In a similar vein, it has been said that when Hindus and Jains restrain from killing insects, they 'show concern for their own spiritual development rather than for the actual lives of those insects.'[200] Some may find the rewards of living in a more beautiful world a powerful incentive to look after, and restore, nature. Yet the benefits might come too late to accrue to us personally.

In E.O. Wilson's *Biophilia*, he argues that nature and other species are important to us because we have an affinity towards the biological world where we originated and in which we evolved.[201] Why do we prefer a city with a park, rather than just a city? A walk in the woods or in a garden has always had a rejuvenating, calming or invigorating effect on us. To be in the great outdoors, hear the song of birds, the rustle of wind in the trees, the trickle of water, the smell of bogs and fungi and sea... But what when we look about us, and see not the wilderness in which we developed, but the wounds we have inflicted on it? When we can no longer experience the world without sensing how we have destroyed it, without contemplating what it could have been still and what we could have seen had we only left it in peace?

> '*Will the things that are being lost – the wilderness, the plants and animals, the skills, and all the others – leave too vast a gap in the human spirit? This is the unanswerable question. In the meantime, we must live in our century and wait, enduring somehow the unavoidable sadness.*'
>
> – David Ehrenfeld[202]

In the absence of a deity with a plan, to give value to things, we have to decide for ourselves what we will care about. My choices will be different from yours. It is not even certain that your choices will be *compatible* with mine. We must select our values, subjectively, all the while acknowledging that we have no means of justifying or defending our decision. They are, and will always be, subjective. I choose to care about tigers, orcas, sharks, wolves, mountain lions, the fish in the sea, nudibranchs, bees and spiders, polar bears, martens and otters, millipedes and pycnogonids, sequoia, oak and mahogany, mangroves, crabs and shrimps. All the critters which humanity daily kills and annihilates, starves, drowns, abuses and tortures.

What are we to think of a species that despoils the ecological conditions that all species depend on for life? What are we worth as individuals if we are helpless to do anything about it? What is our individual worth if the world can only stand one billion people, and we are seven or ten, or twelve? How does it affect us, or our societies, to live in a world where so many of us hate humanity for what it is doing to nature, to other species, and to individuals of those other species? There is nothing magical about humans.

Our old ethic robs us of our future. What does it do to us when we feel we have no future? That we are powerless to shape the future in an acceptable direction? Perhaps the way we treat other species is symptomatic of how we relate to the future as a whole. What can we think of ourselves when we drive millions of other species to extinction, each and all of which are just as valuable as our own – or *more* valuable than our own, simply because they do *not* cause the extinction of a multitude of other species. Does a species that single-handedly exterminates millions of other species have negative value? If you really are a humanist, perhaps you also should strive against anthropocentrism, lest it cause many among the rest of us to hate the human species which is your focus. Humans deflate their own worth by being not very nice, and by being too many. Humans would do well to behave so that we would like them more.

Human dignity crumbles as well, in a future desperation. What are we worth without a future? Of what value are we when we have become vermin, a cancer, threatening not merely our own existence but that of every other species on Earth? Something that there is too much of becomes worthless. Or worse, it becomes pollution. Can you justify your own existence when you are self-destructive? Do you have quality of life when you are suicidal? How much are we worth when we cause so much suffering and death?

What we do to the Earth we also do to ourselves.[203] At least to those of us who care. Perhaps we thereby make ourselves so ill that we are able to heal neither ourselves nor the planet. Are we walking around in a perpetual grief reaction, traumatized by our own destruction of the world?[204] Are we suffering from the cognitive dissonance between what we suspect, in unguarded moments, in our innermost thoughts, is right for the Earth and its inhabitants, and the constructs society presents us in its striving for perpetual economic growth, careerism, relative position, consumerism, and the pressures of family? We may struggle, for instance, with the dissonance between bringing children into this world and the burden we place on the world in which these children are to live, and the quality of life that will be attainable in that world in the future. Being a human that needs to eat, with the consciousness of the cumulative effect of billions upon billions of people who all need to eat, may be a daily burden for anyone who dares to think about it.

'Man always kills the things he loves, and so we pioneers have killed our wilderness. Some said we had to. Be that as it may I am glad I shall never be young without wild country to be young in. Of what avail are forty freedoms without a blank spot on the map?'
— Aldo Leopold[205]

If life as a human being is to have any value we must be 'whole' beings, that do not threaten the world in which we evolved as a species. We cannot afford to let economics dictate ethics. Humanity's conception of the control of nature is even more ludicrous when we ourselves are a species out of control.

An anthropocentric utilitarian might still argue for consideration of other species based on what is good *for us*. As emotional beings, perhaps we have a better life when we *don't* dress in the suffering of others and live off their death. But an ethic based on self-interest, grounded in our own comfort and convenience, is not much of an ethic.[206] Several thinkers have discarded enlightened self-interest and instrumental theories of value as a basis for ethics.[207] Schopenhauer goes so far as to say that '...egoism and the moral worth of an action absolutely exclude each other. If an action has as its motive an egoistic aim, it cannot have any moral worth.' In fact, he makes it one of his axioms in his 'The Foundation of Ethics.'[208] 'Only insofar as an action has sprung from compassion does it have moral value; and every action resulting from any other motives has none.'[209]

We are not to treat someone solely as a means to an end, but also as a goal in itself.[210] In opposition to Kant we could extend this 'someone' to include individuals of other species. Moreover, it is not particularly good ethics to treat others with decency, simply that they may be decent to us in return. One can achieve the same result with purely amoral game theory or evolution.

Actions that pay off, or are to our own advantage from a purely utilitarian point of view, evolution can take care of: they can establish in a population without any form of ethics – at least those behaviors that we stand to gain from in the short term. The things that make sense in the long term our current ethic is apparently also unable to get us to implement. With our intellect and our culture/technology we have the ability, in theory, to think ahead and take account of long-term consequences, while evolution only works on near-term utility. Whether we will manage to get organized to take the necessary steps, even where our survival as a species hangs in the balance, along with the survival of life as we know it, with existing institutions (and in their current state), is, however, not clear. Do we have the ability to control our collective actions? If so, we have a choice. We can *choose* not to drive other species extinct, *choose* not to diminish magnificent phenomena of nature, *choose* not to kill or harm others. In Schopenhauer's terminology, we can *will otherwise*.[211]

Did people manage to stop smoking when the health risks were explained to them? We already have an ethic that values humans, but do we manage to deliver effective development aid or poverty relief because of it? We understand that global climate change will harm our children and grandchildren – those of us who have not avoided having children – but does that knowledge empower us to put an end to a mindless automobile culture, meat consumption, mass tourism, or the perpetual growth economy? Our assumptions about what approaches make good politics do not always hold water.

It would be a platitude, if it did not constantly prove necessary, to remind people that attitudes we today reject were once commonplace. Many of earlier eras' views on slavery, women, children, other races and various other groupings, are abhorrent to us today.[212] Not long ago it would have been perfectly acceptable to consider several of these groups not as humans with rights, but as property. Where humane treatment of slaves prevailed, it rarely reflected ethical niceties. It was 'good business,' on a par with good utilitarian animal husbandry or sound land use.[213] Among abolitionists it was a common stance that although blacks would never attain intellectual or social equality with whites, that was no reason to deny them their natural rights.[214]

Christopher Stone, leaning heavily on Maine,[215] takes on the past status of children:

> We know something of the early right-status of children from the widespread practice of infanticide – especially of the deformed and female. (Senicide, as among the North American Indians,[216] was the corresponding rightlessness of the aged.) Maine tells us that as late as the patria potestas of the Romans, the father had *jus vitae necisque* – the power of life and death – over his children. *A fortiori*, Maine writes, he had the power of 'uncontrolled corporal chastisement; he can modify their personal condition at pleasure; he can give a wife to his son; he can give his daughter in marriage; he can divorce his children of either sex; he can transfer them to another family by adoption; and he can sell them.' The child was less than a person: an object, a thing.[217]

When they first started advocating for the rights of slaves, abolitionists were seen as a small, fanatical minority with laughable and dangerous ethical theories.[218] Children mature ethically just as they do biologically. Humanity may also mature ethical-culturally to attain a new stage of moral development.[219] There may come a day when enlightened people will despise speciesism as much as we today detest racism.[220]

Millions of animal-lovers around the world feel more strongly about the plight of other species than they do about humans. Many of us feel that humans are *the problem*, not the goal. Humans are not a lovable species. We may certainly care for, even love, our friends and relatives. But as a species we are loathsome vermin. It is hard not to despise a crowd of humans that you don't know personally.

As animal-lovers we mourn what humanity is doing to the world and its non-human denizens. Many of us see what humans are doing and hate our own species, and our own membership in it, for the crimes we perpetrate, on the natural world and other species, and for the fact that many of these actions are not even recognized as criminal by our legal system. Some crimes against individuals of other species incur penalties so paltry they are an insult. As such many of us see humanity itself as the problem, not as an end in itself. By placing itself apart from nature, and refusing, so far, to be regulated by it, humanity has come to be viewed by many of us as a disease, or some other kind of scourge, on the biosphere, the beautiful places on Earth, and the animals and plants that we admire and love, and feel a primordial connection to.

It is nearly a truism these days that humanity will not act in time; that a catastrophe must occur, and that most people need to be truly desperate before they will change their ways, for instance to deal with global climate change. But the prevalence of self-reinforcing positive feedback-loops and tipping points in nature means that by the time humanity feels the brunt of it, it will be too late. Of course, we may already be in the midst of a crash. What does a crash look like at human speed?

For other species times are already desperate. They have been up against the wall for a long time already, they have suffered at our hands for decades, not to say millennia, and to a great extent will be long gone before humans will feel the repercussions of their actions. As such, organizing for other species may be our only hope to turn the tide in time. We need a way to get humanity organized to take collective action, *before* people everywhere are desperate. It probably won't be sufficient, but without the passion animal-lovers and nature-lovers bring to bear we will not save life on Earth as we know it, nor as we once knew it. Maybe moving the boundaries of moral consideration is itself more powerful than most interventions attempted to date. Animal-lovers may be more able to overcome paralyzing anxiety about things to come. Because we do not fear for ourselves. We fear for someone else, our loved ones, and that may be a more powerful motivator for action. Many grandparents may feel that they are in the same position. Compassion, caring for others, respect for other species and concern for their habitats may prove a powerful antidote for the narcissism that otherwise seems to threaten life on Earth and citizen activism. One could start perhaps with building strategic alliances with some of those millions, if not billions, of people who love their pets… And anyone who thinks they still remember what nature was like. Those who remember herds of wildlife and real flocks and schools of teeming life. Those who have missed it, and want to bring some of it back. There are still things there to love and cherish if you go to the right place.

We need a society which makes room for other species and nurtures our emotional and spiritual needs, and provides a better quality of life. We need new goals for the great society, a positive vision for how we want to live and what kind of world we want to live in. Modern humans need new experiences of what makes life good. We need to find again some of what we lost when we removed ourself from nature, and erected emotional barriers against other species the easier to exploit them. Meaningful reform of how we treat our surroundings must be founded on changing how we relate to nature, from an economic basis to an ethical basis.[221]

> 'Wild things were taken for granted until progress began to do away with them. Now we face the question whether a still higher "standard of living" is worth its cost in things natural, wild and free. For us of the minority the opportunity to see geese is more important than television, and the chance to find a pasque flower is a right as inalienable as free speech. [...] We of the minority see a law of diminishing returns in progress; our opponents do not.'
> — Aldo Leopold (1949)[222]

Sooner or later there will come a generation, or a number of generations, that will have to pay the price for the shortsightedness and greed of earlier generations. That day is near at hand. It is not fair, but one must take the cards one is dealt. You can't simply stand around proclaiming your rights. The right to a living planet no one can give us but ourselves. If we want it we shall have to take it.

Our political system is not used to dealing with systems with break points, irreversibility – that there is such a thing as too late. It is not so critical to get things right when you can always go back and fix them later. Human rights not withstanding, we can no longer choose freely what kind of world we want to live in. Many options are long gone. Our loss will get greater and greater as more and more possibilities pass beyond our reach. In our struggle for a liveable climate, for instance, we have already left behind many of the cheapest and most comfortable alternatives.

As none of us can achieve much on our own, we need to come together on policies and mechanisms that will keep the system as a whole moving in a better direction. In the words of Dave Foreman: 'These policies and strategies must be part of a bold, hopeful vision, because milquetoast proposals timidly suggested excite no one. It is boldness and hopefulness that grab people's attention and inspire them into action.'[223]

Duties are the flip side of rights. Where rights are social conventions that can change over time, so too our duties are social norms that are shaped and reshaped as our ethics and culture evolve. If human beings have rights, then we also have duties in relation to our impact on ecosystems and our relationship to other species. The next step in our moral development should be to abolish the practice of Might Makes Right in the way we relate to other species.

Change *can* happen. People used to smoke on buses and airplanes, in offices and restaurants... We certainly can change our culture, our ethics, and our laws. But will we? Some of these changes need a little centralized help. Not all matters can be left up to individual free choice and the free market. And all choices and markets have to be constrained to a certain extent. That is why we have laws, regulations, and criminal enforcement. Smoking in offices, restaurants and other public places didn't go away when the public was informed of the risks. No, these activities stopped when we got regulations that forbade them. Even our ethics seemingly need to be inscribed in laws and regulation, or a common tradition, before they become the basis for sound behavior for our society as a whole.

As a fairly conservative endeavor, law lags behind ethics. Where politics comes in the order of things is hard(er) to say, but certainly not first. Politicians do not lead. At least, it is a rarity in world history that politicians are at the forefront, rather than following shifts in popular opinion. Mostly, politicians need to be fairly sure that a new policy will be acceptable to the voters. So in a 'democracy,' however poorly implemented, no one is off the hook for allowing the status quo to persist. It is our responsibility to fix things, there *is* no one else. Even if fixing our problems entails fixing the flaws of our current democratic model along the way. If we are going to stick to the old model of democracy, the general public has to get literate about what's important. That is not to say that we have to take on the task of educating people — it is every voters' own responsibility to ensure that he or she is educated and prepared for their civic duties, or refrains from voting. It is one or the other: either an enlightened set of voters or a new, improved democratic model. And one of the democratic system's duties is to ensure that we have a functioning democratic system.

Political action does require citizens to get involved. As Franklin D. Roosevelt once said to a group of petitioners from his own party: 'I agree with you, I want to do it, now make me do it.' You can't just submit a ballot every four years or so and hope that things will get better. Politicians won't get their act together until somebody forces them to.

Whatever the solutions arrived at, if any, we have to be hard-nosed and realistic about it. Being optimistic is one thing, being naive is something else entirely. Wishful thinking may help some people keep plodding along on a torturous path, but it never really solved anything. Good intentions are not enough. The actual outcomes of policies are more important, and insufficient attention to all the mechanism involved frequently yields outcomes contrary to what was intended. Politicians seem to think that the job is done once they have allocated the money, but the job also has to be done right. And structures sometimes take on a life of their own. We have to be cognizant of the forces and the mechanisms that stand in our way. We're not helping anybody by under-communicating the difficulties involved in getting humanity to act in a rational manner. Facile 'solutions' only make things worse. That being said, one should prepare oneself in the best possible way to be in a position to take advantage of an opportunity when it presents itself. 'Realism' should never keep one from aiming high. To save the world we should take a hard look at what the real, underlying causes are, and exactly why it is that we have not done so before. If we understand the mechanisms that have kept us from taking effective action in the past, we may be able to find ways of getting around them.

When something is important enough, you don't leave it up to chance and happenstance. When we have an important task ahead of us, we actually train for it. Like soldiers. Like engineers. Like a task force. When was the last time you saw someone actually being trained to save the world? Or solving problems in general? For important events and tasks it makes little sense to just show up and wing it.

*

Present-day law is not up to the task of precluding full-scale disruption of planetary ecosystems. Seeing the world as a commodity takes us down a path that ends in a completely different world than if we had viewed the world as sacred. Today's laws spring from such a worldview. Maybe one day we can do better.

Our culture, experiential Deep Ecologists like John Seed argue, robs us of the emotional and visceral experience of that interconnectedness which we had as small children, but which has been socialised out of us by a highly anthropocentric alienating culture.[224] Many would see it as naïve, childlike, to ask why people seem to feel better doing cruel and hideous things to other animals than they would doing those things to humans. Yet it is a question we really should ask ourselves, and take a real, hard look at any answer we may come up with.

New laws often reflect novel values or new insights, or they are simply a consequence of nobody having gotten the job done sooner. A recent initiative aims to recognize (some) whales as 'persons' with rights, and that individuals of certain other species are moral agents.[225] In 2002, the German Bundestag voted to grant animals rights in the German Constitution by adding the words 'and the animals' in a text requiring the State to respect and protect human (and now also animals') dignity.[226] Switzerland has had similar wording in its constitution since 1993 and in 2003 an article was written into the civil code stating that animals are beings, 'not objects.'[227] A committee of the Spanish Cortes Generales concluded, in 2008, that individuals of other species may be granted legal status as a person with rights. The resolution also requires the government of Spain to further a similar decision at the EU level.[228] There is a proposal before the United Nations to make 'Ecocide' — serious crimes against nature, with long-lasting consequences — a fifth International Crime Against Peace, punishable in an international court on a par with genocide and crimes against humanity.[229] The hope is that this will create a sufficient deterrent to keep companies, states and individuals from engaging in activities that cause serious environmental harm.[230] Ecuador has written the rights of 'Mother Earth' into its constitution, and Bolivia has called for legislation in the UN to stop Crimes Against Nature.

In New York, The Nonhuman Rights Project has brought court cases to win legal 'personhood' for captive chimpanzees, and in India the government recently [2013] prohibited the keeping of dolphins in captivity for entertainment or display[231] (Switzerland has had a ban on the import of dolphins and whales since 2012, Bolivia, Chile, Greece, Cyprus, Costa Rica, Croatia, Hungary,

Nicaragua, and Slovenia have similar statutes on their books, while a number of countries, including Brazil, The United Kingdom and Norway, have guidelines so strict that they effectively preclude keeping cetaceans in captivity).[232] In The Netherlands the government has been successfully sued for not doing enough to reduce greenhouse gas emissions, and a similar case is proceeding in Belgium.

Once a cultural change has taken place it becomes second nature. Most people (at least in 'developed nations') would no longer dream of eating whales or dolphins or buying ivory, or displaying it in their home. Such changes can be quite rapid and painless, once they get underway. Veganism seems to be on the rise in many countries. But as of yet, the behavior of individuals seems to have had little effect on society as a whole.

Efforts to make Ecocide a fifth International Crime Against Peace, has been making some headway. The United Nations' International Law Commission 'Draft Code of Crimes Against the Peace and Security of Mankind,' and later working committees, which laid the basis for the Rome statutes, codifying International Crimes that can be prosecuted by the International Criminal Court, did in fact include 'wilful damage to the environment.' However, this language did not make it into the Rome statutes, after opposition from the United States, the United Kingdom, and The Netherlands. In 2010, English barrister Polly Higgins submitted to the ILC a proposal to amend the Rome statutes to add The Crime of Ecocide to the existing list: The Crime of Genocide, Crimes Against Humanity, War Crimes, and The Crime of Aggression. The proposed amendment defines Ecocide as 'the extensive damage to, destruction of or loss of ecosystem(s) of a given territory, whether by human agency or by other causes, to such an extent that peaceful enjoyment by the inhabitants of that territory has been or will be severely diminished.' At the opening of the COP21 in Paris – the twenty-first Conference of the Parties in the international climate negotiations, in December of 2015 – President Correa of Ecuador called for the creation of an International Court of Environmental Justice to punish environmental crimes. Ten countries already recognize Ecocide as a crime in their own national legislation.[233]

Can we design a way of life that will have a better chance of a future? Not just for us, who don't deserve it, but for all the beautiful, wondrous, innocent species, that still live in a way compatible with life? Part of the difficulty, as Skinner would say, is that many of us would no longer be here to reap the benefits, to enjoy the world once it has been restored to us. We have to work hard and bear costs up front, even though we may not be here to sample the rewards of a job well done. Luckily, almost, there is vast room for improvement, and many things we can feel better about along the way if we really get started on the work to create a better world. If we do it for other species, the benefits of a healthier and more beautiful world will be noticeable. With a slight shift in values, some incidental rewards will be ours along the way. If reached in time, parts of nature can recover quickly, if humanity could bring itself to just ease off the pressure. And we may be surprised how much better we can feel if some of our guilt is assuaged. Those of us who love animals, and the natural world, will be able to feel infinitely better about the direction in which things are headed, and life may be worth living again.

> 'When injustice becomes law, resistance becomes duty.'
> — Thomas Jefferson[234]

Are we able to perceive the aggregate outcome from billions of isolated actions and choices in a globalized world? Are we as a species capable of curbing our technology and economy, or do they control us? Has our culture outgrown us? Or will we reach a stage, in time, where we manage to control our own species and choose a path towards a future where one would want to live? Social contagion also means that once we get started we might be able to achieve much more than we ever thought possible.

Is our current ethic adequate in a full world where a single species holds the future in its hands? Are we capable of organizing ourselves differently even if we know how we ought to behave? Can nature-lovers become a political force to be reckoned with? Of course, it would be nice if we could forge functioning alliances with holders of other ethics and ideologies that make people more likely to fight for a beautiful world.

Jean de la Bruyère once said that life is a tragedy for the man who feels, and a comedy for the man who thinks.[235] But for a true tragedy we must both think *and* feel: we have to know what is going on, think about it, and have emotions associated with what we perceive. Our 'democracy,' such as it is, is predicated on those who vote having what it takes to do these things adequately and to make responsible decisions. That, in turn, sets up countless tragedies.

Throughout this book we have come across numerous instances of language that guides and distorts people's conceptions of the natural world and relationships to other species. As Chris Hedges writes in *Wages of Rebellion: The Moral Imperative of Revolt*:[236]

> Revolutions, when they begin, are invisible, at least to the wider society. They start with the slow discrediting and dismantling of an old ideology and an old language used to interpret reality and justify power. Human societies are captive to and controlled by language. When the old ideas are shattered, when it is clear that the official words and ideas no longer match the reality, the institutions that buttress the ruling class deflate and collapse. Our battle is a battle over what the experimental psychologist and linguist Steven Pinker refers to as 'mutual knowledge.'[237]
>
> 'Human beings do not live in the objective world alone, nor alone in the world of social activity as ordinarily understood, but are very much at the mercy of the particular language which has become the medium of expression for their society,' the linguist Edward Sapir writes.
>
> It is quite an illusion to imagine that one adjusts to reality essentially without the use of language and that language is merely an

incidental means of solving specific problems of communication and reflection. The fact of the matter is that the 'real world' is to a large extent unconsciously built up to the language habits of the group. [...] We see and hear and otherwise experience very largely as we do because the language habits of our community predispose certain choices of interpretation.[238]

When you cannot trust to dumb luck, conscious decisions, arrived at through a purposefully designed process, and rational, forceful and timely action, is better. A wider moral mandate than just focussing on humans is a good place to start. Any sound decision hinges on sound values. As George Marshall writes, we have to find ways of engaging our emotional brain and creating institutions that sustain our response.[239]

The sciences can teach us better ways of doing things. But we have to have a *reason* to do things differently, beyond the purely utilitarian.[240] We must have emotions tied to the outcome of our actions. It is our feelings that create the wish that things were otherwise than they are. Feelings move us to act.

> 'If you know wilderness in the way that you know love, you would be unwilling to let it go. We are talking about the body of the beloved, not real estate.'
> — Terry Tempest Williams[241]

In our evolutionary history, we have not been selected for our ability to solve complex tasks for the future, with costs that must be borne in the present, to be solved collaboratively by organizing in societies. It may well be that we are not up to such a challenge, neither as a species or as a society, even if the future depends on it.

The first step is to mobilize enough common will to tackle the challenges we face. This will be a function of how much we care about the other species with which we share this world. If we are not able to mobilize enough collective will to force responsible action, it is likely that humans will stand out as a particularly short-lived species. It is time for a new social contract, compatible with life, lest the state of the world decays into a Hobbesian 'natural' order. Perhaps if we prevail, future humans may see a different kind of full world. Perhaps there is still time to recreate a world full of life, rich nature, beautiful places, healthy and abundant populations of wildlife and plants – a place for real humans to live full, rich lives. A Full World.

Perhaps the fear of calamities that will hit humanity does not impel us to action simply because calamity is what humanity deserves. Perhaps a calamity wiping out humans is widely, if unacknowledged, seen as the only solution to the world's problems. But the other species are innocent. I, for one, will not accept their premature demise while we wait for humanity's misdeeds to catch up with us. Perhaps those who love other species are more willing to act on their behalf, and more able to do so in time. Revolutions, when they come, are sudden and unexpected. So perhaps we are not as far away from doing something as we think.

Of course, for many species it is already too late. They are dying out at a rate of perhaps 70 per day, or three species per hour.[242] None of us will be able to do much unless we get organized – and even then it is a long shot.

> *'Unless someone like you cares a whole awful lot,*
> *nothing is going to get better. It's not.'*
>
> — Dr Seuss[243]

Afterword: Can We Save The World?

'To build a road is so much simpler than to think of what the country really needs.'

— Aldo Leopold

None of us can do much on our own. In isolation all who want to save the world feel hamstrung to the point of dejection and passivity. Few things are more painful for someone burning to make a real difference in the world than the frustration of being unable to do anything meaningful and the feeling of impotence in the face of crisis. Moving mountains requires organizing. We need to connect with a critical mass of allies and confederates and act in ways that leverage further action by ourselves and others, setting off chain reactions of complementary activity and collaboration.

If anything I've written strikes a chord with you and you are committed to making the world a place with a viable future for species large and small, *please* contact me. My information can be found on tvburkey.org/contact_info.htm. I also write occasionally on ThorsHammer.blogspot.no, and notes can be left there. One can also contact me there through links to e-mail, my Facebook account, and Twitter. As one who has struggled my whole life with the frustrated drive to 'save the world' and its species, I need to hear from potential allies and about promising initiatives, connect with like-minded partners in action, and find out if there are more like us out there. We need to work together, communicate what we want, find potential comrades in arms, get a better idea of how many we are, and take it from there.[244]

*

The task that is foremost in my mind, and my actions, lately, is to institute, and bring together key people, from a variety of disciplines and experiences, for a seminar/workshop series to result in an edited book with the title 'Can We Save The World?' Alternatively, 'Can The World Be Saved?'

As stated above, 'Saving The World' is just a shorthand for finding and effecting real solutions to large, complicated problems that involve tipping points and international aspects. These are problems that threaten the multitude of life forms on Earth; issues such as climate change, biodiversity loss, over-harvesting and over-exploitation of 'natural resources' (like fish populations and forests, aquifers, soils, marshes and wetlands, etc.), ocean acidification, and so on. What are the problems we need to overcome to enable humanity to act? Is it possible to get humanity to take necessary and sufficient action in time, given a somewhat unclear deadline? If not, what institutions are needed? In trying to answer the question 'Can we save the world?' to the best of our abilities, we would compile, in one place, what it is that we think we know about what exactly our limitations, challenges and barriers to solving these kinds of problems are. Identifying the causes of inertia and inaction is the first step to doing something about it.

One might think that this was a rather central issue of our times, a prominent feature of public discourse, but, oddly, it is not. A negative answer to this all-important question is not an invitation to fatalistic despair and passivity: if the conclusion is that we cannot move humanity to necessary and sufficient action in time (with existing institutions), that too is a powerful and important message. As long as we don't see how it would be possible, we would have extremely strong reasons to think deeply and exhaustively, without constraint or limitations on the steps to be considered, about what it would really take to Save The World. What institutions, with what powers and mandates, would be needed to get the required steps implemented? What processes need to be embarked upon? What processes are possible, or desirable? What can we say about our

AFTERWORD: CAN WE SAVE THE WORLD? | 139

ability to solve such problems? If it turns out we have no idea, that knowledge is powerful too.

Many of us today answer with a simple 'No,' when asked whether the world can actually be saved. Subjecting this question to rigorous and exhaustive analysis may actually re-energize some of us and give us hope — or failing that, perhaps a measure of acceptance and a last taste of the joy of life after we have given up. Or perhaps once our despair at achieving anything within existing social structures is complete, we may derive a renewed will to fight for a new world, with different power structures.

We will start from the premise that the world needs saving, while not worrying overly what the specific challenges facing us are (biodiversity meltdown, climate crisis, human population size and growth with exploding consumption, fisheries crises, etc.), and analyze whether we really could solve the problems that needed to be solved, if we really wanted to and needed to. Political scientists and other professionals from the humanities and natural sciences, mechanistic thinkers with complementary skill-sets, people with experience of past and present efforts, and people from a variety of walks of life, would be key to a broad and in-depth assessment of this question.

A book or a seminar series may seem a pathetic response compared to the scale of the challenges ahead of us if we are to fight for what we love, but the truth is that in the frenzied lives of professionals, that many people assume are out there trying to save the world on our behalf, asking such a simple question falls by the wayside. And at the moment I am not aware of any endeavors that I, personally, could get involved with or be invited to join, that I might find more promising. Everybody is too busy struggling to keep up with their assigned tasks to take a hard look at whether what we are doing is necessary and sufficient — to take the broader overview required. No one, and no group, at present has the time and resources to take this comprehensive view, or to take a deep look for real solutions. And by 'solutions' we mean a set of necessary and sufficient mechanisms that are actually implemented; not only the changes needed, but how we can actually see them through. Nobody has brought adequate time, focus and resources to bear on this overarching question. How do we get humanity to *actually* take the necessary and adequate steps?

When mathematicians are working on a particularly difficult problem, they sometimes try to show whether or not a solution exists at all before trying to find it. This can be a very powerful exercise. With concrete world-threatening problems, we could, like mathematicians exploring a difficult proof, explore whether a solution is indeed possible, and perhaps what the requisite preconditions might be. Then, afterwards, we can work on finding the actual solutions. And perhaps having undergone this preliminary analysis will help us get dedicated initiatives in place where we can work with all possible focus, brain-power, and available resources, on identifying those solutions and the processes we need to embark upon.

Unfortunately, our political system is not used to tackling problems with potentially irreversible damages, the kinds of problems where it may (suddenly) be too late. People are not trained problem-solvers. Our schools do not teach problem solving. It is quite possible to train people to become good problem-solvers, but we don't. (Why is that?) Of course, no real solution can be definitively specified in advance. Adaptive management, trial and error, and false starts, must necessarily be involved when we are dealing with complex processes. Our path will be more convoluted and chaotic than anyone would like. Yet, this momentous question cannot be ignored. When the world is at stake, one does not simply blunder along in the dark, without seeking as much illumination as can reasonably be found. Let us not proceed in a haphazard or casual way, without a true grasp of the challenges ahead, but study the tools and resources we have at our disposal, in a conscious and structured manner, and use the results to design a coherent approach. At least a structured and deliberate approach should be a complementary effort to the haphazard and uncoordinated approach. The question is a matter of life or death writ large, and must be studied thoroughly in order that we may know where we stand and what tools and options we have — we must have a firmer grasp on the situation.

All the more urgency to get started. Like Archimedes, we need a firm point on which to stand and a long enough lever to move the world. What new institutions might we need? What is our state of preparedness for the tasks at hand? What internal and external resources do we have? We may be able to identify classes of problems that are solvable, and problems that are not. The actual problem to be addressed may actually prove not to be all that important to the analysis (as long as it is a system with tipping points, and international dimensions, as these are the interesting and important problems). The real issues involve humanity's readiness and abilities, degree of cohesion, and willingness to do what it takes. One might even work on hypothetical, unspecified, problems — to imagine issues without scientific uncertainty, for instance. Can we get enough people to agree about the nature of the problems and what needs to be done? Are a great many people really required, or are there better ways? Can we solve a complex problem when we know we have to?

Of course an alternative approach is to try all possible options for saving the world. That often proves a good way to go about it when we are dealing with complex processes that we do not fully understand. With the amount of effort, resources and focus that humanity is currently directing at the questions that will determine our common future, however, blind trial and error would not seem to be a feasible path to take in our current predicament.

Subtopics for analysis/book chapters might include:

- **Why are we not acting to save the world?** Psychological, evolutionary, game-theoretical, structural, etc. mechanisms that pose challenges to meaningful coordinated action. Can we improve our odds of success by keeping a watchful eye towards cognitive biases and logical fallacies, and try to use them for good whenever possible and acceptable?

- **How to make good international agreements.** The criteria and mechanisms for meaningful treaties: compliance, encourage participation, discourage free-riders, censure, side-payments, and other measures that make some treaties effective while others are not.
- **Acting unilaterally in a connected world.** It is hard for anyone to act unilaterally; much more expensive (and perhaps impossible), than to act as part of a larger group. In the absence of global consensus, how can one start in smaller groupings while exploiting mechanisms that encourage others to join?
- **Our current democratic system: designed so nothing much will change, so what do you do when something really needs to change?** Checks and balances were built into our systems so major upheaval (and abuses of power) would not occur, but in the kinds of problems addressed here you actually need some major action to be taken at times... The Dunning-Kruger effect: people don't know that they are incompetent.[245] Can we get a system that works even in the face of widespread ignorance, stupidity and greed? Can a weak democracy fix itself?
- **Our Future Democratic System: What are the characteristics of a system that works when you need it to?** Democracy is a matter of degree, not simply that you have it or you don't. What measures can we put in place to improve our democracy? Can we have democracy also at a global level? For instance, ought our representatives in global fora be elected directly?[246]
- **War-time economies and how we got things done when we needed to.** Partial suspension of democracy; mandates for meaningful action, without too many checks and balances; rationing; small groups empowered, etc. Are any of the tools from war-time and states of emergency applicable for us now?
- **An international system that works: What is needed in (a) super-national institution(s) to save the world?** Currently the only international system is the UN. Can it be altered to function

effectively as a real system of global governance, or does an entirely new institution need to be created?
- **Time constraints: Can we make it in time? How to deal with irreversible damage and systems with break points, tipping points and positive feed-back loops.** People, and our political system, are not used to situations where things can be irreversibly damaged, and there is such a thing as too late. Can we make it in time? Do tipping points pose an insurmountable obstacle for our (current) democratic system? Can enough people be made aware of impending tipping points while there is still time?
- **Everyone doing their little bit: What when there are not enough doing it?** Can we get enough people involved in time? How could you ever know what is necessary and sufficient? What about all the people and agents pulling in other directions? And overpowering societal forcing mechanisms? Are there alternatives to 'everyone doing their little bit'? Can all the little projects add up to a solution, or are we fooling ourselves? Does fooling ourselves in such a way make a real solution more unlikely?
- **Is inter-disciplinary research/collaboration possible? What models work best for teams that want to get things done?** Can natural scientists and social scientists and politicians/bureaucrats work together to save the world? Are there good ways to get the general populace involved?
- **What role for different disciplines?** Getting people from different backgrounds to work together. What role for the different professions? Can we get society to use the knowledge and the experience that we already have? What role for 'common folks'?
- **Black swans and hopeful monsters: Can we plan in complex systems?** If complexity, unknown unknowns, social contagion, accidents of history, punctuated equilibrium[247], and our proneness to a diversity of fallacies limit our power to predict, what hope for planning? Can we know in advance what approaches are likely to work? Is it actually rational to not plan for saving the world, because we don't know how to plan such complex 'projects'? If so, what kinds of approaches hold promise? Are we better off trying to position ourselves to take advantage of happy acci-

dents and staking the future of the world on a diversity of diffuse and distributed processes? If we cannot plan for success, does focussing on process rather than results actually help?

- **Super wicked problems and general approaches to solving them.** What do we know about how to solve super wicked problems? The original coiners of the term suggested that we need present means of restraining our future selves (path dependent policy interventions), and that interventions should be *sticky*, should *entrench* support over time, and should *expand* to include greater population sets as they progress.[248] What else have we learned that may prove useful?

- **A Law of Ecocide: What role for the legal system, international or domestic?** Law is usually pretty conservative. Can it lead? What is lacking in current legal systems to help us save the world?

- **A new economy: Are real solutions compatible with our current economic and monetary systems?** Will any advances be eaten up by continued growth? Is increased efficiency all we can hope for? Does this mean staking all our hopes on technofixes? What are the traits of an economic system where we actually could save the world?

- **Dealing with uncertainty: Can we act responsibly under uncertainty?** Will science ever get to the point where politicians and bureaucrats will/can take meaningful action? How can we deal responsibly with uncertainty?

- **A role for coercion? How would it work?** Are there feasible and acceptable ways to coerce our own populace, or that of other nations? Or ways of working around them, or leaving them out of the equation? Are there positive ways to involve the populace that are part of necessary and sufficient measures?

- **What will China do?** When China and India are both 1.4 billion people, and the Chinese economy is three times the size of the US economy, what will happen then? Will they be focused on saving the world? Will that happen soon enough?

- **Trans-border problems.** To what extent can a problem be effectively addressed within a single nation or other administrative boundary? What do we know to be useful when we have to solve trans-border or multinational problems?

- **Communication: How to communicate effectively for action.** How to mobilize people to action, rather than just disseminating information. What do we know about social movements?
- **The strategic mindset: Tools for strategic and tactical organizing.** How to win the battle *and* the war. Do we know how it can be done? What do we know about planning? What lessons can we learn, or have we learned, from history?
- **What difference does a problem make?** Is the solution different if the problem is climate change/biodiversity crisis/resource crises/demographic crisis/food crisis/over-exploitation (overfishing)/economic crisis? Do solutions to some problems require a different economic system (e.g. a steady-state economy) while others do not? Are more narrow problems (how to stop bottom trawling/deforestation, removing harmful subsidies, overfishing) different from wider problems (global climate change/human population size/building a more appropriate economic system)?
- **Interactive problems.** Can we fix the biodiversity crisis without fixing the climate crisis? Can we fix the biodiversity crisis and the climate crisis without changing the economic system? Can we solve large problems given the weaknesses of our democracy? Can we build better institutions within the existing framework or do we need to go beyond the existing framework? Can smaller questions like overfishing/over-harvesting, invasive species, strife and poverty be fixed without fixing the larger problems of climate, biodiversity crisis, economic crisis, population crisis, institutional crises, and the weaknesses of our current (democratic) model? Can you save one species, without saving a host of other species that it interacts with, and solving the problems of habitat loss and over-exploitation?
- **Technofixes: Is this all we can hope for?** Some issues lend themselves to technofixes, others do not. Technofixes tend to be partial and have unintended consequences/side-effects. Can we deal with the initial problem as well as the secondary effects of the 'solution'? Are the intransigencies of our system such that technofixes are all we can realistically hope for? Given what humans can do, would it not be odd if we cannot solve a problem of our own making?

- **Exploitable social tipping points in solutions.** Sometimes, when change comes it comes rapidly and unexpectedly. Can we use our knowledge of the dynamics of social systems to exploit the nature of tipping points and social trigger points in our quest for solutions?
- **A new story for our existence.** Do we need a new narrative for humanity in order to make fundamental changes in our lives, communities and mentalities necessary to address root causes of the threats we are facing?

The details of contents, focus, structure and format, methods, facilities, required resources, recruitment and participation, preparation, etc. would of course be worked out during the process.

This effort needs key collaborators, the right set of participants with complementary skill-sets and experiences, funding, an institutional affiliation, appropriate venue(s), facilitation, a good editor and sympathetic publisher, and then perhaps: *readers*. Readers with a drive to revolutionize the way we deal with the natural world, rectify past wrongs, catalyze action, and create a better world.

*

I hope that such a seminar-series and book may serve as a precursor to the creation of a think tank/task force, to be called 'The Solutions Center' or something like that, to work at identifying necessary and sufficient, real-world, actually implementable, solutions to the major challenges of our times. Having ascertained that it should still be possible to save the world (if indeed that were our findings), and identified the kinds of institutions that would be needed to do so, we could set about finding real solutions and outlining the real institutions we would need to make it happen. I would personally love to be a participant at such a think tank, and will be looking into ways to make it a reality. The necessary steps for making it happen are similar to those for the seminar-series/book, only that the commitment of core staff and required funding would be much greater. Ideally, a variety of initiatives and measures could run concurrently, and one wouldn't have to wait for the completion of one to work hard on another.

To make headway with such complex issues it seems to make sense to make a concerted effort to come up with and assess practical solutions. Small teams of dedicated, smart people could be hand-picked to deal exclusively with a single issue, for a specified period of time — for instance two years — after which they should submit their recommendations. Teams would be constructed to provide the necessary combinations of knowledge, intelligence, experience, creativity and specific skill-sets — not only in the academic sense, but in terms of knowledge and experience of how the world actually works, currently (or doesn't work, as the case may be): both broad and specific knowledge and understanding, access to information and networks, definitive problem-solving skills, analysis and modeling skills, overview, and the ability to work in teams as well as independently. Such teams should be housed at politically independent think tanks — something which, oddly, seems to be in short supply in today's world. The teams should have access to anyone who could help shed light on, or analyze, sub-components of the analysis (specific knowledge, modeling capacity, analyses, brain-storming). They should be isolated enough to give their complete attention to the work at hand, yet have sufficient resources in terms of access to information, communications, people, modeling resources and computing power, institutions and support teams/assistance from associated personnel with specific skill-sets, as needed. At times they would be able to invite others to provide specific information or inputs, participate in seminars/workshops and brain-storming sessions, assist with particular tools or provide any knowledge or experiences not adequately covered within the team itself.

The recommendations of such teams/think tanks would of course not be taken up automatically by national or international institutions such as governments. However, their recommendations would be out there for all to see. They would be available for public scrutiny. They would be hard to ignore, as they would state explicitly what approaches will not work, or will be inadequate in isolation, and they would be backed by the most comprehensive thinking and analyses of the issue available. (Though people are extremely adept at ignoring what they want to ignore.) At the very least, governments and other institutions would be pressured on whether or not they had any ideas better than the ones proposed by the think tanks, why they were not implementing the recommendations if there were no better ideas out there, and what, if anything, was being done. Simply documenting a feasible approach to such important issues would be powerful. Moreover, if feasible solutions were not found that could be implemented in our current system, this would provide a powerful impetus to analyzing what kind of structures and institutions (systems) would have to be created in order for practical and realizable solutions to exist. More powerful still, would be the demonstration that none of the measures currently on the table or being discussed are up to the task. This might help clear away the endless bickering about minutiae and the political posturing over half-measures and inane diversions from the real issues. For the public it would be a useful counterpoint to what they are hearing from the politicians, bureaucrats, NGOs and special interest groups.

If someone wished to dispute the findings of such a team, they would have to conduct their own analysis and make it available for scrutiny. At the very least, the discourse would shift to comparing competing comprehensive analyses, their inputs, methods and limitations, rather than what we have now, which is simply a confusion of more or less half-baked and unsupported opinions. Such opinions are typically thrown out there with very limited analysis, and certainly without a thorough modeling of whether or not the steps suggested are necessary or sufficient. And they are often colored by ideology and careerism more than a real desire to solve the real problems.

All this is not to say that there should be one team, or one think tank, where the participants alone are holding the fate of the world in their hands. The more the merrier. Anyone would of course be free to set up competing think tanks or related efforts. Harnessing the power of competition ought to be a boon in this area as in many others. All I am saying, is that someone should be taking such a focussed and in-depth look at the challenges we face, and we should be throwing the requisite amount of resources, of all kinds, at this most vital task. I believe the most limited resource to date has been *focus*: the ability for a large enough group of people to dedicate enough time and brain-power to a single issue, without distraction, to make real progress towards an adequate solution.

An alternative, and perhaps a complementary effort, might be to crowd-source thinking about these matters. This could be enabled by internet technology and collaborative software, such as wikis and groupware. Personally, I think this ought to be a complementary, and preferably parallel, approach. The key requirement is to be able to allocate more focus, time, brain-power, tools, creativity, critical thinking, and hard-nosed analysis to the most important issue of all, than anyone has been able to do before.

Largely, we know what needs to be done, but have no idea how to get humanity to do it. The truth is, nobody knows how to get people to act when we need people to act. Pretending, or imagining, that we do only makes matters worse. Our political systems are rigged so that no major changes will occur. This is OK as long as things can generally bumble along as they always have, but it is a disaster in a crisis situation when you really need to get something done – and something major! Typically, when nations really needed to get something done, as in the case of major wars, they have tended to suspend elements of democracy and instate executive rule. Coming up with solutions does not just require good ideas about things that can be done, but has to include how to get them implemented. It is not a solution unless it is carried out – and in time! The teams involved in such think tanks would likely operate, in part, as a microcosm of all of the categories of actors in our society: as politicians, civil servants, academics/scientists, citizens, activists, conferences/workshops, and NGOs. And of course, they should collaborate with such groups as best they can.

Typically, potential solutions will be conditional: 'If we can get enough politicians to do x, then...', 'If we can get enough countries to enact y, then...', 'If we can get people to support z, then...'. The real question is always: how do we get people to do x, y and z? No analysis is complete before this core conundrum is resolved. Real solutions have to be modeled to demonstrate that they will be adequate, and to uncover any weaknesses and limitations and allow for modifications. Even then, implementation has to be subject to adaptive management. Solutions will have to be smart, in the sense that they incentivize countries and other actors to join in, rather than remain on the outside, disrupting. This kind of analysis is all too rare in our society, and absent from current discourse. Something major has to change, and no stone should be left unturned in order to solve the hard problems that are threatening life on Earth. We are the ones who have to make those changes.

Great problems are not to be taken lightly. One cannot simply keep plodding along in one's daily life as if nothing were amiss, blindly hoping that things will be OK, one way or the other; that someone, somewhere, will fix it in time. Finding real solutions is often a function of what you are willing to do, and that, in turn, depends on how difficult you feel the situation to be — on your level of desperation. When you are desperate enough you may finally take the no-holds-barred approach to solutions that the situation requires. Many may not know it or feel it, because of the time delay involved, but the desperation of our situation is currently as high as it can get. On a personal level many will become more desperate later, but our collective do-or-die moment is now. Can we instill the appropriate sense of desperation, and agency, in people, before it is too late?

What are we willing to do?

Notes

1. Daniel G. Kozlovsky 1974. *An Ecological and Evolutionary Ethic.* Prentice-Hall: New Jersey, p. x.
2. My translation.
3. Rachel Carson 1962. *Silent Spring.* (fortieth Anniversary Edition, 2002) Mariner Books, Houghton Mifflin Company: New York, p. 297.
4. Charles Darwin 1859. *On the Origin of Species by Means of Natural Selection, or the Preservation of Favoured Races in the Struggle for Life.* John Murray: London. Perhaps a case can be made for Thomas Malthus' *An Essay on the Principle of Population*, as Darwin himself attributed to Malthus the key inspiration that enabled him to put it all together.
5. Roderick F. Nash 1989. *The Rights of Nature: A History of Environmental Ethics.* The University of Wisconsin Press, p. 160.
6. My translation, p. 96 in Haagen Ringnes 1998. *Reflekser i trylleglass: stemmer fra vårt århundre.* JW Cappelens Forlag: Oslo.
7. Charles J. Krebs 1985. *Ecology: The Experimental Analysis of Distribution and Abundance.* Harper & Row: New York.
8. And genetic drift, which occurs primarily in small populations. Genetic mutations would still occur, but there would be no evolutionary *adaptation*. Things that kill you late in life have little evolutionary effect, and little selection pressure against it. Most of the residual selection pressure we are faced with in today's world may be sexual selection rather than external pressure from 'nature.' And most of the sexual selection we are subject to may primarily affect the timing of reproduction more than whether or not you actually reproduce. Seems like nearly everyone reproduces, and those that choose not to probably don't have particular genes that affect this choice.
9. Nash, p. 156.

    And before you say that it is not the number of humans that is critical, but consumption: who do you think is doing the consuming? Yes, we can certainly have more equitable distribution of wealth and eat less meat, but once humans are born it is hard to control their behavior – including their reproductive choices. We could each reduce our ecological footprint, but the only way to reduce that footprint to zero is not to be born. And as a parent, you have no idea how large your extended footprint will be, or for how many generations it will last after you are gone.

True, consumption is currently increasing faster than population, and one might conceivably be able to cut consumption faster than population, but clearly both are important. As is technological efficiency, up to a point. Efficiently cannot increase indefinitely, and per capita consumption cannot go to zero. It makes little sense to be concerned about how much we consume, yet not be concerned about the number of consumers. Of course, human impact on the biosphere need not go all the way to zero, at least not if humans can learn to behave themselves. However, we are in the midst of a number of global crises, some of which have been ongoing for quite a while, all of which would be less severe if we were fewer humans and behaved better. Have you noticed that we are in the throes of a climate crisis, a biodiversity crisis, an overfishing crisis, a soil crisis, and a number of lesser crises? Yes, the global human population growth rate may be declining, but that does not solve the problem if we are already too many. As a rich, first-world consumer, creating another consumer, who may in turn create more consumers, is the single most consequential decision you will make in your lifetime. No other decision has nearly as much effect on your ecological footprint.

10. Paul J. Crutzen 2002. *Geology of mankind: The Anthropocene.* Nature 415:23 [DOI:10.1038/415023a].
11. King James version.
12. Johan Rockström, Will Steffen, Kevin Noone, et al. 2009. *Planetary Boundaries: Exploring the Safe Operating Space for Humanity.* Ecology and Society 14(2):32. [URL: http://www.ecologyandsociety.org/vol14/iss2/art32/]. And references therein.
13. Jørgen Randers 2012. *2052: A Global Forecast for the Next Forty Years.* Chelsea Green Publishing: White River Junction, VT, p. 139.
14. Alison Mood and Phil Brooke 2010. *Estimating the Number of Fish Caught in Global Fishing Each Year.* Fishcount.org.uk. [URL: http://fishcount.org.uk/published/std/fishcountstudy.pdf, accessed December 15, 2015].
15. J. Matthew Roney 2012. *Taking Stock: World Fish Catch Falls to 90 Million Tons in 2012.* Earth Policy Institute (online). [URL: http://www.earth-policy.org/indicators/C55, accessed December 15, 2015].
16. Daniel Pauly and Dirk Zeller 2016. *Catch reconstructions reveal that global marine fisheries catches are higher than reported and declining.* Nature Communications 7:10244 [DOI: 10.1038/ncomms10244; URL:

http://www.nature.com/ncomms/2016/160119/ncomms10244/pdf/ncomms10244.pdf, accessed February 22, 2016]. See also Chelsea Harvey, January 19, 2016. 'Why we've been hugely underestimating the overfishing of the oceans'. Washington Post [URL: https://www.washingtonpost.com/news/energy-environment/wp/2016/01/19/why-weve-been-hugely-underestimating-the-overfishing-of-the-oceans/?tid=sm_fb, accessed February 22, 2016].

17. The number 100 million is commonly cited, but it is hard to get good references for this estimate. Clarke et al. (2006) give a median estimate of 38 million sharks killed per year (26 to 73 million) just for the shark fin trade, but many murdered sharks do not enter the shark fin trade. Huge numbers are killed as by-catch, others in non-commercial fisheries, and there are enormous hidden numbers. Dogfish are caught in vast numbers, among other things for fish and chips, although this number has declined as dogfish species have become endangered. 100 million is therefore perhaps not a bad estimate of the total number of sharks we kill per year. It is commonly stated that all shark species are currently endangered. IUCN's red data lists yield a lower proportion, but there are many reasons why IUCN is commonly conservative.
Shelley C. Clarke, Murdoch K. McAllister, E. J. Milner-Gulland, et al. 2006. *Global estimates of shark catches using trade records from commercial markets.* Ecology Letters 9:1115–26 [URL: http://cnso.nova.edu/ghri/forms/clarke06.pdf, accessed December 15, 2015].

18. Ransom A. Myers and Boris Worm 2003. Rapid worldwide depletion of predatory fish communities. Nature 423:280-3 [URL: http://www.fmap.ca/ramweb/papers-total/nature01610_r.pdf, accessed December 15, 2015].

19. Daniel Pauly, Reg Watson and Jackie Alder 2005. *Global trends in world fisheries: impacts on marine ecosystems and food security.* Philosophical Transactions Royal Society B 360:5-12 [DOI: 10.1098/rstb.2004.1574, URL: http://rstb.royalsocietypublishing.org/content/360/1453/5.full.pdf+html, accessed December 15, 2015].

20. Scott R. Loss, Tom Will and Peter P. Marra 2013. *The impact of free-ranging domestic cats on wildlife of the United States.* Nature Communications 4(1396) [DOI:10.1038/ncomms2380, URL: http://www.nature.com/ncomms/journal/v4/n1/full/ncomms2380.html].

21. Daniel Jason Lebbin, George H. Fenwick, and Mike Parr 2010. *The American Bird Conservancy Guide to Bird Conservation.* The University of Chicago Press: Chicago.

22. Peter Singer 2009. *Animal Liberation* (Updated Edition). Harper Perennial: New York.
23. Alison Mood 2010. *Worse things happen at sea: the welfare of wild-caught fish.* Chapter 19. *How many fish are caught each year?* Fishcount.org.uk [URL: http://www.fishcount.org.uk/published/std/fishcountchapter19.pdf, accessed December 15, 2015].
24. Robert M. May 2010. *Ecological science and tomorrow's world.* Philosophical Transactions Royal Society B 365:41–47; Rockström et al. 2009; and references therein.
25. Jared M. Diamond 1989. *The present, past and future of human-caused extinctions.* Philosophical Transactions Royal Society B 325:469–77.
26. Michael E. Soulé and Bruce A. Wilcox (eds.) 1980. *Conservation Biology: An Evolutionary-Ecological Perspective.* Sinauer Associates: Sunderland, MA. p. 8.
27. That is, the 'Living Planet Index' which summarizes population sizes of 10,380 supposedly representative species of wild (not domesticated) vertebrates (mammals, birds, reptiles, amphibians and fish), has declined by 52% over this time interval. WWF Living Planet Report 2014 [URL: http://wwf.panda.org/about_our_earth/all_publications/living_planet_report/, accessed February 25, 2016].
28. Vaclav Smil 1991. *General Energetics.* John Wiley: New York.
29. Vaclav Smil 2011. *Harvesting the Biosphere: The Human Impact.* Population and Development Review 37(4): 613–636 [URL: http://www.vaclavsmil.com/wp-content/uploads/PDR37-4.Smil_.pgs613-636.pdf, accessed December 15, 2015].
30. 'Positive' in this setting does not relate to the value of an effect, i.e. whether it is good or bad, but to its self-reinforcing effect, whereby the bigger something gets the more it grows. 'Positive' refers to the sign of the coefficient in front of the variable in question in a dynamic systems equation. It is the coefficients in the equation(s) that determines the feedback.

    Negative feedback is like a thermostat. Positive feedback is things like: trees dying and releasing their stored carbon when carbon-induced global warming gets too high for them. Permafrost melts and releases methane, a very powerful greenhouse gas. People fly more to get to skiing areas when snow disappears from their usual haunts. And we use more energy for air-conditioning as it gets hotter. Warmer air holds more water vapor, which in itself is a powerful greenhouse gas. Land without snow or ice, or snow covered with dust or soot, reflects less incoming sunlight, retaining more heat in the atmosphere. Higher temperatures increase the activity of soil microbes that break down carbon in the soil and top-soil, releasing it to the atmosphere. Higher temperatures and shifting climate zones will lead to an increase in invasive species and new diseases, heat stress and droughts which may cause forest death and increased break down of stored carbon. See Rockström et al. 2009, and references therein.

31. On a 20 year time scale methane has a global warming potential about 80 times greater than that of carbon dioxide. And at this point in time, we should be really concerned with what happens in the near term.
32. Lance H. Gunderson, Craig R. Allen and C. S. Holling 2010. *Foundations of Ecological Resilience*. Island Press: Washington DC.
33. One version included in *A Sand County Almanac*, 1949, but uttered in numerous contexts from about 1930.

    Aldo Leopold 1949. *A Sand County Almanac: And Sketches Here and There*. Oxford University Press.

    The full quote as it appears in *A Sand County Almanac*, reads: 'One of the penalties of an ecological education is that one lives alone in a world of wounds. Much of the damage inflicted on land is quite invisible to laymen. An ecologist must either harden his shell and make believe that the consequences of science are none of his business, or he must be the doctor who sees the marks of death in a community that believes itself well and does not want to be told otherwise.'
34. Cited in Benjamin J. Cohen 2004. *The Future of Money*. Princeton University Press.
35. E. F. Schumacher 1973. *Small is Beautiful: Economics as if People Mattered*. Blond & Briggs: London, Chapter 1.
36. Herman E. Daly 1999. *Uneconomic growth and the built environment: in theory and in fact*. pp. 73–86 in Charles J. Kibert (ed.), *Reshaping the Built Environment: Ecology, Ethics, and Economics*. Island Press: Washington DC.
37. Callum Roberts 2007. *The Unnatural History of the Sea*. Island Press: Washington DC, p. 133.

    Though this was likely due to the conflict with other fishermen, using traditional gear, rather than any consideration of the natural world and the other species in it.
38. As quoted in Robert McAfee Brown 1988. *Spirituality and Liberation: Overcoming the Great Fallacy*, p. 136. The attribution of this quote to St Augustin seems, however, to be disputed [see Wikiquote on 'Augustine of Hippo'; URL: https://en.wikiquote.org/wiki/Augustine_of_Hippo, accessed December 15, 2015].

39. As uttered by then Norwegian Prime Minister, Jens Stoltenberg, when introducing the Norwegian Forest and Climate Initiative which was to give three billion US dollars for tropical forest conservation as a climate mitigation effort. In the same vein we could stop taking airplane trips or stop eating meat, but unless other people do it, too, it doesn't amount to anything. Then we are either reduced to doing it as a merely symbolic act or as a signal to others, or because it makes us feel better (about ourselves) or for some direct benefit to ourselves or someone we care about (like the piece of meat in question – although someone was going to kill that cow or pig in any case).
40. B. F. Skinner 1987. *Upon Further Reflection*. Prentice-Hall: Englewood Cliffs, NJ, p. 2.
41. Rockström et al. 2009, Gro Harlem Brundtland, Paul Ehrlich, José Goldemberg, et al. 2012. *Environment and Development Challenges: The Imperative to Act*. Blue Planet Synthesis Paper, UNEP [URL: http://www.unep.org/pdf/pressreleases/Blue_Planet_synthesis_paper.pdf, accessed December 15, 2015].
42. Frances Cairncross 2004. *What makes environmental treaties work?* Conservation in Practice 5(2): 12–19. [URL: http://conservationmagazine.org/2008/07/what-makes-environmental-treaties-work/, accessed August 25, 2015].
See also Scott Barrett 2005. *Environment and Statecraft: The Strategy of Environmental Treaty-Making*. Oxford University Press.
43. Barrett 2005, p. xi.
44. Barrett 2005, p. xii.
45. Barrett 2005, p. xii.
46. James Hansen 2009. *Storms of My Grandchildren: The Truth About the Coming Climate Catastrophe and Our Last Chance to Save Humanity*. Bloomsbury Publishing: London.
47. Barrett 2005, p. 356.
48. It is always difficult to establish whether or not a treaty has made a difference, because we do not have a control: we do not really know what would have happened anyway, in the absence of a treaty. Countries might have had internal reasons to act on their own, or they might have made bilateral agreements or collaborated in smaller groups, or technological improvements may have continued at pace regardless.
49. Barrett 2005, p. 229.
50. Substitutes already existed for most of the uses of CFCs – although the substances that were to replace chlorofluorocarbons, hydrochlorofluoro-

carbons and hydrofluorocarbons, also have significant global warming potential.
51. Perhaps particularly part IV.
Francis Fukuyama 2014. *Political Order and Political Decay: From the Industrial Revolution to the Globalization of Democracy*. Farrar, Straus and Giroux: New York.
52. E.g. Bryan Caplan 2007. *The Myth of the Rational Voter: Why Democracies Choose Bad Policies*. Princeton University Press. Note, however, that Caplan's focus is on economic mechanisms, and these pertain only to the situation within a given context, notably the confines of a particular economic theory and its limitations.
53. Nassim N. Taleb 2007. *The Black Swan: The Impact of the Highly Improbable*. Random House: New York.
54. Source: Wikipedia, entry on 'The Black Swan (2007 book),' accessed 21 August 2015. The same source suggests discussion of the concept goes back to Aristotle.
55. Figure 14, chapter 17; Location 5419 in Kindle edition.
56. Popularized as the 'Bell Curve'; there are of course a number of other important statistical distributions, like the Poisson, Gamma (Chi-squared), the Pareto distribution, etc., with other properties and determinants.
57. Taleb 2007, p. 43: 'If they [the banks] look conservative, it is because their loans only go bust on rare, very rare, occasions. There is no way to gauge the effectiveness of their lending activity by observing over a day, a week, a month, or ... even a century! In the summer of 1982, large American banks lost close to all their past earnings (cumulatively), about everything they had ever made in the history of American banking – everything.'
This sort of thing is not as outlandish as it might first appear. In systems with exponential growth (growth with a constant rate of increase), the entity in question (money in the bank, the size of the economy, or the global human population, as long as it remains in exponential growth) will double approximately every 69/r years, where r is the rate of increase, in percent. So if the rate of increase is 7 percent annually, a financial asset or a population size will double every ten years. Moreover, every doubling means an increase equal to all previous growth combined (cumulatively, throughout history, for as long as the exponential growth has been going on). Consequently, a loss of 50% entails a loss equal to all cumulative growth, through all time, up until the onset of the final doubling. That is, if the quantity has been doubling every decade until 1980, and then loses 50%, it will be back to where it was in

1970, and the losses will be equal to all historical growth up until 1970. This can also be seen from the (decadal) time series 1, 2, 4, 8, 16, 32, 64, 128, 256, 512, 1 024, 2 048, 4 096, 8 192, 16 384, 32 768, 65 536, 131 072, 262 144, 524 288, 1 048 576, 2 097 152, 4 194 304, 8 388 608, 16 777 216, 33 554 432, 67 108 864, 134 217 728, 268 435 456, 536 870 912, 1 073 741 824; for instance.

58. Wikipedia, 'Black swan theory' [URL: https://en.wikipedia.org/wiki/Black_swan_theory, accessed October 13, 2015].
59. Lewis Carroll 1871. *Through the Looking-Glass, and What Alice Found There*. Macmillan and Co: London, Chapter II.
   The Red Queen's exact words were actually 'Now, *here*, you see, it takes all the running *you* can do, to keep in the same place. If you want to get somewhere else, you must run at least twice as fast as that!'
60. Karl Popper 1957. *The Poverty of Historicism*. Routledge & Kegan Paul: London.
61. Karl Popper 1971. *The Open Society and Its Enemies*. Princeton University Press.
62. Slavoj Žižek 2012. *The Year of Dreaming Dangerously*. Verso Books: London.
63. Thomas Homer-Dixon 2000. *The Ingenuity Gap*. Alfred A. Knopf: Toronto, p. 1.
64. David Ehrenfeld 1978. *The Arrogance of Humanism*. Oxford University Press: New York, p. 241.
65. Raymond F. Dasmann 1975. *The Conservation Alternative*. Wiley: New York (cited by David Ehrenfeld, *The Arrogance of Humanism*, p. 240).
66. FAO 2016. *The State of World Fisheries and Aquaculture 2016. Contributing to food security and nutrition for all.* Rome
   [URL: http://www.fao.org/3/a-i5555e.pdf, accessed November 1, 2016].
67. Rob Dietz and Dan O'Neill, 2013. *Enough Is Enough: Building a Sustainable Economy in a World of Finite Resources*. Berrett-Koehler: San Fransisco.
68. Homer-Dixon, p. 102.
   Like the depiction of the year 2015 in the movie *Back to the Future 2*, with its proliferation of fax machines, this passage is a little dated. Like our difficulty with history, we have great limitations when it comes to imagining the future and what innovations, or social conditions, lie ahead. Most of us have seen similar effects in our daily work, where the advent of computer technologies has obliterated a lot of the support workers used to have from other workers. Whereas the housewife once received services from an ecosystem of specialists, most of us now have to be our own secretaries, travel agents, librarians,

analysts, editors, publishers, etc. In other ways, a lot of jobs have become much more specialised, as new niches arise and complexity begets more complexity.

69. George Monbiot 2003. *Manifesto for a New World Order*. The New Press: New York.
70. Homer-Dixon, p. 5.
71. Homer-Dixon, p. 4.
72. Christopher Stone 2010. *Should Trees Have Standing? Law, Morality and the Environment*. Oxford University Press, chapter 8, footnote.
73. Kelly Levin, Benjamin Cashore, Steven Bernstein, and Graeme Auld 2012. *Overcoming the tragedy of super wicked problems: constraining our future selves to ameliorate global climate change*. Policy Sciences 45(2):123-152.
74. Horst W. J. Rittel and Melvin M. Webber 1973. *Dilemmas in a General Theory of Planning*. Policy Sciences 4:155-169.
75. Levin et al., p. 125.
76. Thomas Pynchon 1973. *Gravity's Rainbow*. Viking Press: New York.
77. Amos Tversky and Daniel Kahneman 1974. *Judgment under Uncertainty: Heuristics and Biases*. Science 185:1124-31 [URL: http://psiexp.ss.uci.edu/research/teaching/Tversky_Kahneman_1974.pdf, accessed December 15, 2015].
78. This quote, or variants thereof, is often attributed to Joseph Stalin, but the provenance is unclear [see https://en.wikiquote.org/wiki/Joseph_Stalin]. The behavioral bias is also known as the 'identified victim' effect: Tehila Kogut and Ilana Ritov 2005. *The 'Identified Victim' Effect: An Identified Group, or Just a Single Individual?* Journal of Behavioral Decision Making 18:157-167 [DOI:10.1002/bdm.492].
79. A convenient list with a good set of references: https://en.wikipedia.org/wiki/List_of_cognitive_biases.
80. Daniel Kahneman and Amos Tversky 1973. *On the psychology of prediction*. Psychological Review 80(4):237-251.
81. Justin Kruger and David Dunning 1999. *Unskilled and Unaware of It: How Difficulties in Recognizing One's Own Incompetence Lead to Inflated Self-Assessments*. Journal of Personality and Social Psychology 77(6):1121-1134 [URL: http://www.jerwood-no.org.uk/pdf/Dunning%20Kruger.pdf, accessed December 15, 2015].
82. George Marshall 2014. *Don't Even Think About It: Why Our Brains Are Wired To Ignore Climate Change*. Bloomsbury: New York.
83. See e.g. Michael Shermer 2002. *Why People Believe Weird Things: Pseudo-

science, Superstition, and Other Confusions of Our Time. Henry Holt: New York, p. 22–23.
84. Tar De livsløgnen fra et gennemsnitsmenneske, så tar De lykken fra ham med det samme (Dr Relling, Act V., *Vildanden (The Wild Duck)*, 1884).
85. Clive Hamilton 2010. *Requiem For A Species: Why We Resist The Truth About Climate Change*. Earthscan: London, p. 48–49. The species that is the subject of Hamilton's requiem is the human species, as Hamilton argues that we will prove unable to stop catastrophic climate change – although multitudes of other species will inevitably die out before global climate change brings an end to humanity.
86. E.g. Charles G. Lord, Lee Ross, and Mark R. Lepper 1979. *Biased Assimilation and Attitude Polarization: The Effects of Prior Theories on Subsequently Considered Evidence*. Journal of Personality and Social Psychology 37:2098–109 [URL: http://synapse.princeton.edu/~sam/lord_ross_lepper79_JPSP_biased-assimilation-and-attitude-polarization.pdf].
Dan M. Kahan, Hank Jenkins-Smith and Donald Braman 2011. *Cultural Cognition of Scientific Consensus*. Journal of Risk Research 14:47–74
[URL: http://www.motherjones.com/files/kahan_paper_cultural_cognition_of_scientific_consesus.pdf].
Ulrike Hahn and Adam J. L. Harris 2014. *What Does It Mean to be Biased: Motivated Reasoning and Rationality*. Psychology of Learning and Motivation 61:41–102 [URL: http://www.ucl.ac.uk/lagnado-lab/publications/harris/Hahn_Harris_L&M2014.pdf, accessed December 15, 2015].
87. Chris Mooney 2011. *The Science of Why We Don't Believe Science*. Mother Jones May/June 2011 [URL: http://www.motherjones.com/politics/2011/03/denial-science-chris-mooney, accessed December 15, 2015].
88. Upton Sinclair 1935. *I, Candidate for Governor: And How I Got Licked*. University of California Press: Berkeley.
89. A number of studies documenting these effects are discussed in Mooney 2011. See also Joe Keohane 2010. *How facts backfire*
[URL: http://www.boston.com/bostonglobe/ideas/articles/2010/07/11/how_facts_backfire/?page=full, accessed December 15, 2015].
Backfire effect: Brendan Nyhan and Jason Reifler 2010. *When Corrections Fail: The Persistence of Political Misperceptions*. Political Behavior (2010) 32:303–330 [DOI: 10.1007/s11109-010-9112-2;
URL: http://climate.engin.umich.edu/figures/Rood_Climate_Change_AOSS480_Documents/Nyhan_Belief_Facts_Politics_PoliticalBehavior_2010.pdf].
90. Mooney, p. 2 (online edition).

91. Shermer 2002, p. 283.
92. Max Planck 1936. *The Philosophy of Physics*. Norton: New York, p. 97.
93. Al Gore 1992. *Earth in the Balance: Ecology and the Human Spirit*. Houghton Mifflin: Boston.
94. Naomi Oreskes and Erik M. Conway 2010. *Merchants of Doubt: How a Handful of Scientists Obscured the Truth on Issues from Tobacco Smoke to Global Warming*. Bloomsbury Press: New York.
   There is also a 2014 documentary, directed by Robert Kenner, based on this book.
95. Shermer 2002, p. 5.
96. Derrick Jensen 2006. *Beyond Hope*. Orion Magazine May/June 2006 [URL: https://orionmagazine.org/article/beyond-hope/, accessed December 15, 2015].
97. E.g. Stuart Oskamp 2000. *Psychological Contributions to Achieving an Ecologically Sustainable Future for Humanity*. Journal of Social Issues 56:373–390 [URL: http://web.stanford.edu/~kcarmel/CC_BehavChange_Course/readings/Additional%20Resources/J%20Soc%20Issues%202000/oskamp_2000_2_generalobstacles_c.pdf, accessed 11 November, 2015].
   Kennon M. Sheldon and Tim Kasser 2008. *Psychological threat and extrinsic goal striving*. Motivation and Emotion 32:37–45
   [URL: http://www.selfdeterminationtheory.org/SDT/documents/2008_SheldonKasser_MOEM.pdf, accessed 11 November, 2015].
   Mark Dowd 2009. 'Fear is not the best motivator.' The Guardian, September 9 [URL: http://www.theguardian.com/commentisfree/belief/2009/sep/09/climate-change-operation-noah, accessed 11 November, 2015].
   George Monbiot 2014. 'An Ounce of Hope is Worth a Ton of Despair.' The Guardian, June 17 [URL: http://www.monbiot.com/2014/06/16/an-ounce-of-hope-is-worth-a-ton-of-despair/].
98. Sheldon and Kasser, p. 37.
99. Oskamp 2000, citing H. Leventhal, D. Meyer and D. Nerenz 1980. *The common sense representation of illness danger*. In S. Rachman (Ed.), *Medical psychology* Vol. 2:7–30. Pergamon: New York.
99a. *A Sand County Almanac*, 1949.
100. Pauly et al. 2005.
101. Derived from an old Chinese proverb.
102. Moisés Naím 2013. *The End of Power: From Boardrooms to Battlefields and Churches to States, Why Being In Charge Isn't What It Used to Be*. Basic Books: New York.

103. Naím, page 18.

Francis Fukuyama has made a similar point about what he calls today's 'vetocracy,' as well as stressing the effect of a society increasingly layered and polarized with the shrinking of the middle class.

Francis Fukuyama 2014. *Political Order and Political Decay: From the Industrial Revolution to the Present Day.* Farrar, Straus and Giroux: New York.

104. Michael Shellenberger and Ted Nordhaus 2004. *The Death of Environmentalism: Global Warming Politics in a Post-Environmental World.* This paper was distributed at the 2004 meeting of the Environmental Grantmakers Association and is available online [URL: http://www.thebreakthrough.org/images/Death_of_Environmentalism.pdf, accessed 30 November, 2015].

105. A fail-safe means of reducing the ecological footprint of billions of humans, is to make humans smaller. *Much* smaller. Think Tom Thumb... Bird-food size. Or, you could just create good plant-based substitutes for meat... Or use contraception...

106. Henry David Thoreau. 1854. *Walden; or, Life in the Woods.* Ticknor and Fields: Boston.

107. Skinner, p. 6.

108. *A Sand County Almanac,* Foreword (signed 1948).

109. Lynn T. White 1967. *The Historical Roots of Our Ecological Crisis.* Science 155:1203–1207.

110. Nash 1989.

111. White, p. 1205.

112. Jens-André P. Herbener 2015. *Naturen er hellig – klimakatastrofe og religion.* Informations Forlag: Copenhagen.

113. Nash 1989.

114. Nash, p. 93.

115. White, p. 1206.

116. Nash, p. 20.

117. I Corinthians 9:9–10.

118. Richard D. Ryder 1989. *Animal Revolution: Changing Attitudes Towards Speciesism.* Basil Blackwell: Oxford, p. 28 (2000 edition).

119. Aquinas, like Aristotle, was of the opinion that only humans had 'rational' souls. Animals had 'sensitive' souls which were not 'rational' [Ryder's footnote].

120. Ryder, p. 28, 2000 edition.

121. Jeremy Bentham 1789. *Introduction to the Principles of Morals and Legislation.* Methuen: London, p. 235.

122. John Muir 1875. *Wild Wool*. Overland Monthly, April, p. 364.
123. John B Cobb Jr. 1972. *Is It Too Late? A Theology of Ecology*. Bruce: Beverly Hills.
124. *The Arrogance of Humanism*, p. 120.
125. Darwin himself concludes *On the Origin of Species* with these words: 'There is grandeur in this view of life, with its several powers, having been originally breathed into a few forms or into one; and that, whilst this planet has gone cycling on, according to the fixed law of gravity, from so simple a beginning endless forms most beautiful and most wonderful have been, and are being, evolved.'

    Given the simplicity of Darwin's evolutionary theory, and its extraordinary explanatory power, Leibniz may have presaged Darwin when it comes to encapsulating this grandeur: 'God, however, has chosen the most perfect [world], that is to say the one which is at the same time the simplest in hypotheses and the richest in phenomena.' (G. W. v. Leibniz, *Discourse on Metaphysics*, sec. 6 in Leibniz, p. 11. G. R. Montgomery trans. 1962. Open Court: La Salle, IL.)
126. Immanuel Kant 1911 [1785]. *Grundlegung zur Metaphysik der Sitten*, Ak 4:420–1 (Academy edition of Kant's *Gesammelte Schriften*, Volume 4).
127. Kant's first formulation of his 'supreme principle' of morality reads: 'Act so that maxima of your action may be adopted as a universal law.' His second formulation (the one Schopenhauer attacks, in *On The Basis Of Morality*) reads: 'Act so as to treat humanity, both in thine own person and in the person of every other, always as an end, never merely as a means.' [See URL: http://www.animal-rights-library.com/texts-c/schopenhauer01.htm].
128. Isaac Bashevis Singer 1972. *Enemies: A Love Story*. Farrar, Straus & Giroux: New York.
129. Nash, Epilogue.
130. Nash, p. 207.
131. Paul W. Taylor 1986. *Respect for Nature – A Theory of Environmental Ethics*. Princeton University Press.
132. In Joel Feinberg's terminology, 'To have a right is to have a claim to something and against someone the recognition of which is called for by legal (or other institutional) rules, or in the case of moral rights, by the principles of an enlightened conscience.' (p. 43) Obviously, such formal claims or the nature of an 'enlightened conscience' are more context specific than objective, invariant, reality. Moreover, if *my* 'enlightened conscience' feels that elephants and elephant shrews have 'rights,' then presumably they do. But it

may not be constructive to talk of 'rights' as more than a mental shorthand for something else.

Joel Feinberg 1974. *The Rights of Animals and Future Generations*, pp. 43–68 in William Blackstone (ed.), *Philosophy and Environmental Crisis*. University of Georgia Press: Athens, GA.

133. Nash, p. 211.
134. In the words of J. Baird Callicott: 'If rights were real natural entities associated with us from birth, it is surprising that they were not sooner or more universally noticed.'

    J. Baird Callicott 1986. *On the Intrinsic Value of Nonhuman Species*. pp. 138–172 in Bryan G. Norton (ed.), *The Preservation of Species: The Value of Biodiversity*. Princeton University Press.
135. This Abbey quote can be found in *Earth Apples: The Poetry of Edward Abbey*, published posthumously in 1994, edited by David Petersen. St. Martin's Press: New York.
136. John Muir 1903. *Our National Parks*. Houghton, Mifflin & Company: Boston, p. 57.
137. [See http://www.wired.com/2009/12/octopus-tools/, accessed December 15, 2015].
138. Vincent G. Dethier 1962. *To Know a Fly*. Holden-Day: San Fransisco, p. 118–19; cited by Shermer, p. 22–23.
139. I have recently found an amusing Victorian-era parallel, in the writing of early Darwinian, Dr Lauder Lindsay:

    > In truth, the physical differences between certain animals and certain men is much less obvious than between different individuals, classes and races of man himself. Thus the difference is not more striking between different ages, sexes, and other conditions of man than between the lowest savage races of man and the anthropoid apes, the dog, or even the ant... Man's claim to pre-eminence on the ground of uniqueness of his mental constitution is as absurd and puerile, therefore, as it is fallacious. His overweening pride or vanity has led to his futile contention with the evidence of facts. He has trusted to a series of gratuitous assumptions.

    Lauder Lindsay 1879. *Mind in the Lower Animals*. In Kegan Paul, vol. 1, pp. 118–25 (cited in Ryder, p. 162).

    Ryder goes on to write: Lindsay, a medical man, claimed that nonhumans are capable of reason as well as religious and moral sense, and went on to argue that since the lower animals 'are unquestionably our fellow-creatures and fellow-mortals' then man is bound to show them kindness: 'In general terms, the treatment of the lower animals by man is to be conducted on the same principles as that of his fellow man, or of the child by his parent or instructor. This is the only rational system or mode of treatment.'

140. *The Arrogance of Humanism*, p. 146.
141. Shermer 2002, p. 47. See also Stephen Jay Gould 1981. *The Mismeasure of Man*. W. W. Norton: New York.
142. Göran E. Nilsson 1996. *Brain and body oxygen requirements of* Gnathonemus petersii, *a fish with an exceptionally large brain*. The Journal of Experimental Biology 199:603–607 [URL: http://jeb.biologists.org/content/199/3/603.full.pdf, accessed December 15, 2015].
Also, some mice have brain-to-body mass ratios similar to that of humans, and small birds and tree shrews have ratios greater than that of humans. Small ants can have brains that make up as much as 15% of their body mass. Marc A. Seid, Armando Castillo and William T. Wcislo 2011. *The Allometry of Brain Miniaturization in Ants*. Brain, Behavior and Evolution 77(1):5–13 [DOI: 10.1159/000322530].
Humans have since started measuring brain-to-body mass allocation as the 'encephalization quotient,' which takes into account body size allometry. See Evan M. Macphail 1982. *Brain and Intelligence in Vertebrates*. Clarendon Press: Oxford.
143. Edward Abbey 1989. *A Voice Crying in the Wilderness (Vox Clamantis in Deserto): Notes from a Secret Journal*. St. Martin's Griffin: NY, p. 13.
144. Having a theory of mind relates to all the business of thinking about what others know or do not know, what they understand, and so on. For instance, various species of birds in the crow family (corvids) show signs of going through the mental arithmetic involved in assessments like the following: 'this individual over there was in a position where he could have seen me hide a food item over here, so he may know where it is and I should hide it again while he is not looking, while that individual over yonder would have had his view of the location obscured by that outcropping, so he does not know what I know...', etc.
See e.g. Nicola S. Clayton, Joanna M. Dally and Nathan J. Emery 2007. *Social cognition by food-caching corvids. The western scrub-jay as a natural psychologist*. Philosophical Transactions Royal Society B 362:507–522;
Joanna M. Dally, Nathan J. Emery and Nicola S. Clayton 2009. *Avian Theory of Mind and counter espionage by food-caching western scrub-jays* (Aphelocoma californica). European Journal of Developmental Psychology 7(1):17–37;

Thomas Bugnyar 2011. *Knower–guesser differentiation in ravens: others' viewpoints matter.* Proceedings Royal Society B 278:634–40.

145. E.g. Derek C. Penn and Daniel J. Povinelli 2007. *On the lack of evidence that non-human animals possess anything remotely resembling a 'theory of mind'.* Philosophical Transactions Royal Society B 362:731–744;

Thomas Bugnyar 2011;

Elske van der Vaart , Rineke Verbrugge and Charlotte K. Hemelrijk 2012. *Corvid Re-Caching without 'Theory of Mind': A Model.* PLoS ONE 7(3): e32904 [DOI:10.1371/journal.pone.0032904].

146. Singer 2009.

147. Bentham, p. 236.

148. Whereas Singer would claim that 'the capacity for suffering and enjoying things is a prerequisite for having interests at all' (*Animal Rights*, p. 148), Feinberg merely notes that 'a being must have *interests* [my emphasis] if he is to be a logically proper subject of rights.' Feinberg's distinction between 'a thing' and someone that can have interests, does not rest on Kant's rationality nor Singer's, Bentham's or Hume's ability to suffer or feel pain (sentience) nor Tom Regan's awareness (being 'subjects-of-a-life'), but focuses instead on conation (the mental faculty of purpose, desire, or will to perform an action; volition [my dictionary]): 'A mere thing, however valuable to others, has no good of its own. The explanation of that fact, I suspect, is that mere things have no conative life; neither conscious wishes, desires, and hopes; nor urges and impulses; nor unconscious drives, aims, goals; nor latent tendencies, directions of growth, and natural fulfillments.' Goodpaster (1978) expands the notion of having interests to plants. Plants should also be granted standing (they are 'morally considerable') because they, in Feinberg's terms, display 'tendencies, directions of growth, and natural fullfillments.' See also Stone (1972, 2010), Hall (2011), and Feinberg (1974) on the interests (and 'rights') of plants.

Kenneth Goodpaster 1978. *On being morally considerable.* Journal of Philosophy 75:306–25.

Christopher D. Stone 1972. *Should Trees Have Standing – Toward Legal Rights for Natural Objects.* Southern California Law Review 45:450–87.

Tom Regan 2003. *Animal Rights, Human Wrongs: An Introduction To Moral Philosophy.* Rowman & Littlefield: Lanham, MD, p. 101.

Matthew Hall 2011. *Plants as Persons: A Philosophical Botany.* SUNY Press.

149. Taylor 1986.

150. Aldo Leopold 1930. *Game Management.* University of Wisconsin Press: Madison, p. 19.

151. John Muir 1916. *A Thousand-Mile Walk to the Gulf*. Houghton Mifflin Company: Boston, pp. 98–99 (cited in Callicott, p 147).
152. David Ehrenfeld 1976. *The Conservation of Non-Resources*. American Scientist 64(6):648–656 [and pp. 207–209 in *The Arrogance of Humanism*].
153. Cited in E. S. Turner 1964. *All Heaven in a Rage*. Michael Joseph: London, p. 162.
154. Mike J. Morwood, Peter Brown, Jatmiko, et al. 2005. *Further evidence for small-bodied hominids from the Late Pleistocene of Flores, Indonesia*. Nature 437:1012–7. *Homo neanderthalensis* survived in a remote area of southern Spain until we wiped them out about 27,000 years ago (Tattersall and Schwartz 2000) – although it has been traditional to treat them as *Homo sapiens neanderthalensis*, and recent evidence regarding the prevalence of Neanderthal genes in our own species would seem to support that view (again), and that perhaps 'breeding them out' was an aspect of their demise. It may also be worth noting that Neanderthals, now extinct, also had larger brains than modern humans.

    Ian Tattersall and Jeffrey Schwartz 2000. *Extinct Humans*. Westview Press: Boulder, CO, p. 220.
155. Joshua D. Greene, R. Brian Sommerville, Leigh E. Nystrom, et al. 2001. *An fMRI Investigation of Emotional Engagement in Moral Judgment*. Science 293(5537): 2105–8 [DOI: 10.1126/science.1062872].
156. Nash, p. 44–5.
157. John Stuart Mill 1871. *Principles of Political Economy, with some of their Applications to Social Philosophy*, Book IV, Chapter IV, §3. John W. Parker: London. This book went through seven editions, the first one 1848, the last 1871.
158. Unless something critical has changed, and a species and its environment are on their way to a new equilibrium – in which case time scale is a factor. In this context, stable oscillations and a stable domain in state-space is considered equilibrium.
159. Cf. WWF 1999, Boudron et al. 2009, and references therein.

    Frédéric Baudron, Marc Corbeels, François Monicat, Ken E. Giller 2009. *Cotton expansion and biodiversity loss in African savannahs, opportunities and challenges for conservation agriculture: a review paper based on two case studies*. Biodiversity and Conservation 18(10):2625–44.

    WWF 1999. *The impact of cotton on fresh water resources and ecosystems*. WWF Background Paper [URL: http://awsassets.panda.org/downloads/impact_long.pdf, accessed December 16, 2015].

160. Interested readers might start their digging in one or more of these classic pieces:
William D. Hamilton 1963. *The evolution of the altruistic behavior.* American Naturalist 98:353-356.
William D. Hamilton 1964. *The genetical theory of social behavior.* Journal of Theoretical Biology 7:1-32.
Robert L. Trivers 1971. *The evolution of reciprocal altruism.* Quarterly Review of Biology 46:35-57.
Edward O. Wilson 1975. *Sociobiology: The New Synthesis.* Harvard University Press: Cambridge.
Elliott Sober and David Sloan Wilson 1998. *Unto Others: The Evolution and Psychology of Unselfish Behavior.* Harvard University Press.
See also Charles Darwin 1871. *The Descent of Man and Selection in Relation to Sex.* John Murray: London.
161. Taylor, p. 285.
162. Tom Regan 1983. *The Case for Animal Rights.* University of California Press.
163. Kant 1911 [1785], p. 420-1.
164. John Rawls 1971. *A Theory of Justice.* Belknap Press (Harvard University Press): Cambridge MA.
165. Immanuel Kant 1913 [1788]. *Kritik der praktischen Vernunft,* Ak 5:776.
166. King James version.
167. Arthur Schopenhauer 1840. *Über die Grundlage der Moral.* Unless otherwise noted, the actual wording repeated here is from *Arthur Schopenhauer, Philosophical Writings,* 1994. Edited by Wolfgang Schirmacher. Continuum: New York (Schirmacher, p 210-11).
168. The obvious exception is real science, which by definition provides something new, either testing past results, presenting new data, providing new interpretations, or new analysis. Then there is also room for writing about this new insight, or writing based on it, with re-evaluations of past claims. But in the political realm, most decisions don't really require new insight. Mostly, it is a matter of using the knowledge that we already do have.
169. *Über die Grundlage der Moral,* 1840. Schirmacher, pages 232-234. In the translation of E. F. J. Payne it becomes *The Foundation of Ethics,* and the wording is as follows.
170. Elsewhere, in a different translation: The assumption that animals are without rights and the illusion that our treatment of them has no moral significance is a positively outrageous example of Western crudity and bar-

barity. Universal compassion is the only guarantee of morality. [Schopenhauer, *On The Basis Of Morality*. My footnote.]

171. My emphasis. Note, again, that this was written some 20 years before Charles Darwin's *On the Origin of Species* was published. It is said that great ideas are often a product of their time, and the seeds to their eventual elucidation may be found all over, and indeed Darwin dragged his feet for 20 years before he had the impetus to publish. His chief insight was also independently and simultaneously arrived at by Alfred Russel Wallace [Alfred Wallace 1858. 'On the Tendency of Varieties to Depart Indefinitely From the Original Type'; letter sent to Darwin in March of 1858. URL: http://people.wku.edu/charles.smith/wallace/S043.htm, accessed November 1, 2016]. However, Darwin's greatest contribution was not the identification of descent with modification or that species evolve from a common ancestor, but the *means* by which they do so, the mechanism of evolution: natural selection. (He also played the pivotal part in the acceptance of evolutionary thinking by making the case so forcefully, and convincingly, with a wealth of convincing examples.) Note also that Schopenhauer used 'identity' in the mathematical sense of 'identical' and 'oneness,' not in the more common modern sense of 'identification' and ego.

172. Translator's note: Rudolph Wagner (1805–1864), physiologist and anthropologist, professor at Erlangen and Göttingen. [Not my footnote.]

173. Schirmacher, p 233–4.

174. Nash 1989, Ryder 1989.

Note, however, that Ryder (on p. 34), along with a variety of others, seems to have fallen prey to, and thus help to propagate, a twentieth century prank apparently designed to give a more sympathetic impression of the ancient Church's regard for animals. Otherwise St Basil and certain other representatives of the ancient Church might have been seen to presage both Schopenhauer and Darwin. If we, following Ryder, are to believe C. W. Hume (1962), Schopenhauer seems to echo St John of Chrysostom, one of several pre-Fransiscan saints who preached kindness to animals and 'a powerful influence in the Byzantine Church,' who (according to C. W. Hume) said 'The Saints are exceedingly loving and gentle to mankind and even to brute beasts... Surely we ought to show them great kindness and gentleness for many reasons, but above all, because they are the same origin as ourselves.' (Allegedly Homily 39, on the Epistle to the Romans, quoted in C. W. Hume 1962. *The Status of Animals in the Christian Religion*. Universities Federation for Animal Welfare Bulletin 2.)

Ryder claims that in the ancient Church, there was a long tradition of saints, even before St Francis, that preached kindness to animals, and includes this prayer (allegedly) from the Liturgy of St Basil:

> The Earth is the Lord's and the fulness thereof. O God, enlarge within us the sense of fellowship with all living things, our brothers the animals to whom thou has given the earth as their home in common with us. We remember with shame that in the past we have exercised the high dominion of man with ruthless cruelty, so that the voice of the earth, which should have gone up to Thee in song, has been a groan of travail. May we realise that they live, not for us alone, but for themselves and for Thee, and that they love the sweetness of life. (Citing quote in C. W. Hume 1962. Universities Federation for Animal Welfare Theological Bulletin 2, p. 3.)

But, as Philip Johnson has discovered, and describes on his blog, this prayer does not stem from St Basil in the fourth century at all, but rather from an early twentieth century book of prayers by a Walter Rauschenbusch. [See URL: http://animalsmattertogod.com/2012/05/01/st-basils-animal-prayers-are-a-hoax-part-one/, accessed September 22, 2015].

175. Schirmacher, p. 156. The preceding passage reads:

> Now if, as a rare exception, we come across a man who possesses a considerable income, but uses only a little of it for himself, and gives all the rest to persons in distress, while he himself forgoes many pleasures and comforts, and we try to make clear to ourselves the action of this man, we shall find, quite apart from the dogmas by which he himself will make his action intelligible to his faculty of reason, the simplest general expression and the essential character of his way of acting to be that he *makes less distinction than is usually made between himself and others*. This very distinction is in the eyes of many so great, that the suffering of another is a direct pleasure for the wicked, and a welcome means to their own well-being for the unjust. The merely just person is content not to cause it; and generally most people know and are acquainted with innumerable sufferings of others in their vicinity, but do not decide to alleviate them, because to do so they would have to undergo some privation. Thus a strong distinction seems to prevail in each of all these between his ego and another's. On the other hand, to the noble person, whom we have in mind, this distinction is not so significant. The *principium individuationis*, the form of the phenomenon, no longer holds him so firmly in its grasp, but the suffering he sees in others touches him almost as closely as does his own. He therefore tries to strike a balance

between the two, denies himself pleasure, undergoes privations, in order to alleviate another's suffering. He perceives that the distinction between himself and others, which to the wicked man is so great a gulf, belongs only to a fleeting, deceptive phenomenon.

[Regrettably, the passage is marred by a footnote, not adequately moored in empiricism, concerning the relative suffering of 'man' and 'animals' and 'Man's right over the life and power of animals.']

176. As in *An Inquiry Concerning the Principles of Morals*, 1777.
177. Schirmacher, p. 228.
178. Schirmacher, p. 228-9.
179. Schirmacher, p. 229.

Schopenhauer continues: On the other hand, if we attempt to say, 'This man is virtuous but knows no compassion,' or, 'He is an unjust and malicious man yet he is very compassionate,' the contradiction is obvious.

180. Schirmacher, p. 235.
181. Schirmacher, p. 225.

Schopenhauer substitutes the 'will-to-live' for Kant's reason as the essence of the self, and it should not be a great leap to substitute such a will-to-live to having interests, and moral considerability, or 'standing.' I leave it to the reader to think for herself which organisms on our planet exhibit such 'will-to-live,' such striving for life.

Arthur Schopenhauer, *The World as Will and Idea*; see also *Transcendent Considerations Concerning the Will as Thing in Itself, The Will to Live: Selected Writings of Arthur Schopenhauer*, Richard Taylor (ed.). Frederick Unger: New York.

On the Will in Nature:

> ...what Kant set as the *thing-in-itself* over against mere *appearance*, more definitely called by me *representation* [*Vorstellung*], and regarded as absolutely unknowable, that this *thing-in-itself*, I say, this substratum of all appearances and consequently of the whole of nature, is nothing but what we know immediately and very intimately and find within ourselves as *will*. Accordingly, far from being inseparable from, and even a mere result of *knowledge*, as all other previous philosophers assumed, this *will* is fundamentally different from, and wholly independent of knowledge, which is quite secondary and of a later origin. Consequently, the will can exist and manifest itself even without knowledge, as is actually the case in the whole of nature from the animal kingdom downward. As the one and only thing-in-itself, that

which alone is truly real, the only original and metaphysical thing in a world in which everything else is only appearance, in other words, mere representation, this will endows all things, whatever they be, with the power by virtue whereof they are able to exist and act. Accordingly, not only the voluntary actions of animals, but also the organic mechanism of their living bodies, even the shape and constitution thereof, also the vegetation of plants, and finally even the inorganic kingdom crystallization, and generally every original force manifesting itself in physical and chemical appearances, in fact gravity itself — all these in themselves and outside the appearance, which merely means outside our head and its representation, are absolutely identical with what we find in ourselves as *will*. Of this will we have the most immediate and intimate knowledge that is at all possible. Further, the individual manifestations of this will are set in motion by motives in the case of knowing, i.e., animal beings, but no less by stimuli in the organic life of animals and plants, and finally by mere cause in the narrowest sense of the word in the case of inorganic nature; such distinctions concern only the appearance. On the other hand, knowledge and its substratum, the intellect, is a mere secondary phenomenon, entirely different from the will and accompanying only the higher stages of the will's objectification, and not essential to the will itself. It is dependent on the will's appearance in the animal organism, and is therefore physical, not metaphysical like the will itself. Consequently, absence of will can never be inferred from an absence of knowledge; on the contrary, the will can be demonstrated even in all those appearances of nature where there is no knowledge, of vegetable as well as inorganic nature. Therefore, will is not conditioned by knowledge, as was hitherto assumed without exception, although knowledge is conditioned by will. (Schirmacher, pp 76–77.)

182. Schirmacher, p. 230.
183. Schirmacher, p. 239.
184. Translator's note: Pausanias, 1:17:1.
185. Translator's note: Stobaeus, *Florilegium* 1:31.
186. Translator's note: The Panchatantra is a collection of fables of Indian origin, in five books, compiled in the fifth century.
187. Schirmacher, p. 240-1.
188. Feinberg 1974, Goodpaster 1978.
189. Feinberg 1974.

Further:

> Now we can extract from our discussion of animal rights a crucial principle for tentative use in the resolution of the other riddles about the applicability of the concept of a right, namely, that the sorts of beings who can have rights are precisely those who have (or can have) interests. I have come to this tentative conclusion for two reasons: (1) because a right holder must be capable of being represented and it is impossible to represent a being that has no interests, and (2) because a right holder must be capable of being a beneficiary in his own person, and a being without interests is a being that is incapable of being harmed or benefitted, having no good or 'sake' of its own. Thus, a being without interests has no 'behalf' to act in, and no 'sake' to act for. My strategy now will be to apply the 'interest principle,' as we can call it, to the other puzzles about rights, while being prepared to modify it where necessary (but as little as possible), in the hope of separating in a consistent and intuitively satisfactory fashion the beings who can have rights from those which cannot.

190. 'My inclination is to construe the notion of rights as more specific than that of considerability, largely to avoid what seem to be unnecessary complications over the requirements for something's being an appropriate "bearer of rights." The concept of rights is used in wider and narrower senses, of course.' Perhaps, as I have suggested, there is something muddled about the whole notion of 'rights' and 'human rights.' 'I doubt whether it is so clear that the class of rights-bearers is or ought to be restricted to human beings, but I propose to suspend this question entirely by framing the discussion in terms of the notion of moral considerability (following Warnock), except in contexts where there is reason to think the widest sense of "rights" is at work. Whether beings who deserve moral consideration in themselves, not simply by reason of their utility to human beings, also possess moral rights in some narrow sense is a question which will, therefore, remain open here – and it is a question the answer to which need not be determined in advance.' (Goodpaster 1978, p. 311)
191. Goodpaster 1978, p. 310.
192. Stone 1972.
193. Edward O. Wilson 2014. *The Meaning of Human Existence*. Liveright: New York.
    Edward O. Wilson 2012. *The Social Conquest of Earth*. Liveright: New York.
194. This may be a paraphrased variant or alternative translation of Hugo's 'On

résiste à l'invasion des armées; on ne résiste pas à l'invasion des idées.' (*Histoire d'un Crime* (The History of a Crime), written 1852, published 1877). Alternatively, the English phrase 'an idea whose time has come' may have been first published in the English translation of Gustave Aimard's *Les Francs-Tireurs* (1861): 'Il y a quelque chose de plus puissant que la force brutale des baïonnettes: c'est l'idée dont le temps est venu et l'heure est sonnée.'

(There is something more powerful than the brute force of bayonets: it is the idea whose time has come and hour struck) [Source: Wikipedia on Victor Hugo [URL: https://en.wikiquote.org/wiki/Victor_Hugo]].

195. The is/ought dichotomy, and the fallacy of extrapolating from the descriptive to the normative, was treated by David Hume, in *A Treatise of Human Nature*, 1777 (first published in 1738). The term 'naturalistic fallacy' stems from G. E. Moore's *Principia Ethica*, 1903.
196. Albert Schweitzer 1931. *Aus Meinem Leben und Denken*. Felix Meiner Verlag: Leipzig, chapter 13. English translation, 1933, *Out of My Life and Thought, An Autobiography*, by C. T. Campion. George Allen & Unwin: Woking.
197. John Muir 1898. *The Wild Parks and Forest Reservations of the West*. Atlantic Monthly, LXXXI:15–28.
198. Immanuel Kant 1914 [1797]. *Die Metafysik der Sitten*, Ak 6:443.
199. Deuteronomy 25:4 reads: 'Thou shalt not muzzle the ox when he treadeth out the corn.' (King James version) The quote from Aquinas is from his *Summa Contra Gentiles*, iii. 113. In *Summa Theologica* [S T II, i, Q. 102, art. 6] he wrote: God's purpose in recommending kind treatment of the brute creation is to dispose men to pity and tenderness towards one another.
200. Bryan G. Norton 1984. *Environmental ethics and weak anthropocentrism*. Environmental Ethics 6(2):131–148 [DOI: 10.5840/enviroethics19846233].
201. Edward O. Wilson 1984. *Biophilia*. Harvard University Press.
202. *The Arrogance of Humanism*, p. 269.
203. Chellis Glendinning 1994. *My Name is Chellis and I'm in Recovery from Western civilization*. Shambhala Publications: Boston.
204. See John Zerzan 2002. *Running on Emptiness – The Pathology of Civilization*. Feral House: Los Angeles.
205. *A Sand County Almanac*, Foreword.
206. White 1967.
207. Lynn White, John Cobb, Joseph Wood Krutch, and others; see Nash 1989, pp. 94, 107, and references therein.
208. Schirmacher, p. 202.

209. Schirmacher, p. 204.
210. Kant 1785. Ak 4:437-8.
211. *World of Will 2*: 646 (Schirmacher, p. xvii).
212. It was not until 1879 that Native Americans were recognized in the United States as persons eligible for federal writs of habeas corpus.
213. Nash, p. 202.
214. Nash, p. 205.
215. H. Maine, Ancient Law 153 (Pollock ed., 1930). Westermarck, supra note 3, at 393-4, was skeptical that the arbitrary power of the father over the children extended as late as into early Roman law [Stone's footnote].
216. Though of course it is always perilous to treat the diversity of North American cultures as a monolithic group [my note].
217. Stone 2010, p. 1.
218. Nash, p. 206.
219. Lawrence Kohlberg 1981. *The Philosophy of Moral Development*. Harper & Row: San Fransisco.
220. Richard D. Ryder 1971. *Experiments on Animals*, in Godlovitch, Godlovitch and Harris (eds.), *Animals, Men and Morals*. Taplinger: New York, p. 81.
221. Nash, p. 201.
222. *A Sand County Almanac* 1949, Foreword.
223. Dave Foreman 2004. *Rewilding North America: A Vision For Conservation In The 21st Century*. Island Press: Washington DC, p. 6.
224. [URL: http://en.wikipedia.org/wiki/Deep_ecology#cite_note-8, http://en.wikipedia.org/wiki/Deep_ecology#cite_note-8].
225. The Economist 2012. 'Whales are people, too: A declaration of the rights of cetaceans.' Feb 25th [URL: http://www.economist.com/node/21548150]. Personhood for whales etc.:
Thomas I. White 2015. *Whales, Dolphins and Ethics: A Primer*. In Denise L. Herzing and Christine M. Johnson (eds.), *Dolphin Communication and Cognition: Past, Present, and Future*. MIT Press [URL: https://uk.whales.org/sites/default/files/twhite-whales-dolphins-ethics.pdf; see also http://us.whales.org/issues/primer-on-non-human-personhood-and-cetacean-rights].
David Neiwert 2015. *Of Orcas and Men: What Killer Whales Can Teach Us*. The Overlook Press: New York [*Salon* (excerpts from *On Whales and Men*): http://www.salon.com/2015/06/27/are_killer_whales_persons_the_more_we_learn_about_orcas_the_more_our_assumption_of_innate_superiority_looks_like_a_presumption/].

There is clear evidence of culture in at least cetaceans and primates, and a group of orcas in the waters between Washington state and British Columbia has acquired legal protection based on its distinct culture. Genetic analyses suggest that cultural differences may even have caused reproductive isolation between different 'types' of orcas, to the point where they may be considered incipient species.

Hal Whitehead, Luke Rendell, Richard W. Osborne and Bernd Würsig 2004. *Culture and conservation of non-humans with reference to whales and dolphins: review and new directions.* Biological Conservation 120:427–437

[URL: http://faculty.washington.edu/wirsinga/Whitehead2004.pdf].

Court ruling on protection of orca culture: Georgia Strait Alliance 2003. *US Court overturns decision not to list Orca population as endangered.* December 18 [URL: https://georgiastrait.org/press/us-court-overturns-decision-not-to-list-orca-population-as-endangered/].

226. John Hooper 2002. 'German parliament votes to give animals constitutional rights'. The Guardian, May 18 [URL: http://www.guardian.co.uk/world/2002/may/18/animalwelfare.uk].

Erin Evans 2010. *Constitutional Inclusion of Animal Rights in Germany and Switzerland: How Did Animal Protection Become an Issue of National Importance?* Society and Animals 18: 231–250 [URL:

http://www.animalsandsociety.org/wp-content/uploads/2016/04/evans.pdf].

227. Margot Michel and Eveline Schneider Kayasseh 2011. *The Legal Situation of Animals in Switzerland: Two Steps Forward, One Step Back – Many Steps to go.* Journal of Animal Law, Volume VII:1–42

[URL: http://www.afgoetschel.com/de/downloads/legal-situation-of-animals-in-switzerland.pdf, accessed August 25, 2015].

Vanessa Gerritsen 2013. *Animal Welfare in Switzerland – constitutional aim, social commitment, and a major challenge.* Global Journal of Animal Law GJAL 1/2013 [URL: http://www.gjal.abo.fi/gjal-content/2013-01/article3/Gerritsen%20FINAL.pdf].

228. Peter Singer, *Animal Liberation*, preface to the 2009 edition.

229. See Polly Higgins 2010. *Eradicating Ecocide: Laws and Governance to Stop the Destruction of the Planet.* Shepheard-Walwyn: London.

230. [URL: http://www.eradicatingecocide.com].

231. While the government said that dolphins 'should' be recognized as legal persons with the capacity for certain legal rights, it fell short of actually granting them such rights or status.

232. David Kirby 2014. *Here's All the Places Around the World That Ban Orca*

Captivity. Take Part, April 10 [URL: http://www.takepart.com/article/2014/04/10/all-states-countries-and-cities-ban-orcas-captivity, accessed August 24 2015].

233. Polly Higgins 2010–15. *What Is Ecocide?* Eradicating Ecocide [URL: http://eradicatingecocide.com/the-law/what-is-ecocide/, accessed December 3, 2015]. See also Higgins 2010.

234. According to The Thomas Jefferson Foundation, 'This statement has not been found in Thomas Jefferson's writings, although it captures some of the ideas that Jefferson expressed in the Declaration of Independence, e.g. '...when a long train of abuses and usurpations, pursuing invariably the same Object evinces a design to reduce them under absolute Despotism, it is their right, it is their duty, to throw off such Government...' [URL: https://www.monticello.org/site/research-and-collections/when-injustice-becomes-law-resistance-becomes-duty-quotation]. (See also [URL: http://www.barrypopik.com/index.php/new_york_city/entry/when_injustice_is_law_resistance_is_duty_when_injustice_is_law_rebellion_is]).

Thomas Jefferson also wrote, 'I hold it that a little rebellion now and then is a good thing, and as necessary in the political world as storms in the physical,' and 'Strict observance of the written law is doubtless one of the highest duties of a good citizen, but it is not the highest [...] To lose our country by a scrupulous adherence to written law would be to lose the law itself.' He is also alleged to have said, 'All tyranny needs to gain a foothold is for people of good conscience to remain silent,' though this latter has not been found in Jefferson's writings either, and is variably attributed to Edmund Burke and others, though the closest quote we have may be from John Stuart Mill.

Henry David Thoreau did write, in *Civil Disobedience*, that 'If the injustice is part of the necessary friction of the machine of government, let it go, let it go: perchance it will wear smooth – certainly the machine will wear out... but if it is of such a nature that it requires you to be the agent of injustice to another, then I say, break the law. Let your life be a counter-friction to stop the machine. What I have to do is to see, at any rate, that I do not lend myself to the wrong which I condemn.' Martin Luther King, Jr. is also attributed the statement 'One has a moral responsibility to disobey unjust laws.'

235. As quoted in J. Raymond Solly 1913. *Selected Thoughts from the French: XV Century-XX Century, with English Translations*. Reprint, Forgotten Books: London (2013), pp. 132–3. Though the quote may be attributable to Horace Walpole.

236. Chris Hedges 2015. *Wages of Rebellion: The Moral Imperative of Revolt*. Nation Books: New York, p. 67.
    See also Monbiot 2014.
237. [Hedges' footnote:] Steven Pinker 2007. *The Evolutionary Social Psychology of Off-Record Indirect Speech Acts*. Intercultural Pragmatics 4:437–461 [URL: http://scholar.harvard.edu/files/pinker/files/evolutionary_social_psychology_of_off-record_indirect_speech_acts.pdf, accessed September 22, 2015].
238. Edward Sapir 1929. *The Status of Linguistics as a Science*. Language 5(4):207–14, p. 210. [Hedges' footnote].
239. Cf. Marshall, p. 229.
240. I use the term 'utilitarian' not in the philosophical sense that Jeremy Bentham and John Stuart Mill were known as 'utilitarians,' and exponents of utilitarianism, although there is a certain amount of overlap, but in the practical sense of arguing for what is useful (to us, and our in-group), i.e. useful to ourselves, not to others (assuming you do not include other species in your in-group, but merely consider what is good for humans). Utilitarianism in the formal sense argues that the best moral action is the one that maximizes utility, where utility is usually considered that which is related to the well-being of sentient beings. Hence, utilitarianism, depending on how it weighs the interests of different species against each other, could in some cases be closer to my own views than what we seem to be practicing today, and in that sense I have no great need to distance myself from the 'utilitarians.'
241. Terry Tempest Williams 1996. *Testimony: Writers in Defense of Utah Wilderness* (with Stephen Trimble). Milkweed Editions: Minneapolis.
242. Background rate: 0.1–1 species/yr/million species. Perhaps 30 million species extant. Natural rate: perhaps 3–30 species pr. year. Present rate, 1000 times higher (May 2010): 3,000–30,000 species extinct pr. year. Per day: 8–82 species extinct. Other sources hold that we may be driving as many as 200 species extinct per day (e.g. UNEP).
    See also Gerardo Ceballos, Paul R. Ehrlich, Anthony D. Barnosky, et al. 2015. *Accelerated modern human-induced species losses: Entering the sixth mass extinction*. Science Advances 1(5): e1400253 [DOI: 10.1126/sciadv.1400253, URL: http://advances.sciencemag.org/content/advances/1/5/e1400253.full.pdf, accessed 22 December 2015;
    Stuart L. Pimm, C. N. Jenkins, R. Abell, Thomas M. Brooks, et al. 2014. *The biodiversity of species and their rates of extinction, distribution, and protection*. Science 344(6187) [DOI: 10.1126/science.1246752].

243. *The Lorax* by Dr Seuss 1971. Random House: New York. Dr Seuss is the pseudonym of Theodor Seuss Geisel, author of children's books *The Cat in the Hat*, *Yertle the Turtle*, etc. [See http://en.wikipedia.org/wiki/The_Lorax].
244. However, if your aim is to be 'militant,' and engage in activities that the establishment can successfully construe as 'illegal' or 'violent,' you are likely better off not getting in touch, and instead operating in a cell structure and being extremely cautious about your lines of communication. In such efforts, I would at this point probably present more of a liability.
245. Kruger and Dunning 1999.
246. Monbiot 2003.
247. In evolutionary theory, an alternative to gradualism, whereby instead of gradual, slow change, we have long periods of stasis punctuated by spurts of rapid change and speciation. Here used as an analogy to sudden change and upheaval in social systems, and the unpredictability of historical events. (See Niles Eldredge and Stephen J. Gould 1972. *Punctuated equilibria: an alternative to phyletic gradualism* in Thomas J. M. Schopf (ed.) *Models in Paleobiology*. Freeman Cooper: San Francisco, pp. 82–115.)

    A non-gradual evolutionary leap, to something entirely out of past experience, a macromutation, was dubbed a 'hopeful monster' by German geneticist Richard Goldschmidt. Perhaps my recollection of such an abomination here is a commentary on the intellectual laxity of wishful thinking...
248. Levin et al. 2012.

Index

Abbey, Edward 66, 86, 90, 95, 164n135, 165n143
abolitionists 84, 124-125,
absorption point 14-16, 99, 103
abstract, scorn of the 51, 159n78
abundance 103, 151n7
accident of history 37, 92, 93, 97, 143
acidification of oceans 2, 20, 44, 49, 74, 138
acting to save the world 4, 25-29, 54-55, 73, 114, 117, 126, 139, 141
action 2-6, 21, 26-28, 31-34, 52, 55, 60-63, 72-73, 114, 118, 123-126, 128, 135-138, 141, 145-146, 163n127
action, individual 2-6, 26-27, 34, 55, 61-63, 114, 118, 128, 137, 163n127
action, unilateral 6, 27, 46, 55-56, 60-61, 127-128
actions, global 21, 24
activism 13-15, 127
activists 13-14, 60, 69, 150
activists, animal rights 13-14
activities, human 11, 14, 20, 21, 31, 129, 131
acts, illegal 22, 77, 179n244
ad ignorantiam 52, 54
adaptation 14, 59, 65-66, 87, 89, 100, 151n8
administrators 34
advice 26, 76, 115
agency 43, 61, 112, 132, 150
agreements, bilateral 156n48
agriculture 2 14, 22-23, 27, 33, 80
Aimard, Gustave 174n194
albedo 17, 154n30
Alexandria Library 65
Alice in Wonderland 41, 158n59
alive, being 112
Allee effect 17
alliances 72-73, 127, 134
allometry 165n142
altruism 101, 168n160
amphibians 154n27
analogy, argument from 89
anchoring 51, 69
anecdotes 54
animal rights 13, 79, 82, 84, 90, 95, 97-98, 101, 105, 111-113, 124-125, 131, 163n132, 166n148, 168n162,170, 172n189, 173n190, 175n225, 176n226,231
animal rights activists 13-14
animal-lovers 3, 95, 115-118, 125-126, 134
animal-lovers, role in saving the world 95, 116-118, 126, 134
animals, humans as 7, 51, 97, 162n119, 164n139
animals, life span of 87-88
animals, social 17, 91, 102, 112-113
animism 79-80
Anthropocene era 11, 152n10
anthropocentric ethics 4, 79, 84-86, 118, 122-123, 130-131, 174n200
anthropocentric principle 40, 54
anthropocentrism/anthropocentric 86
anthropology 111
anti-intellectualism 47-48, 179n247
ants 112, 165n142
anxiety 55, 61, 62, 126
Aquinas, Thomas 52, 80-81, 120, 162n119, 174n199
Archimedes 141
argument 54, 57-59, 86, 88, 89, 94, 101, 108, 111, 114, 119
Aristotle 81, 92, 157n54, 162n119
arrogance 7, 38, 97
Arrogance of Humanism, The 43-44, 82n124, 88n140, 121n202, 158n65, 163n124, 165n140, 174n202
arthropods 103
Asia 107, 111
assumptions 88-89, 114
assumptions, false 13, 39, 124, 164n139, 168n170, 175n225
Athens 111
atmosphere 2, 17, 31, 73, 74, 154n30
atmospheric gas balance 20, 31, 73, 74, 154n30
attraction, basin of 16-17
Australasian ecozone 36
automata 82
automobiles 22, 27, 45, 71
avarice 10

awareness 88, 92, 97, 111, 166n148
awareness, public 1, 16, 33, 48, 51, 52, 62, 75, 143, 159n81
axiomatic systems 94

backfire effect 58–59, 160n87,89,90
bacteria, soil 45
balkanization 34, 44
banks 37, 63, 71, 157n57
Barnosky, Anthony D. 178n242
Barrett, Scott 29–31, 156n42–45,49
barriers, to action 56, 71, 138
baseline, shifting 65, 161n100
basin of attraction 16–17
bees 112–113, 121
behavior 10, 57, 86, 95
behavior, automatic 59
behavior, irrational 49, 54, 62, 68, 116
Behring Breivik, Anders 67–68
belief/beliefs 51–52, 54, 57–59, 61, 70, 80, 82, 87–89, 93, 94, 155n33, 160n87,88
belonging 66, 95
benefit, short term 27
benefits, personal 28, 75–76, 123–124
Bentham, Jeremy 82, 91, 135n240, 162n147,148, 178n240
bias, confirmation 51, 59
bias, normalcy 52
biases, cognitive 37, 39, 51–53, 58–59, 89, 142, 159n77–79, 160n86
Bible, The 9, 80, 152n11, 168n166
BINGOs (Big International NGOs) 64–65
biocentrism 118
biodiversity crisis/loss 2, 14, 32, 49, 64, 136, 138–39, 145, 178n242
biological diversity/biodiversity 2, 14, 18, 19, 30, 32, 67, 68, 92, 178n242
biology 7–8
biology, evolutionary 7–8, 40, 95, 101, 169n171, 179n247
biomass 9, 13, 15, 112–13
Biophilia 120, 174n201
bioregionalism 118
biosophy 2
biosphere 28, 90, 112, 126, 151n9, 154n29
birds 13, 65, 120, 153n21, 154n27, 165n142,144
birth 14–15, 101, 164n134
Black Swan 36–39, 143, 157n53–54,58
blame 11, 19, 53, 68–69, 111, 116
Bolivia 131
bottom trawling 22, 145, 155n37
Boudron, Frédéric et al. 167n159
brain size 88–89, 107, 165n142, 167n154

brain-to-body size ratio 88, 165n142
brain, the 47, 53, 107, 115, 135, 159n82
Brooke, Phil 152n14
Brown, Robert McAfee 155n38
Brundtland, Gro Harlem et al. 156n41
Bruno, Giordano 81–82
Bruyère, Jean de la 134
bubbles, financial 38
Bugnyar, Thomas 165n144–45
Bundestag, German 131
bureaucracies/bureaucrats 33, 41, 46, 114, 143, 144
Burke, Edmund 177n234
business as usual 27–28, 117
business interests, role of 33–34, 54–55, 57
by-catch 13, 152n16, 153n17
by-products 26, 74

Cairncross, Frances 156n42
Callicott, J. Baird 164n134
Campephilus imperialis 99
Canada 8, 45
cancer 26, 31, 76, 122
capital 20–21, 71
capital, human 33
capital, natural 20
Caplan, Bryan 157n52
carbon dioxide 2, 17, 30, 45, 73, 154n30–31
carbon, soil 45, 154n30
careers/careerism 142, 148
Carroll, Lewis 158n59
cars 22, 27, 45, 71
Carson, Rachel 7, 32, 115, 151n3
cascade effects 2, 99, 145
cat, domestic 13, 153n20
catch(es), fish, global 12–13, 152n15–17
Categorical imperative 83, 104, 163n126, 168n163
Cathars 81
Catholicism 81
cats 82
Ceballos, Gerardo 178n242
center of the universe 7
central limit theorem 37
CFCs 31, 156n50
challenges 1–3, 8, 26, 28, 32, 35, 43–44, 46, 49–50, 63, 135, 138–41, 146, 149
challenges, structural 4, 75
change, major 41, 43–44, 149, 150
change, meaningful 25, 27, 43, 46, 60, 74, 110, 132, 142, 146
cheaters 27, 29, 142
checks and balances 27, 72, 142

chickens 103
children 8, 51, 53, 55, 66, 85, 122, 124–25, 151n9
chimpanzees 131
China 8, 110, 144
Chinese torture 18, 32
chlorofluorocarbons 31, 156n50
choice 19–20, 23, 51, 65, 118, 121, 124, 128, 133, 151n9, 157n52
choices, life-style 28, 44, 118, 128, 133, 151n9
Christianity 79–82, 94, 107–9, 169n174
Church, the ancient 169n174
Church, the Byzantine 169n174
Churchill, Winston 33
circular arguments 88
citizens 1, 42, 48, 127, 129, 150, 177n234
civilization, Western 7, 36, 43, 60, 79, 98, 119, 174n203-4
civilized society/person 99, 119
Clarke, Shelley C. et al. 153n17
Clayton, Nicola et al. 165n144
clientelism 34
climate 20, 44, 128
climate change 2, 11, 14, 16–18, 30–32, 49, 53, 56, 68, 73, 115–16, 124, 126, 138, 139, 145, 151n9, 156n46, 159n73,82, 160n85, 162n112
climate mitigation 156n39
climate negotiations 30–32, 132
climate, predictable 11, 32
co-option 55–56
Cobb, John B., Jr. 82, 163n123, 174n204
cod 45, 86, 103
coexistence 23, 118
cognition 160n86, 165n144
cognitive abilities of other species 87–88, 90, 97–98, 107
cognitive biases see biases, cognitive
cognitive dissonance 59, 118, 122
cognitive errors see biases, cognitive
collaboration 27, 63, 64, 135, 137, 143, 156n48
collective action problems 31, 55, 56, 60, 63, 66, 79, 124, 126, 135
Commager, Henry Steele 72
commodities 130
communication 5, 35, 45, 130, 134–35, 137, 145, 179n244
communities 10, 43, 62, 146
community, ecological 8, 66, 99, 104
companies 20, 71, 131, see also corporations
compartmentalizing 44, 52

compassion 62, 91, 103, 105, 108–11, 119, 123, 126, 168n171, 171n179
competence 33, 52, 142, 159n81
competition/competitors 10, 11, 14, 17, 56, 68, 100, 149
complex systems 16, 18, 28, 39, 45, 47, 140, 143
complexity 1–2, 28, 42, 44, 46–47, 140–41, 143, 158n68
compliance 29–30, 50, 142
conation 166n148
concepts 10, 19, 79, 81, 123, 134
concern 19, 34, 42, 53, 68, 81, 95, 114, 116, 118, 126, 151n9, 155n31
conditionality 92, 119, 150
confidence, false 18, 39, 47, 52–53, 142, 159n81
confirmation bias 51, 59
conflicts 70, 76, 83, 94, 95, 104
connection to nature 66, 103, 126, 130
conscience 60, 106, 110, 111, 163n132, 177n234
consciousness 2, 58, 87–88, 90, 92, 110, 166n148
consensus agreement 30, 142
consequences 2, 10, 18, 21, 22–23, 24, 29, 31, 32, 37–41, 52, 76, 99, 101, 118, 126
consequences, immediate 76, 118
consequences, remote 10–11, 18, 22, 26, 60, 76, 83, 93, 124, 131
consequences, unintended 145
conservation 49, 53, 63, 73, 93, 114, 154n26, 156n39, 158n65, 167n152, 175n223,225
conservation biologists 14, 63
conservatism 55, 73, 95
consideration of other species 3–4, 21–22, 28, 34, 73, 79–81, 83–86, 94–95, 101, 104, 108, 113, 116–17, 123, 125–28, 135–36
constraints 9–11, 71, 83, 128, 143, 159n73
consumerism 23, 68, 112, 151n9
consumers, number of 151n9
consumption 23, 45, 55, 57, 66, 81, 103, 124, 139, 151n9
contraception 162n105
convenience 7, 62, 66, 100–101, 123
convention, social 85
Conway, Erik M. 161n94
cooperation 17, 27, 29, 84
COP/Conferences of the Parties 132
Copernicus 7, 81, 98
coping strategies 56
coral reefs 18, 75, 116

corals 83, 88
corporate relations 64-65
corporations 31, 36, 54-55, 68, 69, 71, 74, 95
correlation 54
Cortes Generales, Spanish 131
corvids 90, 165n144, 166n145
cost benefit analysis 20, 28, 29, 31, 57, 76, 114, 123-124
cost overruns 39
costs 16, 20, 21, 28, 30-32, 34, 55-56, 71-72, 74, 76, 93, 116, 123-124, 127, 133, 135
cotton 101, 167n159
countries see nation states
courage 25, 61
courts 33, 69, 131-33, 175n225
crash 33, 126
creation 7, 79, 82, 94, 174n199
crime 69, 109, 125-26, 131, 133
crimes against humanity 131-132
Crimes Against Nature 131-133
Crimes against Peace, International 131-132
crises 26, 27, 32, 49-50, 116, 137, 139, 145, 149, 151n9, 162n109
crisis, financial 37-38
critical mass 5-6, 55, 60, 70, 137
crocodile 107
crowd, wisdom of 35, 48
crows see corvids
cruelty 106, 109, 111, 119-20, 131, 169n174
Crutzen, Paul J. 152n10
Cuba, missile crisis 67
cultivated ignorance 52
cultural phenomena 38
culture 10, 19, 24, 76, 80, 84, 87, 89, 93, 98, 99, 102, 103, 111, 124, 128, 130, 133, 175n225
culture, Western 79, 105
cumulative stresses 18, 122
curiosity 87
cycles 2, 10, 16

da Vinci, Leonardo 81
daily lives 1, 9, 10, 52, 101, 150
Daisy World 17
Dally, Joanna M. et al. 165n144
Daly, Herman E. 155n36
damage, environmental 5, 11-12, 16, 22, 83, 99, 132, 155n33
damage, irreparable see irreversible damages

Darwin, Charles 3, 7-8, 53, 97, 99, 101, 105, 106, 151n4, 163n125, 168n160, 169n171,174
Dasmann, Raymond 44, 158n65
data 12-13, 49, 58, 70, 168n168
death 15, 26, 31, 51, 61, 68, 87, 98, 122, 123, 141, 155n33
death by a thousand cuts 18, 32
Death of Environmentalism, The 73, 162n104
death penalty 22, 155n37
decentralization 72-73
decisions, responsible 32, 34-35, 42, 44, 48, 52, 72, 134-35, 151n9
decisions, strategic 65
declines 9, 12, 15, 17, 151n9, 152n16, 153n17, 154n27
Deep Ecology 100, 130, 175n224
democracy, system of, weaknesses 27, 33-35, 43, 46-48, 72, 129, 134, 142-43, 145, 149, 157n51,52
denial 56, 160n87,89
density dependence 9, 103
dependence 2, 8, 10, 30, 40, 41, 58
dependence, statistical 36-38
dependency 22, 30, 65, 66
depression 4, 53
Descartes, René 80, 82, 93, 106
descent 90-91, 95, 98, 100, 102, 169n171
Descent of Man 53, 168n160
desire 6, 88, 92, 148, 166n148
despair 138-39, 161n97
desperation 47, 63, 74, 122, 126, 150
determinism 39
Dethier, Vincent G. 87, 164n138
Deuteronomy 81, 120, 174n199
development aid 46, 95, 115, 116, 124, 145, 156n41
Diamond, Jared M. 154n25
dichotomies, false 54
Dietz, Rob 158n67
diffuse systems 27, 32, 39, 144
dignity 122, 131
disaster 52-53, 75, 126, 136, 149, 156n46, 160n85
discounting, hyperbolic 51
discounting, irrational, the future 49, 51, 116
disease 17, 79, 126, 154n30
disinformation campaigns 59
displacement activities 62
disruption 37, 150
dissemination of information 58, 60, 113, 145

distinctions, between species 8, 84, 86–90, 92, 105–107, 171n181
distributions, statistical 36–38, 157n56
diversity, biological see biological diversity
diversity, genetic 92
Dobzhansky, Theodosius 7
dogfish 153n17
dogmatism/dogma/dogmatic systems 94, 109, 170n175
dolphins 88, 131, 132, 175n225, 176n231
domestic cat 13, 82, 153n20
Dowd, Mark 161n57
droughts 26, 53, 154n30
dualism 80, 82
Dunning-Kruger effect 52–53, 142, 159n81, 179n245
Dunning, David 52–53, 142, 159n81, 179n245
duty 48, 87, 104, 108, 111, 119, 133, 177n234
dynamic systems theory 1, 16–18, 35, 39, 50, 154n30
dysfunctionality 33, 34–35, 47

Ecclesiastes 105
ecocide 69, 131–33, 144, 176n229–30, 177n233
ecological footprint 5, 101, 151n9, 162n105
ecological functional role 15, 99
ecological limits 2, 9–11, 21, 24
ecological systems 7, 16, 18, 23, 42, 47
ecologist 13–14, 19, 155n33
ecology 8, 14, 16–18, 21, 23, 49, 63, 82, 151n7, 163n123
ecosystem 10, 14–18, 27–28, 59, 99, 104, 128, 130–32, 153n19
economic growth 21, 45, 54, 55, 56–57, 69, 117, 122, 124, 144
economic interests 33–34, 57, 92
economic system 20–21, 32, 144, 145
economics 20, 23, 101, 123, 155n35
economics, behavioral 114
economy 20–21, 23, 27, 55–57, 69, 133, 144, 145
economy, size of 45, 69, 117, 124, 144, 145, 151n9, 157n57, 158n67
ecosystem services 79, 99, 114
ecosystems 10, 14–16, 18, 28, 59, 99, 104, 128, 132, 153n19
ecosystems, global 27, 130
Ecuador 131, 132
education 70, 93, 129, 155n33
effects, disproportional 36–38
efficiency, technological 21–22, 45, 144, 152

egotism 110, 123
Egypt 107, 109
Ehrenfeld, David 43–44, 82, 88, 94, 121, 158n64, 167n152
Ehrlich, Paul R. 156n41, 178n242
Eldredge, Niles 179n247
elephant shrews 163n132
elephants 74, 89, 132, 163n132
emergency, states of 142
emergent properties 48, 84, 118
emissions, greenhouse gases 30, 45, 132
emotions 3–4, 15, 57–58, 66, 73, 79, 87, 97, 101, 103, 110, 114, 123–27, 130–35
empathy 66, 87, 91, 108, 119
empiricism 92, 106, 170n175
employment 65, 74
empowerment 27, 46, 70, 124, 142
encephalization quotient 165n142
energy 9, 17, 20, 75, 154n30
enforcement 15, 29–30, 128
engagement 3, 28, 61, 114–15, 179n244
environment 9–11, 26, 45, 49, 55, 73, 83, 100, 114, 116
environmental movement 73, 118
environmentalism 73, 118, 162n104
environmentalists 53, 62, 73, 75, 162n104
epistemic arrogance 38
error, cognitive see biases, cognitive
errors 37, 39–40, 44, 53, 62, 73
estimate, (in)ability to 36–39, 50, 53, 152n16
eternity 14, 56, 81, 99
ethical objects 97–98
ethical subjects 97–98, 104, 166n148
ethics, anthropocentric see anthropocentric ethics
ethics, biocentric 118
ethics, instrumental 104, 119, 123, see also utilitarianism
ethics, non-anthropocentric, role in saving the world 73, 95, 116–118, 126, 134
European Union 131
eusociality 112
Evans, Erin 176n226
events, extreme/rare 36–39, 41, 42
events, independent/random 37
evidence 43, 57, 58, 82, 94, 105–106, 160n86, 164n139
evils 19, 41, 98
evolution 2, 7, 9, 20, 26, 50, 58, 84, 92, 93, 100, 101, 120, 123–24, 151n8, 168n160, 169n171
evolution, human 55, 97–98, 120, 135, 167n154

evolution, moral 93, 101, 113, 123
evolutionary biology 8, 40, 95, 101
evolutionary theory 40, 163n125, 179n247
evolved, highly 8, 100
experience 11, 21, 29, 32, 36-37, 40, 66, 99, 113, 119, 120, 127, 130, 143
experts 36, 42, 47
explanations 26, 51, 69, 70, 163n125
exploitation 2, 11, 29, 49, 67, 79, 84, 115, 117, 127
extinction 2, 14, 16, 18, 19, 20, 99, 102-103, 121-22, 154n25
extinction, anthropogenic 2, 14, 18, 19, 121-22, 124, 178n242
extinction, drivers of 14, 18, 20, 23, 121, 154n25
extinction, mass 19, 23
extrapolation 23, 37, 54, 113, 174n195
Ezekiel 25

facts 51, 57-59, 60, 160n89
failure 45, 50, 63, 73, 77, 89
fairness 33, 127
faith 94, 108-109
fallacies, logical 51-54, 73, 83, 113, 142
fallacy, narrative 37, 51, 70
false assumptions 13, 39, 88, 89, 114, 124, 164n139, 168n170, 175n225
FAO 12, 13, 158n66
fate 9, 22, 61, 82
fault 11, 17, 19, 53, 68-69, 111, 116, 117
fear 61, 63, 68, 72, 101, 108, 115, 126
fear, as motivator 61-62, 136, 161n97
fear, irrational 68
feedback loops/mechanisms 17-18, 40, 45, 126, 154n30
feedback, negative 17, 40, 154n30, see also regulation
feedback, positive 16-18, 40, 126, 143, 154n30
feelings see emotions
Feinberg, Joel 111, 163n132, 166n148, 172n188-89
Fertile Crescent 80
fight or flight response 26, 55, 58, 59, 62
finance 33, 69, 72
financial crisis 37, 38, 54
financial system 38, 54
first mover disadvantage 55
fish 12, 21, 22, 65, 88-89, 91, 92, 109, 121, 131, 154n27, 165n142
fish catches 12, 152n14-16, 153n17-19, 158n66

fish catches, historic 12, 152n16, 153n17-19
fish farms 12
fish, number of, killed 12, 21, 152n14, 153n17, 154n23
fisheries 27, 33, 34, 45, 49, 139, 145, 154n23
fisheries, collapse 2, 14, 16, 45, 49, 139, 145, 151n9, 158n66
fisheries, industrial 12, 13, 154n23
fisheries, subsistence 13
fisheries, techniques 13, 21, 45
fishing, illegal 13
fitness, evolutionary 91
flocks 15, 65, 127
fluctuations, natural 10, 16
focus, lack of 34, 62, 69, 74, 140, 141, 149
food 9, 11, 13, 20, 67, 75, 100-103, 106, 115, 122, 145, 153n19, 158n66
Food and Agricultural Organization 12, 13, 158n66
food chain 8, 13, 102
food production 13, 115
forcing mechanisms 143
Foreman, Dave 128, 175n223
forest death 154n30
forest ecosystems 16
forestry 14, 23, 33
fossil fuels 22
Foucault, Michel 57
Foundation of Ethics, The 110, 123, 168n169
fragmentation, habitats 14, 32
fragmentation of collective will 34, 44
framing 51, 69, 73
free will 83, 87, 128
free-rider problems 27, 29, 142
freedom 8, 32, 43, 63, 83, 109, 123
frequency dependence 103
frontier economy 21
frustration 6, 137
Fukuyama, Francis 34, 157n51, 162n103
full world 1-2, 21, 23, 24, 115, 118, 134, 136
functional role, ecological 15, 99
funding/fundraising 64-65, 146
future 1, 6, 14, 26-28, 37, 40-41, 43, 49, 51, 54, 61-62, 67, 72, 76-77, 87, 93, 98, 99-100, 102, 115-16, 118, 121-22, 133-34, 135-36, 137, 141, 142, 143, 154n24, 158n68, 159n73, 161n97, 163n132
future of life on Earth 6, 14, 69, 93, 98, 126, 150

Gaia hypothesis 17
game theory 26, 27, 29, 55, 93, 101, 123, 141
Gandhi, Mohandas K. 63
Gates, Bill 38
Gaussian distribution 36
Geisel, Theodor Seuss 136, 179n243
gene frequencies 9
generalization, hasty 54
genetic drift 151n8
genetics 7, 9, 14, 74, 84, 92, 168n160, 175n225
genocide 131, 132
geoengineering 74
germination 11
Gerritsen, Vanessa 176n227
Gibbons, John H. 67
Glendinning, Chellis 174n203
global ecosystems 27, 130
global human population (size) 83, 121–122, 151n9, see also population size
global species 2, 9–10, 21, 24, 27, 42, 46, 63, 118, 142
global warming see climate change
globalized world 2, 8, 21, 24, 28, 35, 46, 55, 133, 142–43, 157n52
Gnathonemus petersii 88, 165n142
goal in itself 123, see also inherent value
goals, extrinsic 62, 161n97,98
God 7, 54, 80–82, 94, 97, 99, 113, 121, 163n125, 174n199
Golden Rule 104
Goldschmidt, Richard 143, 179n247
good 3, 28, 36, 41, 53, 73, 76, 93–94, 103, 108–109, 110, 115, 142, see also inherent value
good, public 31, 33, 73, 118
good intentions 28, 129
good life 20, 23, 127
Goodpaster, Kenneth 111–12, 166n148, 172n188, 173n190–91
goods 20
Google 37
Gore, Al 60, 161n93
Gould, Stephen Jay 165n141, 179n247
governance 28, 34–35, 48, 56–57, 72, 117, 176n229, see also institutions
governance, global 117, 143, 176n229, see also institutions, global level
governments 28, 65, 77, 131–32, 147–48, 177n234
gradualism 40–41, 179n247
Grand Banks 45

Greece 72, 79, 111, 131
Greene, Joshua et al. 98n155, 167n155
greenhouse gases 132, 154n30, see also carbon dioxide; methane; CFCs; HCFCs; emissions
groupware 149
growth machine 56–57, see also economic growth
growth rates 151n9, 157n57
growth, economic see economic growth
growth, exponential 157n57
growth, uneconomic 21, 155n36
Gunderson, Lance H. et al. 18n32, 155n32

habitat destruction/loss 14, 32, 145
habitat fragmentation 14, 32
habitats 14, 20, 44, 126
Hahn, Ulrike 160n86
Hall, Matthew 166n148
Hamilton, Clive 56, 160n85
Hamilton, William D. 168n160
hamstrung 6, 27, 60, 63, 137, see also passivity
Hansen, James 30, 156n46
happiness 3, 66, 92, 100
harm 22, 28, 45, 91, 103–104, 119, 124, 131, 172n189, see also damage
Harris, Adam J. L. 160n86
harvesting 2, 21–22, 49, 154n29, see also overharvesting
Harvey, Chelsea 152n16
hate 121–22, 125
HCFCs 156n50
heat stress 154n30
heat waves 26
Heaven 80, 94
Hedges, Chris 134–35, 178n236
Hegel 41
heliocentrism 81, see also Copernicus
Herbener, Jens-André P. 80n112, 162n112
herds 15, 127
herring 103
hierarchical worldview 80, 81, see also dualism; Bruno; St Francis
Higgins, Polly 132, 176n229, 177n233, see also ecocide
higher lifeforms 8, 100, see also descent
hindsight 37
Hindus 110, 120
history 30–31, 37, 40, 68, 70, 129, 143, 145
history, evolutionary 26, 35, 50, 97, 135
Hitler, Adolf 63
Hobbesian natural order 136
holistic worldview 104

Homer-Dixon, Thomas 42, 46, 158n63,68
Homo erectus 97
Homo floresiensis 97, 167n154
Homo neanderthalensis 97, 167n154
Homo sapiens 8, 90, 97, 98, 99, 103, 167n154, see also humans
honor 108–109
Hooper, John 176n226
hope 25, 39, 47, 55, 60–63, 81, 128, 129, 139, 145, 161n96,97
Hopeful monster 143, 179n247
Hosea 80
households 20
hubris 80, 97
Hugo, Victor 113, 173n194
human activities 11, 14, 20, 21, 31, 129, 131
human factor, the 41
human population see population
human rights 35, 60, 83–86, 90, 97–98, 99–100, 124–25, 127–28, 164n134, 173n190, 177n234
humane treatment 84, 111–112, 119, 123–24, 169n174
humanism/humanists 43–44, 81–82, 95, 122, 158n64, see also Arrogance
humanity 6, 7, 10, 19, 20–21, 23, 43, 54, 95, 121, 126, 136
humans 2–4, 7–15, 19, 33, 34, 51, 69, 79, 80–84, 86–92, 99, 101, 115–16, 121–27, 131, 135–36, 151n9, 162n105, 167n154
Hume, C. W. 169n174
Hume, David 108, 166n148, 174n195
humility 80
hunting 14, 22
hydrochlorofluorocarbons 156n50
hypocrisy 107
hypothesis testing 88-89, 90, 94

ibis 107
Ibsen, Henrik 56, 160n84
idealism 63, 93
ideas 44, 57, 59, 62, 70, 80, 98, 113, 117, 134, 148, 169n171
identified victim effect 51n78, 159n78
identity 57–58
ideology 31, 51, 58, 72, 134, 148
ignorance 30, 52–53, 54, 104, 142
ignorance, cultivated 52
life-lie 56
illegal fishing 13
impact, environmental 40, 83, 100, 115, 128, 151n9, 154n29, see also damage

impacts 4, 7, 9, 18, 36, 118, 151n9, 153n19,20, 157n53
implementation 2, 25, 28, 50, 124, 138, 140, 146, 149
import duties 30
impotence 137, see also hamstrung; passivity
impoverishment 10, 15, 66, see also damage
in-group 57, 58, 84, 95, 99, 100
inaction 72, 77, 138, see also inertia; passivity; hamstrung
incentives 29, 72, 75, 120, 128
incompetence see Dunning-Kruger effect
India 131, 144
indicators, socioeconomic 23
individual action see action, individual
individual worth 80, 97, 100, 115, 121–22
inertia 27, 44, 138, see also inaction
infanticide 125
infinity 21, 56, 81, see also eternity
influence in politics 33–34, 54, 71, see also lobbying
information 5, 51, 55, 58–59, 62, 69–70, 104, 145
information squeeze 42
information theory 18
infrastructure 14
Ingenuity Gap, The 42, 47, 158n63
inherent value 82, 84, 86, 90–92, 94, 103, 104, 123, 126, 164n134, 166n148, 172n189
initiative, personal 156n39, see also action, individual
injustice, historical 84, 95
innocence 133, 136
innovation(s) 19, 22, 41, 59, 72, 158n68
insects, social 112
insight 70, 131, 168n168
institutions 4, 8, 24, 27, 44, 47, 77, 93, 124, 134, 135, 138, 141, 145, 146
institutions, political 72
institutions, global level 27, 46, 49, 142–43
instrumental value 104, 119, 123, see also utilitarianism
intelligence 19, 26, 54, 87–89, 93, 97, 107, 124–25, 165n142, 171n181
intentions, good 28, 129
inter-dependence 8
interaction 8, 14, 30, 40, 51, 145
interests, having 81, 108, 111–12, 166n148, 171n181, 172n189
interests, special 34, 73, 148, see also lobbying

international agreements 29–32, 85, 117, 142, 156n42,48
international arena/level 41, 63, 117, 142, 144
International Court of Environmental Justice 133
International Criminal Court 69, 131–132, see also ecocide
international dimensions 1–2, 49, 138, 141
International Whaling Commission (IWC) 31
internet 37, 116, 149
interventions 39, 41–42, 74, 126, 144
intractability, mathematical/social 50
intrinsic value see inherent value
introduced species 14, 18, 32
intuition 35, 50, 59, 98
invasive species 14, 18, 32
invertebrates 16, 87, 100
invisible hand 84, 93
irrational outcomes 34, 62, 68
irreversible damages 14, 16, 99, 128, 140, 143, see also tipping points; absorption
is/ought dichotomy 89, 113, 174n195
Isaiah 11, 25, 80
island biogeography 14
isolation 6, 25, 60, 66–67, 137, see also critical mass
IUCN red data lists 153n17
ivory trade 74, 132

Jains 120
Jefferson, Thomas 133, 177n234
Jensen, Derrick 61–62, 161n96
Jesuits 105
Jesus 54, 104
Jews 105, 108
Judaism 105, 108, 111
Judeo-Christian tradition 79–80, 93–94, 108
justice 84, 95, 104, 109–110, 112, 133, 168n164, see also crime; penalties
Juvenal 36

Kahneman, Daniel 52, 159n77
Kant, Immanuel 82, 83, 104, 105, 108, 119, 120, 123, 163n126-27, 166n148, 168n163,165, 171n181, 174n198, 175n175
Kasser, Tim 62n97-98, 161n97-98
Keohane, Joe 160n89
Keynes, John Maynard 57
Kibert, Charles J. 155n36
killed, numbers 12–13, 14, 152n14, 153n17

killing 12, 14, 22, 100–102, 103, 113, 120, 123, 124
kindness 110, 164n139, 169n174
King, Martin Luther, Jr. 177n234
Kirby, David 132n232, 176n232
knowledge 4, 23, 27, 35, 39, 41, 46–49, 52–53, 69–70, 87, 107, 107, 113, 124, 139, 143, 146, 171n181
knowledge by acquaintance 26–27, 65
knowledge by description 26–27, 65
knowledge of death 87
knowledge, incompleteness of 36, 41, 51, 52
Kogut, Tehila 159n78
Kohlberg, Lawrence 175n219
Kozlovsky, Daniel 1, 151n1
Krebs, Charles J. 151n7
Kruger, Justin 52, 142, 159n81, 179n245
Krutch, Joseph Wood 174n207
Kyoto Accord 30, see also international agreements

labor 20, 21, 46
Lake Wobegon effect 52–53
Land Ethic 104
land use 14, 23, 44 see also agriculture; forestry; infrastructure
language 84, 87, 97, 105, 106–107, 117, 134–35
law(s) 15, 22, 53, 85, 93, 94, 97, 118, 126, 128–29, 130, 131–133, 144, 159n72, 162n121, 176n225,227,229
laws of nature 84
leaders 33, 44, 57, see also politicians
Lebbin, Daniel Jason et. al. 153n21
legal system 77, 84, 126, 131–32, 144, 163n132, see also law(s); illegal fishing; standing
Leibniz, Gottfried Wilhelm 80, 106, 163n125
Leopold, Aldo 19, 25, 63, 79, 93, 104, 123, 127, 137, 155n33
lessons 29, 37, 40, 46, 145
Levin, Kelly et al. 49–50, 159n73,75, 179n248
liberalism 8, 43, 83
Library of Alexandria 65
life 7, 10, 20, 66, 79, 118, 119, 127, 134, 136, 141, 150, 163n125
life on Earth 6, 7, 14, 15, 19, 69, 93, 95, 102, 116, 124, 126–27, 138, 150
life span of animals 87–88
life span, average 43
life-lie 56

life-style 27–28, 43, 50, 65, 66, 101, 118, 133
life, quality of 3, 10, 20, 23, 122–23, 127, 133, 139
life, subject of a 104, 168n162
life, tree of 19
life, web of 20
likelihoods 36, 38–39, 51–52
limitations 39, 42, 56, 63, 71, 100, 115, 138, 143, 150, 158n68
limiting resources 2, 10, 21, 43, 149
limits to human activity 2, 11, 21, 43, 83, 84
limits, critical 2, see also ecological limits
limits, ecological 2, 9–11, 21, 24
Lindsay, Lauder 164n139
literacy 48, 129
livestock 13, 15
Living Planet Index 154n27
lobbying 33, 72, see also influence
local 2, 9, 10, 21
logic 51, 73, 83, 113, see also fallacies
logical contradiction see categorical imperative
Long Term Capital Management (LTCM) 38
longevity 26, 43, 87–88
Lord, Charles G. et al. 160n86
Loss, Scott R. et al. 153n20
love 3, 4, 6, 66, 86, 94, 95, 103, 114–18, 123, 125–27, 133, 135–36, 139
loving-kindness 110
lower lifeforms 8, 100, see also descent
luck 39, 40, 41, 43, 135
lynx 92

Macphail, Evan M. 165n142
macroeconomics 20–21
magical thinking 54, 121
Maine, Henry James Sumner 125, 175n215
Malthus, Thomas 75, 151n4
mammals 13, 15, 88, 89, 154n27
Man 4, 7, 8, 20, 53, 80, 81, 82, see also humans
management, adaptive 40–41, 140, 150
Mandeville, Bernard 110
mangroves 121
manipulation 29, 54, 94
Marine Mammal Protection Act, US 15
market bubbles 38
market economy 34, 36–38, 55, 117, 128
markets, financial/stocks 34, 36–38, 54–55, 117, 128
Marshall, George 53, 115, 135, 159n82
mass extinction (drivers of) 19, 23
materials, raw 20

mathematics 35, 50, 140
maximum sustained yield 45
May, Robert M. 154n24
meaningful action 6, 27, 60, 137, 141–42, 144, see also change
meaningful change see change, meaningful
means of production 20
meat, consumption of 8, 81, 124, 151n9, 156n39, 162n105
mechanisms 6, 7, 18, 20, 23, 26, 32, 35, 44, 45, 49, 55, 56, 59, 60, 70, 89, 93, 94, 117–18, 128, 130, 140, 141, 142, 143, 169n171
mechanisms, positive feedback 16–18, 40, 126, 154n30, see also tipping points
mechanisms, stabilizing 17–18, 103, see also feedback, negative; regulation
mechanistic thinking 28, 139, see also mechanisms
media, role of 36, 56, 67–72
medicine, modern 9, 27
mental abilities of other species see cognitive abilities
methane 17, 154n30, 155n31
mice 165n142
Michel, Margot 176n227
micro-powers 71–72
microbes 45, 154n30
middle class 71, 162n103
Might Makes Right 83–84, 97, 99, 104, 113, 128
migration 11
Mill, John Stuart 100, 167n157, 177n234, 178n240
misnomer 7
mobilization 135, 145, see also organize
modeling 39, 49, 147, 148, 150
models 17, 27, 39, 49, 143
molluscs 88, 91, 103
Monbiot, George 159n69, 161n97, 178n236, 179n246
monetary system 21, 48, 54, 144
money 20, 31–32, 33–34, 37, 54, 64–65, 66, 71–72, 114, 130, 155n34, 157n57
Montaigne, Michel de 81
Montreal Protocol 29–31
Mood, Alison 152n14, 154n23
Mooney, Chris 58n87, 160n87,89,90
Moore, G. E. 174n195
moose 22, 113
moral agents 87, 90, 98, 104, 112, 113, 131
moral considerability 80, 82, 84, 86, 90, 94, 95, 97–98, 99–100, 104, 108, 110–12, 116, 123, 126, 166n148, 173n190

moral rights see rights; moral considerability
morals 60, 82, 87, 119, 162n121, 171n176, 175n220
mortality 68, 105, 108–111, 159n72, 163n127, 168n170
Morwood, Mike J. et al. 167n154
mosquitoes 103
motivated reasoning 57–59, 160n86,87,89
motivators 27, 62, 126, 128, 161n97
movies 62, 66, 117, 158n68
Muir, John 82, 94, 119, 163n122, 164n136, 167n151, 174n197
mussels 88, 91, 103
mutations 151n8, 179n247
mutualists 8, 10
Myers, Ransom 13n18, 153n18

Naím, Moisés 70–72, 161n102
naïveté 28, 129, 131
narcissism 127
narrative fallacy 37, 51, 69–70
Nash, Roderick 108, 151n5,9, 162n110,113–14,116, 163n129–30, 164n211, 167n156, 169n174, 174n207, 175n213–14,218,221
nation states 12, 27–33, 46, 55, 60, 71, 144, 149–50, 156n48
national security 33, see also terrorism
Native Americans 125, 175n212, 175n216
natural 10, 11, 19, 118, 136
natural capital 20
natural fluctuations 10, 16
natural phenomena 15, 19, 47, 67, 84
natural process 19, 82, see also processes
natural resources 2, 9, 20, 21, 49, 138, 145
natural sciences 35, 111, 143, see also science
natural selection 3, 7, 9, 26, 89, 151n4,8, 168n160, 169n171
Naturalist's/Naturalistic Fallacy 89, 113, 174n195
nature 7–10, 11, 16, 18, 20–23, 43, 45, 48, 66–67, 79–85, 95, 98, 102, 104, 108, 113, 114, 116, 119–20, 124, 126–26, 133, 136
nature-lovers 115–16, 117–18, 126, 134, see also animal-lovers
nature, control of 7, 123
nature, outside of 9–11, 126
nature, part of 8–10, 19
Nazis 83
Neanderthals 97, 167n154
necessary 25, 29, 55, 93, 100, 102, 112, 118, 124, 138, 139–40, 143, 144, 146, 148

needs 57, 88, 100, 122, 127
negative feedback 17, 40, 154n30, see also regulation
negotiations 29–32, 117, 132, 142
negotiators 29, 32
Neiwert, David 175n225
neoconservatives 95
neoliberalism 31, 72
Netherlands, The 132
neurology 89, see also brain
neuroscience 51, 57
New Synthesis 7
news 36, 56, 67–72
NGOs 60, 64–65, 72, 117, 148, 150
Nilsson, Göran E. 165n142
nitrogen cycle 2, 20–21
Noah principle 94
nobody remembers... 34, 65, 67, 117, 127
noise 22, 34, 69–70
Nonhuman Rights Project, The 131
nonlinear dynamics 1, 98, see also dynamic systems
Nordhaus, Ted 73, 162n104
Normal distribution 36–37, 38
norms, social 44, 84, 93, 102, 118, 128, 174n195
North Pacific Fur Seal Treaty 31
Norton, Bryan G. 164n134, 174n200
Norway 2, 8, 67, 132, 156n39
Norwegian Forest and Climate Initiative 156n39
nuclear power 74
numbers killed 12–13, 14, 152n14, 153n17
nutrient cycles 2, 20–21
Nyhan, Brendan 1690n89
Næss, Arne 100

O'Neill, Dan 158n67
ocean acidification 2, 20, 44, 49, 74, 138
Oceania 36
octopus 87n137, 164n137
omnivory 10, 11, 21
On The Tragic 3
opinion 57, 97, 115, 148, 162n119
opinion, popular 115, 129
opportunities, making the most of 39, 41, 53, 130
optimism 28, 43, 129
orcas 83, 121, 175n225, 176n232
Oreskes, Naomi 161n94
organize, need to 60, 93, 95, 113–15, 124, 126, 134–37 passim, 145
Origin of Species (On the) 3, 7, 105, 106, 151n4, 163n125, 169n171

oscillations, stable 167n158
Oskamp, Stuart 161n97,99
ostrich effect 52, 59, 62
outdoors 66, 120
over-exploitation 11, 14, 16, 49, 67, 138, 145, 151n9, 152n16
over-fishing see over-exploitation
overconfidence 18, 39, 47, 52–53, 142, 159n81
overharvesting see over-exploitation
overpopulation 9, 10, 23, 100, 145, 151n9
overshoot 11
oysters 91
ozone layer 29, see also Montreal Protocol

pain 88-89, 90-92, 112, 166n148, see also sentience; suffering
pantheism 80-82
paradigm shift 8, see also Planck
Paradise 79, 80, 94
parsimony 88–89, 91, 163n125
participation 29–31, 33, 34, 48, 114
passion see love
passivity 6, 27, 42, 44, 60, 63, 72, 77, 137, 138
past 2, 19, 21, 23, 28, 36–37, 40, 43, 54, 65, 87, 130
path dependence 144
Pauly, Daniel 152n16, 153n19, 161n100
penalties/sanctions 22, 77, 93, 101, 108–109, 126, 131, 133, 155n33
Penn, Derek C. 166n145
people see humans
permafrost 16, 154n30
perpetrators 116, 125
personal tragedies 3, 4, 6, 114, 134, 150
personhood 95, 104, 125, 131, 166n148, 175n212,225, 176n231
perspective 84
pets 13, 66, 127
phenomena, cultural 38
phenomena, natural 15, 19, 47, 67, 84
phenomena, physical 36, 38, 171n181
phenomena, statistical 26, 50, 76
philosophy 1, 7, 8, 48, 56, 80, 82, 93, 98, 105–106, 115
philosophy of science 41, 49
phosphorous cycle 2, 20–21
photosynthesis 100–101
phylogeny 7, see also taxonomy
Pimm, Stuart et al. 178n242
Pinker, Steven 134, 178n188
Planck, Max 59, 161n92

Planetary Boundaries 11, 152n12, see also full world
planning, central 40–41
planning, inability to plan 38–39, 41, 44, 143, 145, 159n74
plants 11, 91, 108, 114, 121, 126, 136, 166n148
pleasure 56, 66, 112, 139, 170n175, see also suffering
poaching 13, 74
point of no return see tipping points
polar bears 8, 115–16, 121
policy 30, 49–50, 54, 73, 128–30, 144, 157n52
political influence see influence in politics
political reasons 13
political science 4, 29, 57, 139
politicians 28, 35–36, 41, 46, 56, 60, 68–69, 70–72, 74, 114, 129–30, 143, 144, 148, 150
politics 13, 24, 33–35, 36, 39, 41, 43, 47–48, 56–59, 71–72, 75, 115, 124, 128–29, 134, 140, 143, 149, 168n168
pollutants/pollution 21, 22, 32, 122
Popper, Karl 41–42, 50, 158n60,61
populace, general 30, 48, 54, 68, 74, 143, 144
population 2–3, 9, 10, 14, 28, 32, 38, 40, 43, 49, 50, 54, 100, 103, 144, 154n27
population fluctuations 8, 16, 17
population genetics 14
population growth (human) 2, 9, 55, 100, 139, 145, 151n9, 157n57
population size (human) 9, 10, 12, 13, 15, 83–84, 100, 118, 121–122, 139, 145, 151n9, 157n57
populations, small 9, 14, 17, 151n8
post hoc ergo propter hoc 54
poverty alleviation 46, 95, 115, 116, 124, 145, 156n41
Povinelli, Daniel J. 166n145
power 27, 35, 39, 55, 56–57, 59, 60, 61, 63, 70–73, 97, 121, 134, 138, 142, 143
power of definition 115
power structure 35, 55, 60, 117, 139
Power, The End of 70, 161n102
precautionary principle 39, 44, 53–54
predators 10, 92, 102, 153n18
predictable climate 11, 32
prediction 18, 26, 35, 36–40, 41–42, 50, 53, 61, 143, 159n80, 179n247
predictive sciences 18, 35
prehistory 20, 40, 97
prejudice 87, 92

preparedness 26, 34, 41, 50, 69, 129, 130, 141
present 23, 26, 66, 93, 97, 116, 130, 135, 144, 178n242
pressure 28, 122, 133, 148
prevention 40, 75, see also precautionary principle
prey species 8, 10, 17, 102
pricing mechanisms 23, 30, 32, 34
primates 107, 175n225
prisoner's dilemma 29, 55, 101
probability theory 35, 50, 98
probability, neglect of 51
problem solving 2, 56, 116, 130, 138, 140, 144, 145, 147
problems 1-3, 6, 22, 25-26, 42-49, 51, 55-56, 63, 65, 73-76, 95, 98, 116, 125-26, 129-30, 138-45, 151n9
problems, global 2, 27, 28-32, 136, 138, 145, 150
problems, interactive 145
problems, super wicked 49-50, 52, 62, 144, 159n73
problems, trans-border 1-3, 28-32, 138, 144
processes 39, 43, 49, 54, 135, 138, 40, 141, 144
processes, historical 28
processes, natural 7, 8, 16, 19, 82, 99, 100
processes, political 32, 33-34, 48
production, means of 20
products 20, 30, 32
professionalism 33-34
progress 23, 32, 44, 46-47, 127, 149
property 31, 55, 124
psychology 26, 51, 57, 62, 141, 159n80, 160n86, 161n97
public awareness see awareness
public choice theory 34
public goods 31, 33, 73, 118
public opinion 115, 129, 148
punctuated equilibrium 40, 143, 179n247
punishment see penalties/sanctions
purpose 82, 85, 90, 100, 135
Pynchon, Thomas 51, 159n76
Pythagoras 109

quotas 13, 45, see fisheries

races, human 87, 105, 124, 164n139
racism 125
rage 4, 25, see also emotions
rainforest 18, 156n39, see also forest
Randers, Jørgen 152n13
randomness 37-39
rarity 36-38, 103, 129, 157n57
rational/rationality 20, 23, 53, 54, 61, 94, 98, 111-12, 116, 130, 135, 143, 157n52, 160n86, 166n148
rational beings 81, 87, 92, 104, 105, 162n119, 166n148
rationalization/rationalize 52, 88
Rauschenbusch, Walter 169n174
ravens see corvids
raw materials 20
Rawls, John 104, 168n164
realism 129-130, 145
reality 8, 11, 65, 88, 91, 94, 134, 163n132
reason 32, 57-58, 83, 89, 91, 107-108, 110, 112, 164n139, 170n175, 171n181
rebellion 134, 136, 177n234, 178n236
reciprocity 29, 101, 168n160
recovery 2, 16, 45, 64, 133, 174n203, see also resilience; irreversible damages
recycling 20-21, 114
recycling capacity 2, 20-21, 31, 49
Red Queen hypothesis 40, 158n59
Regan, Tom 104, 166n148, 168n162
regulation, population 9-10, 126, 151n9
regulation(s) 29, 63, 84, 128-129
Reifler, Jason 160n89
religion 57, 77, 79-82, 93-94, 104, 106, 108-109
remote consequences see consequences
Renaissance 81
repercussions see consequences
representation 33, 34, 35, 57, 172n189
reproduction 9, 11, 26, 83, 100, 102, 151n8,9, 175n225
reptiles 154n27
research 13, 90, 97, 143, see also science
resilience 18, 155n32, see also recovery
resource constraints/limitations 2, 9-10, 21, 43, 149, 158n67
resource use 20, 45
resources 2, 9, 17, 31, 33, 43, 83
resources, common property 31
resources, natural 2, 9, 20, 21, 49, 138, 145
respect 31, 47, 85, 103, 104, 126, 131, 163n131
responsibility 13, 19-20, 26, 35, 42, 48, 63, 68, 129, 134, 135-36, 144, 177n234
restoration 120, 133
reverence for life 110
revolution 41, 47, 71-72, 117, 134, 136, 162n118, 178n236
rewards, immediate 76, 93, 116
right (from wrong) 63, 113

rights see animal rights; human rights
rights of nature 79, 82, 108, 151n5
rights, animal see animal rights
rights, human see human rights
risk 17, 26, 41, 53–54, 62, 63, 68, 79, 124, 129
Ritov, Ilana 159n78
Rittel, Horst W. J. 159n74
Roberts, Callum 155n37
robustness to extreme deviations 40
Rockström, Johan et al. 152n12, 154n24,30, 156n41
Rolston, Holmes 104
Rome 65, 79
Rome Statutes 132
Roney, J. Matthew 152n15
Roosevelt, Franklin Delano 129
root causes 1, 73, 146, 162n109
Rousseau, Jean-Jacques 82, 110
Rowling, J. K. 38
rules 30, 44, 57, 59, 83–84, 93, 104, 113, 163n132
ruling classes 39, 134
Rumsfeld, Donald 52
Ryder, Richard D. 81, 108, 162n118,120, 169n174, 175n220

sacrifice, personal 27, 55–56, 95, 109, 115
sacrilege 94, 130
sadness 4, 64, 121, see also tragedy
sanctions, social 77, 93, see also penalties
Sand County Almanac see Leopold, Aldo
Sapir, Edward 134, 178n238
Satan 79
Save the world 3, 4, 25–27, 48, 54–55, 63–64, 73, 116, 117, 126, 130, 137–46
scala natura 80
scale 2, 3, 9, 11, 21, 41, 114, 118, 139
scale, global 2, 45, 46, 118
scale, human activity 20–21, see also activities
scale, large 2, 9, 11, 23, 27
scale, time see time scale
Schirmacher, Wolfgang 168n167
Schneider Kayasseh, Eveline 167n227
schools 15, 127
Schopenhauer, Arthur 105–111, 123–24, 168n167,169, 171n181
Schor, Juliet 46
Schumacher, E. F. 20n35, 155n35
Schwartz, Jeffrey 167n154
Schweitzer, Albert 110, 117, 174n196
science 7, 22, 31, 35, 43, 47, 49, 54, 58, 87, 90–91, 98, 105, 113, 135, 144, 155n33, 160n87, 168n168
science of choice 20, 23
science, political 4, 29, 57, 139
science, predictive 18, 35
sciences, social 25, 42, 46, 47, 64, 143
scientific process 8, 49, 54, 59
scientists 4, 27, 29, 51, 57, 59, 65, 139, 143
Scripture 80, 120
scrub-jays see corvids
sea 14, 21–22, 66, 120, 154n23, 155n37, see also ocean
Sea Shepherd 69
security, national 33, see also terrorism
Seed, John 130
Seid, Marc A. et al. 165n142
selection pressure 9, 151n8
selection, natural see natural selection
selection, sexual 151n8, 168n160
self-censorship 114–15
self-consciousness 87, 90, 92, 97
self-deception 97, see also Dunning-Kruger
self-enforcement 29–30
self-interest, power of 62, 95, 108, 123
selfishness 80, 102, 114, see also altruism
senicide 125
senses 91, 135, see also pain
sentience 87, 90, 108, 111, 166n148, see also emotions; suffering
September 11, 2001 37, 67
serendipity 9, 41, 53, 130, 144
services 20, 79, 99, 114, 158n68
Sessions, George 100
Seuss, Dr. 136, 179n243
shark fin trade 13, 153n17
sharks 13, 83, 88, 121, 153n17
Sheldon, Kennon M. 161n97,98
Shellenberger, Michael 73, 162n104
Shermer, Michael 59, 159n83, 161n91,95, 165n141
shifting baseline 65, 161n100
shopping 56, 66
shortcuts, mental 59, 163n132
shrimp 91, 103, 121
side payments 29, 31, 142
signal to noise ratio 70
Silent Spring 7, 32, 151n3
Simon, Paul 83
Sinclair, Upton 58, 160n88
Singer, Isaac Bashevis 83, 163n127
Singer, Peter 90–91, 154n22, 166n146,148, 176n228
Skinner, B. F. 25–27, 76, 93, 115, 118, 133, 156n40

slavery 84, 124–25
slaves 19, 57, 81–82, 84, 124–25
Sloan Wilson, David 168n160
smart people 43, 48, 59
Smil, Vaclav 15, 154n28,29
Smith, Adam 84, 93, 95
smoking 26, 76, 124, 128
snow 11, 17, 154n30
snow leopards 83
Snowball Earth 17
Sober, Elliot 168n160
social animals 17, 91, 102, 112–113
social cohesion 38
social contagion 39, 133, 143
social contract 73, 99, 136
social convention 85
social engineering 41
social hierarchy 55, 62
social interactions 30, 40
social movements 145
social sciences 25, 42, 46, 47, 64, 143
social systems 27, 30, 37, 40, 41, 47, 114, 117, 139, 146, 179n247
sociology 42, 95, 103
soil crisis 138, 152
Solly, J. Raymond 177n235
solutions 1–2, 4, 25, 28, 31, 32, 44, 46–47, 49–50, 64, 74, 114, 129–30, 136–50
soul 80, 81, 82, 87, 88, 162n119
Soulé, Michael 15, 154n26
sovereignty, national 29
Soviet Union 37, 85
Soylent Green 75
space 9, 20, 26, 32, 66, 68, 95
space ship economy 21
special interests 33–34, 74
speciation, 14, 19, 179n247
species loss see extinction, anthropogenic
species, introduced 14, 18, 32
species, prey 8, 10, 17, 102
speciesism 108, 125, 162n118
speed 42, 46–47, 83, 94, 100, 126, 132–33, 145, 152n9, 158n59
Spinoza, Baruch 80
squid 83
St Augustine 25, 155n38
St Basil 169n174
St Francis 80, 81, 169n174
St John of Chrysostom 169n174
St Paul 81
stabilizing effect/mechanism see mechanism, stabilizing
Stalin, Joseph 51

standing (legal) 79, 98, 112, 159n72, 166n148, 171n171
stasis 40, 179n247
state-space 16, 167n158
statistical distributions 36–38, 157n56
statistical knowledge 26, 50, 54, 176
statistics 12, 23, 35, 51, 69–70
status quo 63, 64, 129
steady state economics 21, 69, 145, 158n67
Stein, Gertrude 20
sticky interventions 144
stock markets 34, 36–38, 54–55, 117, 128
Stoltenberg, Jens 156n39
Stone, Christopher 112, 125, 159n72, 166n148
strategy/strategic 29–30, 56, 59, 65, 73, 101, 114, 115, 127, 128, 145, 156n42
stress 22, 154n30
stresses, cumulative 18, 42
structural challenges 4, 75
structures 8, 10, 33, 35, 44, 49, 57, 60, 75, 117, 130, 139, 141, 148
subject of a life 104, 168n162
subsidies 44, 145
subsidies, perverse 34, 145
substitutes 2, 21, 31, 156n50, 162n105
success 28, 29, 38–40, 43, 55, 60, 61, 62, 64, 74, 75, 112–13, 142, 144
succession 19
suffering 4, 12, 89, 90–92, 98, 108, 113, 119, 122–23, 126, 166n148, 170n175
sufficient 28, 47, 55, 64, 112, 126, 129–30, 138, 139–40, 143, 144, 146, 148
suicide 66, 101, 122
Sun, the 9, 17, 20, 74, 81, 82
super wicked problem 49–50, 52, 62, 144, 159n73
survival traits 58, 89, 91
sustainability 12–13, 21, 23–24, 45, 79, 99, 135
Switzerland 131, 176n226
Sydney Opera House 39
sympathy 99, 101, 108, 116
systems 1, 2, 16, 23, 33, 35, 38, 42, 47, 63, 64, 94, 128, 143
systems change 25, 27, 41, 142, 146
systems theory 1, 16–17, 35, 39, 50, 154n30
systems, complex see complex systems

Taleb, Nassim Nicholas 36–39, 51, 157n53,57
Tattersal, Ian 167n154
tautology 54
tax and dividend 30

taxa/taxonomy 16, 84, 91, 102–103, 110
Taylor, Paul W. 91, 104, 163n131, 168n161
teams, working in 143, 147–48
technical solutions/technofixes 31, 74, 144, 145, 162n105
technocratic competence 33, 73
technology 8, 10, 13, 21, 22–24, 43, 45–47, 55, 60, 73, 83, 87, 93, 97, 115, 124, 133, 151n9, 156n48
technology, environmental 45, 47, 54–55, 83, 151n9, 156n48
temperatures 154n30, see also global warming
termites 112
terrorism 67, 68, 69
Testament, Old see Scripture; Bible; Hosea; Isaiah; Deuteronomy;
theory 16, 18, 26–27, 29–32, 35, 45, 50, 55, 57, 75, 93, 101, 123, 124, 125, 141
theory of mind 90, 165n144, 166n145
thermodynamics 21, 102
thing-in-itself 108, 171n181, see also inherent value
things 79, 81, 82, 103, 104, 107, 125, 166n148
think tanks 146–49
thinkers 25, 123, 139
thinking 51, 56, 58, 65–66, 88, 104, 121, 124, 134, 138
thinking, long-term 23, 118, 124
thinking, magical 54, 121
thinking, mechanistic 28, 139, see also mechanisms
thinking, wishful 52, 62, 129, 179n247
Thoreau, Henry David 76, 162n106, 177n234
thought, independent 62
threshold 16–18, 23, 30, 31, 37, see also tipping point
tigers 83, 92, 106, 121
time 20, 25, 26, 27, 35, 45, 46, 49, 50, 54, 55, 63, 65, 66, 67, 68, 70, 82, 84, 85, 86, 87, 92, 95, 97, 98, 99, 102, 103, 104, 113, 115, 118, 126, 128, 133, 136, 138, 149, 150
time constraints 65, 75, 133, 136, 138, 139, 140, 143, 149
time lags 47, 129, 150
time scale 8–9, 10, 16, 92, 93, 155n31, 167n158
time scales, geological 9
time series 157n57
time squeeze 42, 54–55, 65, 75, 139, 149
timing 36, 117, 151n8

tipping points 1, 16–17, 23, 28, 46, 49, 55, 63–64, 126, 128, 138, 141, 143
tipping points, social 30, 146
tit for tat 101, see also game theory
tool use 87, 164n137
tools 42, 45, 89, 94, 104, 115, 118, 140–41, 142, 145, 149
tortoises 88
traffic 22, 27, 45
tragedy 2–3, 6, 51, 68, 99, 114, 119–136
tragedy of the commons 34, 55
training 35, 48, 51, 54, 59, 130, 140
transportation 22, 27, 44, 45, 137
trauma 66, 122
treaties, international 29–32, 85, 117, 142, 156n42,48
treatment of other species 77, 84, 86, 88–90, 95, 97, 102–104, 108–109, 111–112, 119, 121, 123, 127, 164n139, 168n170, 169n174, 174n199
tree of life 19
tree shrews 165n142
trees 25, 48, 65, 79, 80, 90, 120, 154n30, 159n72
trends 23, 70, 94, 117, 153n19
trends, long term 69, 117, see also time scale
trial and error 35, 140, 141
Trimble, Stephen 178n241
Trivers, Robert L. 168n160
trogons 83
trust 35, 48, 58, 135, 164n139
truth 56, 66–67, 71, 87, 115, 138, 149, 160n85, 161n94
tuataras 83, 88
Tversky, Amos 52, 159n77,80
tyranny 82, 177n234

ultimate good, greatest 41
uncertainty 26, 52, 53, 55, 62–63, 141, 144, 159n77
understanding 4, 7, 28, 31, 35, 37, 42–43, 47–48, 50–54, 58, 60, 70, 92, 114, 130, 141, 147, 165n144
uneconomic growth 21, 155n36
unexpected, the 37–38, 117, 136, 146
uniqueness 87–88, 90, 92, 164n139
United Nations 73, 85, 131, 142
United Nations, Environment Programme 156n41, 178n242
United Nations, Food and Agricultural Organization 12, 13, 158n66
United Nations, International Law Commission 132

United Nations, World Trade Organization (WTO) 30
United States 13, 31, 37, 43, 47, 48, 132, 157n57, 175n212
United Kingdom 132
unknown unknowns 36, 52, 143
unnatural 11, 155n37
unpredictability 11, 37–38, 40, 41, 42, 61, 143, 179n247
US see United States
USSR 37, 85
utilitarianism 86, 100, 101, 108, 119, 123–24, 135, 178n240, see also ethics, instrumental
utility 26, 80, 93, 119, 124, 173n190, 178n240

value 82–84, 97–98, 100, 103, 109, 114, 121–24, 164n134
value-neutral process 99, 100
value, inherent see inherent value
value, instrumental 104, 119, 123, see also utilitarianism
values 62, 73, 83, 93, 95, 131, 133, 135
value(s), subjectivity of 82–86, 121
van der Vaart, Elske et al. 166n145
variability/variation 9, 11, 12, 33
veganism 102, 132, see also meat
veil of ignorance 104
vertebrates 89, 165n142
vetocracy 162n103
victims 10, 53, 116, 159n78
violence 66, 86, 179n244
virtual reality 74–75
virtues 80, 109, 110–11
vital needs 100
Voltaire 82
voting/voters 35, 46, 47, 68, 129, 134, 157n52

Wallace, Alfred Russel 169n171
Walpole, Horace 177n235
war 37, 50, 60, 63, 71, 86, 98, 114, 115, 132, 145, 149
war-time economies 142, 149
Warsaw Ghetto Uprising 61
waste see efficiency
waste products see pollutants
water 20, 120, 154n30, 167n159
web of life 20
Webber, Melvin M. 159n74
welfare 8, 21, 154n23, 176n226,227

Western civilization see civilization, Western
Western world 36, 43, 67, 79, 98
wetlands 138
whales 31–32, 88, 131–32, 175n225
White, Lynn T. 162n111,115, 174n206,207
White, Thomas I. 175n225
Whitehead, Hal et al. 175n225
wicked problems 49, see also super wicked
Wikipedia 157n54, 158n58, 159n79, 175n224
wikis 149
Wilcox, Bruce 15, 154n26
wilderness 66, 79, 114, 119, 120, 121, 123, 135
wildlife 15, 73, 127, 136
wildness 66, 114
will to live 108, 110, 171n181
will, collective 26, 34, 55–56, 63, 135, 136, 139, 141, 150
will, free 83, 87, 128
will, political 26, 49, 63, 135, 141, 150
will, the 107, 124, 171n181, 175n211
Williams, Terry Tempest 135, 178n241
Wilson, Edward O. 112, 120, 168n160, 173n193, 174n201
wishful thinking 52, 62, 129, 179n247
wolves 80. 86, 92, 121
women 87, 105, 124
work 4, 5, 28, 34, 46, 55, 61, 64, 65, 69, 133, 140
World Trade Organization, WTO 30
World War I 37
world, globalized 2, 8, 21, 24, 28, 35, 46, 55, 133, 142–43, 157n52
world, political 24, 33, 35, 75, 168, 177n234
world, state of the 4, 20, 23, 27, 75, 119, 136
worldview 7–8, 43, 55, 60, 63, 80, 90–91, 93–94, 98, 130, see also ideology
Worm, Boris 153n18
worry 19, 51, 53, 77, 104, see also fear; anxiety
worth see value
wounds 19, 120, 155n33
WTO 30
WWF 15, 73–74, 154n27

Zapffe, Peter Wessel 2–3, 8
Zeller, Dirk 152n16
Zerzan, John 122n204, 174n204
Žižek, Slavoj 41n62, 158n62
zoology 107